Penn Traffic Forever

DELUXE EDITION

By Robert Jeschonek

pie press publishing

Other Johnstown and Cambria County
books by Robert Jeschonek

A Glosser's Christmas Love Story
Christmas at Glosser's
Easter at Glosser's
Halloween at Glosser's
Long Live Glosser's
Death by Polka
Fear of Rain
The Masked Family

DEDICATION

To the people of Penn Traffic, whether they are with us in body or in our hearts. Without them, there would be no store and no story. Thanks to them, we will never forget.

Introduction

You might have heard this story before. Once upon a time, a grand old department store towered at the heart of daily life in a classic downtown environment. Shopping there became a tradition for generations of local residents. The town's yearly calendar revolved around the store's sales and special events. Its sights, sounds, smells, textures, and flavors were inextricably woven into the memories and dreamscapes of thousands of shoppers.

And then it died.

As people moved to the suburbs, the center of the retail trade went with them. Business became more precarious, such that the company could no longer withstand a shock like a financial setback or a natural disaster. And one day, it was all over.

This same story has played out again and again in towns and cities across the United States. Name a city, and someone who lived there or still does will tell you about a great old store they loved and lost. It's all part of the giant wave of demographic and economic change that swept through the country in the mid-to-late twentieth century.

Johnstown, Pennsylvania has its own version of this story, one that doesn't seem so different on the surface from all the rest. The Penn Traffic Department Store operated in Johnstown for 123 years. Generations of area residents shopped at the store, making it the center of their lives in a multitude of ways. But by the mid-1970s, population shifts and changes in shopping habits took a toll. Business pulled away from downtown Johnstown, weakening the store...and a massive flood in 1977 delivered the death blow. The store died, end of story.

1

Sounds the same as what happened elsewhere, doesn't it? But the details that matter most are so much different. Because the truth is, no other store anywhere was quite like Penn Traffic in downtown Johnstown.

Ask anyone who shopped there, and they'll tell you. Penn Traffic's dresses were a cut above the rest. You'll never find a finer men's suit or pair of shoes than you could find in that store. The hats, lingerie, furs, jewelry, perfume, and cosmetics were all top of the line.

And the *food*, there hasn't been anything like it since. The Penn Traffic bakery made the best pies, cookies, pastries, fresh bread, and rolls. The restaurant on the first floor of Penn Traffic served the most delicious breakfasts, lunches, dinners, and desserts you've ever tasted. And could any candy past or present ever measure up to the glorious Penn Way candies, handmade on marble slabs by elite craftspeople in the famous candy kitchen?

Speaking of employees, Penn Traffic had some of the friendliest and most helpful you could imagine. They provided world-class service, guiding and supporting shoppers as if they were all members of the same family. They celebrated our triumphs, shared our losses, and always helped us find exactly what we were looking for whenever we entered the store.

Photo by Philip Balko

Photo from Penn Traffic 1971 Annual Report

It was some of those very employees, all these years after the store's closing in 1977, who helped bring it back to life for this book. It was their stories and photos and artifacts that brought back the magic we all love so well and miss so dearly. We owe them a debt of gratitude, these faithful keepers of the flame. Without them, countless details would have been lost forever. The full story of Penn Traffic would have faded into history, and future generations would have been denied an important part of their heritage.

Now, at least, those generations will be able to see what they missed out on. They'll be able to learn about the store that meant so much to so many for so long. They'll be able to share our memories of what made Penn Traffic special, and carry forward the best parts of its legacy into the future...the hopes and dreams that came to life within its walls.

Those, of all the goods and services provided by Penn Traffic, are perhaps its greatest gifts. When we walked through its doors, we had hope--hope of finding just what we wanted or needed to make our lives better. Hope of enjoying a respite from our troubles in a palatial refuge where everyone greeted us with a smile. Hope that every surprise we found, from the bargain basement to the top floor, would be a good one.

And we had dreams there, too. Dreams of better things for ourselves and our families. Dreams of happier times and brighter futures that we might someday make a reality.

These dreams, and these hopes, are what made Penn Traffic great. They survive to this day, in this book, in our hearts, because they're something we'll always need.

Because it doesn't matter that the store has been closed for over 38 years. It doesn't matter that the building has been carved up and converted to serve other purposes. It doesn't matter that the company itself has been gone since 2010, its assets sold off to new owners who care nothing for the Penn Traffic legacy.

As long as someone yet lives who shared the Penn Traffic experience, whether directly or indirectly, from memory or listening to stories or reading this book, the store survives. Women in their Sunday best still sip tea on the mezzanine and watch shoppers on the first floor below. Fathers and daughters still share lunch in the restaurant, laughing over burgers and sundaes. Mechanical reindeer and elves still frolic in the big display windows at Christmas time, as children press their noses to the glass and snowflakes flutter down all around.

Can you see it? Hear it? Feel it? I told you so. I told you Penn Traffic is still alive. And we're never letting it die, are we? We're never letting it fade away.

Like the title of this book says, Penn Traffic will live forever if we want it to. And why wouldn't we? If there's one thing that hasn't changed since the store first opened over 160 years ago, it's the motto on the Sign of Quality seal that appeared on much of its merchandise.

Photos by Philip Balko

"Johnstown's Greatest Store." That's what they used to call it. And that's how many of us think of it still, isn't it?

Say it with me now, before you turn the page. Tell the world how you really feel about Johnstown's Greatest Store and how long we'll keep it in business in our hearts and lives and memories. Say it together, because working together is how we make magic happen around here:

Penn Traffic Forever!

Courtesy of John Kriak

Chapter One

A Reunion on Washington Street

"Penn Traffic Employee Reunion." That's what the ad in the *Johnstown Tribune-Democrat* said. "If you worked for the Penn Traffic company, join this historic reunion and be part of the new book *Penn Traffic Forever*."

It was an ambitious invitation, considering the Penn Traffic Department Store in downtown Johnstown had been closed since 1977, the PT department stores had been sold in 1982, and the Penn Traffic Company as a whole had ceased to exist in 2010.

How many Penn Traffic employees were still around? How many of them would see or hear about the ad? And how many of those would want anything to do with a reunion, especially on a sunny Sunday afternoon when there so many other outdoor activities to be found?

According to the ad, the event would take place on Sunday, June 7 at 1:00 PM, rain or shine. And it would happen where the heart of Penn Traffic had always been, at the Penn Traffic Building at 319 Washington Street. Other than that, no details were given.

And none were needed. The dedicated keepers of the Penn Traffic flame appeared as if by magic, coming together in front of the very building where they'd spent so many working hours together in years gone by.

A Historic Reunion

Two dozen men and women made their way across Washington Street and assembled at the corner of the building where the menswear entrance and famous Christmas display window had once been, adjacent to the Johnstown Public Safety Building.

There were plenty of hugs and tears to go around. Laughter filled the air as people who'd worked together decades ago--some of whom hadn't seen each other since-- reminisced about old times, caught up on new times, and just generally enjoyed each other's company.

It didn't matter what job they'd worked in the company or where they'd been in the corporate hierarchy. These two dozen people were like family to each other, just as they'd been in the old days. And all together like that, with all their memories of how things had been, they held the keys to the story of Penn Traffic. No one could tell that story like they could.

There was Barbara Baxter, who worked for 26 years as a women's clothing buyer, beginning in 1951; David Ickes, who worked 5 and a half years in maintenance and the furniture department; Lois Robinson, a 15-year veteran of the misses' department; and Ann Snyder, who worked 13 years at various

locations in the company, from downtown Johnstown to Westmont to Richland and beyond.

Shirley Blough worked for a decade as a waitress in the Penn Traffic restaurant. Eleanor Kohan was the head pie maker in the bakery for

Photos by Philip Balko

years. Michael Molnarko worked in the fifth floor receiving department for 5 years, starting in 1966. Betty Scott worked 11 years in the meat department, and her sister Pansy was a cashier at the Penn Traffic grocery store for 8.

Then there was Marie Neff, who went to work selling gloves at Penn Traffic in 1945. She worked at the downtown store for 37 years, witnessing everything from the store's 100th anniversary to its destruction in the 1977 flood. Her work in the accounts payable office ended only when the department store division was sold in 1982.

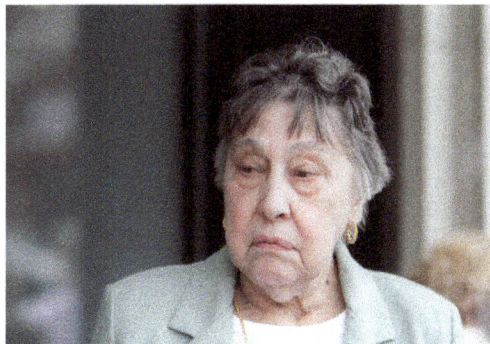

Marie had the greatest longevity with the company, but only one man could claim that he was still working in the Penn Traffic Building after all those years. Former Penn Traffic executive John Kriak worked for the company from 1976 to 1993, then returned years later to run a consulting firm based in the Penn Traffic Building. Of all the reunited attendees, John had the shortest trip from his current workplace to the site of the reunion.

A Real Cross-Section

So very many employees were unable to come to Washington Street that day. Many of them had moved away and couldn't travel back for the event. Many wanted to be there but had other obligations. And many had passed away through the years.

But those who attended represented a real cross-section of the company--men and women of various ages who'd worked in different departments and offices during different eras. From cashiers and waitresses to a top executive, they showed the full spectrum of Penn Traffic's history from the postwar boom of the 1940s to the end of the department stores in the 1980s.

Photos by Philip Balko

Their stories became the foundation of this book. By 2015, precious little documentation of the stores and company still existed. Most records and artifacts had been thrown away long ago. Without the memories in the minds of these witnesses, the details of Penn Traffic's history might have soon disappeared forever.

Just as importantly, these people were the keys to other parts of the story. They provided information that led to other employees and friends of the store who had important stories to tell though they hadn't come to the reunion. And those people pointed the way to other Penn Traffic witnesses and resources that fleshed out the story further.

That story continues to grow. It was once in danger of being lost forever to future generations, as the old guard died out and the few remaining artifacts crumbled away. But the spark that was lit at the reunion on June 7, 2015 brought back the magic. It brought this book to life and energized interest in the store and company that once played such a huge part in the lives of so many people.

Though on that day, sustaining a cultural legacy was probably the last thing on their minds. Marie Neff, John Kriak, Barbara Baxter, and all the rest were mostly interested in restoring old bonds of love and friendship, remembering good times when life seemed brighter and

Photos by Philip Balko

8

simpler, and reconnecting with something bigger than themselves, something they'd helped build and make great even as it fed contentment and security back into their own lives.

Something called Penn Traffic, which no longer physically existed, but would always exist as a force and a feeling in their hearts...and now, thanks to them, in the hearts of generations to come.

Photos by Philip Balko

Yearly mail subscription: Local area, $18; beyond area, $21   Johnstown Tribune-Democrat, Tuesday, November 30, 1965   3

PUT YOUR BEST FOOT FORWARD

in any one of 90 styles in shoes and slippers

Where but at Penn Traffic do you find a selection of 90 dress, casual and slipper styles? Where but at Penn Traffic do you find a collection of famous names as Bostonian, Mansfield, Pedwin, Hush Puppies® and Evans? All quality-crafted shoes with precise finishing, hand detailing and a whale of a lot of comfort, good looks and quality for your money. Come in and let us help you put your best foot forward, whatever the occasion.

Store for Men, Main Floor

Penn Traffic

For dress or business

(top to bottom)

Mansfield Wing-Tip Brogue 20.95
Bostonian Grained Moccasin 23.95
Bostonian Llama Calf 26.95
Bostonian Corfam® Plain Toe 25.95

For casual or sports outfits

(top to bottom)

Pedwin Huddle Moccasin 11.95
Bostonian Hand-Sewn Moccasin . . . 16.95
Bostonian Hand-Sewn Moccasin . . . 13.95

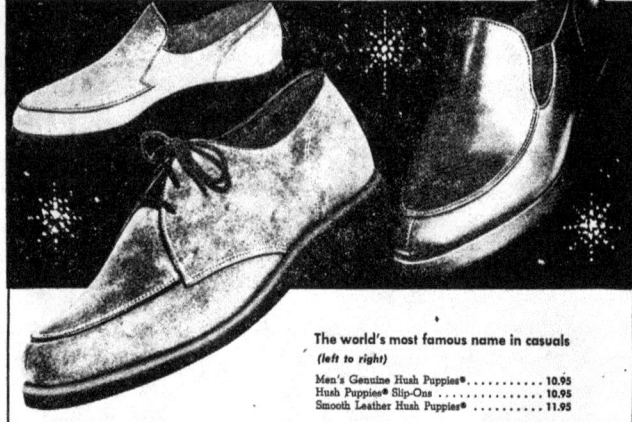

The world's most famous name in casuals

(left to right)

Men's Genuine Hush Puppies® 10.95
Hush Puppies® Slip-Ons 10.95
Smooth Leather Hush Puppies® 11.95

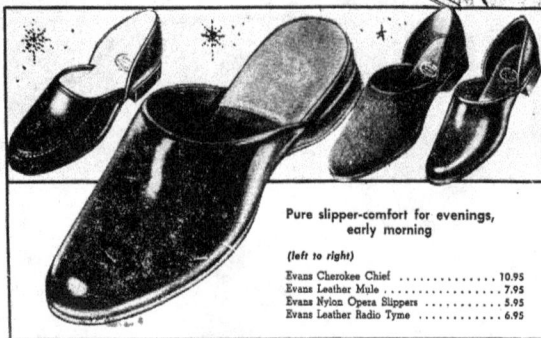

Pure slipper-comfort for evenings, early morning

(left to right)

Evans Cherokee Chief 10.95
Evans Leather Mule 7.95
Evans Nylon Opera Slippers 5.95
Evans Leather Radio Tyme 6.95

Give a Bostonian or Mansfield Gift Certificate

SHOP TODAY AND TOMORROW 9:30 to 5; THURSDAY and SATURDAY TO 9 P. M. DIAL 535-3581 FOR PERSONAL SHOPPERS!

Penn Traffic VIP

SAMUEL H. HECKMAN
PRESIDENT AND GENERAL MANAGER
YEARS OF SERVICE 57
1901-1958

Penn Traffic was, in retrospect, Johnstown's version of Saks or Macy's in New York. It made shoppers feel as though they were big city people. My mother, my sister Lynn, and I were frequent shoppers there while we were growing up. We were always clothed in Penn Traffic fashions.

Holidays were always a special event there. I remember the delicious coconut cream pigs that the candy shop sold, which invariably found their way into our Easter baskets.

My sister and I enjoyed watching the woman behind the counter in the hosiery department, gently sliding her hand through the stocking to show to a perspective buyer.

The restaurant area was also a favorite of my sister and me. Here we would enjoy sitting in the booth like big-time shoppers, enjoying our delicious burgers. During the Christmas season, our family would always treat ourselves to purchasing a new Christmas decoration for the house, from the wide array of new decorations for sale that came out every year. We felt like children in a candy store.

It was a very sad day when we found out that the store was closing forever. Penn Traffic was and is still a part of Johnstown's history. It should be lauded as such.

Dorothy Holtzman

One of my best memories was the excitement and anticipation every Christmas waiting for the unveiling of the holiday window at Penn Traffic. My Dad was a city policer officer at that time, and sometimes we would pick him up. We knew it was getting close to the holiday season when we drove by one day in November and saw the main window was covered. After that, we would always check to see if the window was uncovered. Checking that window after the Christmas parade was a big deal for a little boy who couldn't wait for Christmas to come. Any time we went to town during the Christmas season, a stop at the Penn Traffic window was mandatory.

Jim McMonagle

Sounds silly, but my favorite dish was a stuffing ball with gravy, then a nice piece of pie, I think either coconut custard or egg custard.
Karen Burns Kormanik

When I was a little girl, I often went to Penn Traffic with my grandmother. It was always a very special experience. We ate lunch in a quaint little restaurant off the mezzanine. They served my favorite drink, called the orange blossom, which had 7up soda blended with orange sherbet. After lunch, we would sit in the wooden chairs on the mezzanine and look down at the main floor of the store below, where people were shopping. We would see what everyone was doing and what was on sale, and we would plan our own day of shopping.
Karen Brubaker, President and Owner, O'Shea's Candies

I remember in the good old days, they would play a player piano. Penn Traffic also had a machine in the shoe department that let you look in and see the bones in your feet. My grandma bought my sister and me camel hair coats at Penn Traffic. The first hardback book I ever owned was *Stormy, Top Horse of Cresent Mountain*, which I bought there.
Mary Elizabeth Clark Margerum

I bought my wedding gown and veil at Penn Traffic. My parents always took my sister and me there for our Easter dresses every year.
Toni Schuller

I was a member of the Penn Traffic Teen Advisory Board for two years as a junior and senior. I represented Ferndale Area High School. We did a lot of community service as well as the fashion show. Great store and great memories.
Carol Unice

Chapter Two

Before it was Penn Traffic

1854

Penn Traffic's roots reach all the way back to the pre-Civil War era in 1854, though the store had a different name in those days. It started as Stiles, Allen & Co., a small general merchandise store established by pioneer merchants Augustus Stiles and George D. Allen on the bank of the old Portage Canal in downtown Johnstown.

Photo from Penn Topics

The original store was set up in an unpainted wooden building, a far cry from the massive, five-story structure that would someday occupy the site. In those early days, customers often bartered or provided services in exchange for goods, though the founders apparently had a commitment to providing quality merchandise.

Times were changing for the fledgling general store, though. On June 7, 1854, Stiles, Allen & Co. was bought by local merchant George S. King, the founder and general manager of Cambria Iron Works. King converted the operation to a company store for Cambria Iron Works, managed by John S. Buchanan under the name King, Buchanan & Co.

Such company stores were often set up by the owners of a dominant employer in a town to sell goods to employees, who were encouraged to do all their shopping in that one location. Often, employees were issued scrip, vouchers, or credit to pay for purchases, keeping them dependent and sometimes indebted to their employer.

Company stores were immortalized in Tennessee Ernie Ford's song, "16 Tons," in which the singer talks about selling his soul to one.

Photo courtesy of Johnstown Area Heritage Association

13

War Footing

King, Buchanan & Co. stayed part of Cambria Iron Works, but went through a name change within a year. A group of investors from Philadelphia, led by Charles S. Wood and Daniel Morrell, bought Cambria Iron Works and received the company store in the bargain. They quickly renamed the store Wood, Morrell & Co., though John Buchanan did stay on as manager until he was replaced by James McMillen in 1860.

Soon, there was talk of expanding the store...but the Civil War got in the way. Cambria Iron Works turned its attention to supplying Union forces, and Wood, Morrell & Co. focused on taking care of the families of Union soldiers from the Johnstown area. During the war, the store offered extensive credit to Union soldiers' families and dependents, handing out company scrip that could be exchanged for merchandise.

Photo from Penn Topics

A Big New Building

When the war ended, and the surviving soldiers came home to Johnstown, it was time for the store to grow again. In 1867, Wood, Morrell & Co. replaced the original wooden structure with a big new store on the same site.

The new three-story building, which cost $100,000 and was designed by Sloan and Hutton, converted the business from a low-key general store to a full-fledged department store.

The grand new structure featured L-shaped north and south wings, each 101 feet long, connected by a one-story first floor that formed the common foot of the wings. The bearing walls and façade were brick, with projecting arches, cornices, and moldings. The façade had an iron cornice and big display windows, and the hipped slate roof had four cross gables.

It was the largest building of its kind in a hundred-mile radius, a giant for its time...and it was just as grand on the inside. The stairways, wainscoting, and window moldings were crafted from white and black walnut, white and yellow ash, and chestnut. Mantles throughout the store were made of slate that resembled Italian or Grecian marble, granite, or brown stone.

Once the store opened for business, staffed by twenty-five employees, customers flocked to buy its many wares, including clothing, shoes, dry goods, hardware, and groceries. The building also housed manufacturing rooms, administrative offices, sleeping rooms for clerks, and private rooms for the manager and superintendent.

Photo from Penn Topics

It was a true shopping mecca, the perfect store to take advantage of the postwar increase in business anticipated by the owners and operators of Wood, Morrell & Co.

Hell with the Lid Off

The next two decades brought steady growth to the store and its hometown, not to mention technological improvements. Gas lights were added to key downtown streets in 1872, illuminating the city at night. Telephone service started on March 27, 1878, with the first call transmitted over a private line in Johnstown--a conversation between the Wood, Morrel store and Woodvale Woolen Mills.

And the iron and steel industry forged ahead, driving the local economy. An 1885 article in *The Washington Chronicle* referred to Johnstown as the home of the leading iron and steel plant in the country, a factory it described as "Hell with the lid off."

But all the change and progress were about to grind to a halt. None of it could stand up to the terrifying disaster roaring toward Johnstown in 1889.

WOOD MORRELL CO. EMPLOYEES OF 1885

The above photo shows a large part of the employees of the old Wood-Morrell Company store (now the Penn Traffic) in the middle 1880's. Many oldtimers will recognize most of them and particular the book boys, most of whom are still living.

Shown in the photo are, standing back row, left to right: J. H. Young, Phil Beauky, Jerry Ellwood, Stewart Hill, Jack Edwards, the writer,

Charley Byers, Frank Howard, bookkeeper; Jack Parsons, Al C. Berry, credit department, Billie Happle and James Taylor.

Third row, left to right: Ezra Mock, R. Z. Replogle, Lew Frick, Carrie Lewis, Ella Tremellon, Ida White, Carrie Higson, Ben Devine, John Maley, Lew Raab.

Second row, left to right: Henry Schwing, Ed Crouse, Frank Singer, John Berry, Sh., P. C. Bolsinger, J.

H. Apple, Michael Maley policeman, and Edward Barr.

Front row, sitting on floor, are a group of book boys, left to right: Stem, Howlett, Huff, Savering, Maier, Schmurr and Barnhart. I do not recognize the others. The book boys, in case you young readers do not know, were employed to take the customer's credit book from the clerk to the credit department for O. K. before the customer was allowed to take the merchandise.

Riding the Storm Out

When the South Fork Dam on the Little Conemaugh River let go on May 31, 1889, it sent 20 million tons of water hurtling toward Johnstown. The resulting wave of destruction smashed much of the city to bits, laying waste to the thriving industrial center and killing over 2,200 people.

Courtesy of Darrel Holsopple

The Great Flood heavily damaged the Wood, Morrel store, wiping out the entire east wing of the building. The north corner, which housed the business office and the store's safe, also sustained damage...but the store's accounting books and important papers were saved by an employee, Joseph H. Berlin.

Before the first wave struck Johnstown, Berlin learned floodwaters were rising toward the safe. He got a ride to the store in the horse and buggy of Dr. J.M. Cooper and reached the safe in time to salvage the books and documents. Berlin was unable to leave before the big wave hit, though he did ride out the disaster on the building's roof, holding on to the flagpole mounted there.

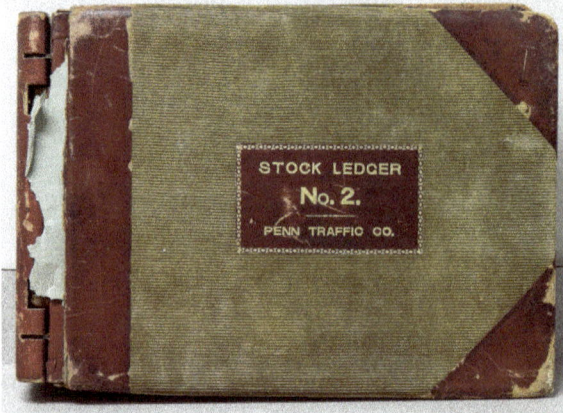

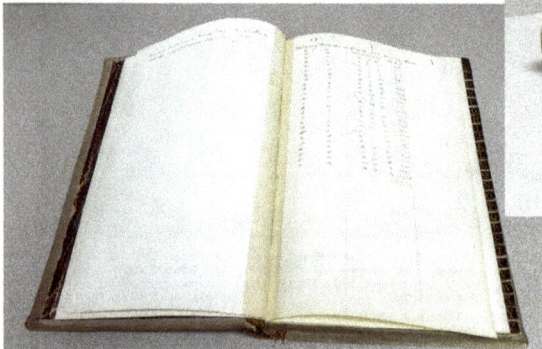

Road to Recovery

Not all the store's employees were as lucky as Berlin. Many department heads and assistants died in the flood, including Alex Kilgore, Jacob Hamilton, Mary Purse, and Annie White.

The toll in human life and property was steep, but Wood, Morrell & Co. rebuilt the store and reopened it weeks later. Improvements were made to the building, and business soon returned to normal.

It wouldn't be the last time disaster struck the place, and its owners brought it back to life... though, 88 years later, another flood would finally put an end to it for good.

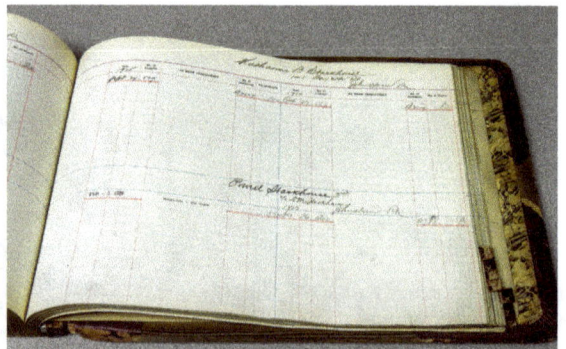

Photos by Philip Balko

Chapter Three

What does "Penn Traffic" Mean, Anyway?

1891-1894

Two years after the Great Flood of 1889, 37 years after the company store on Washington Street first opened, the name "Penn Traffic" finally entered the picture.

In July, 1891, Wood, Morrell & Co. separated from the Cambria Iron Company and became Penn Traffic Limited. The new company was founded as a limited partnership because Pennsylvania had no laws at the time for a mercantile business to become a corporation.

Six of the new partnership's founders were from Philadelphia, the source of the capital controlling Cambria Iron Works in those days. A seventh investor hailed from Johnstown.

But what about that name? Where did they ever come up with "Penn Traffic," and what exactly does it mean, anyway?

Good question.

The Name That Almost Was

To this day, no one knows for sure exactly how the name "Penn Traffic" came to be. One theory, described in printed materials from the company's 100th anniversary celebration in 1954, claims that "Penn" was chosen because it was short for "Pennsylvania." "Traffic," according to the theory, was used because of its definition meaning "trade" or "business."

Another theory holds that the store's name was chosen because of its location along the main traffic route of the Pennsylvania Canal between Pittsburgh and Philadelphia.

But there's another, more complicated theory...one with a connection to a late nineteenth century scandal. According to an interview published in the *Tribune-Democrat* newspaper in June 1958, longtime Penn Traffic employee Bill Kohler, who worked at the store on the day of the Great Flood of 1889, said that the new limited partnership was originally supposed to be called the Penn Trading Company. In fact, Kohler said that the initials "PT" were applied to numerous signs, bags, and other materials, plus carved into the building's date stones... but then, the company's owners decided to make a change.

Apparently, a big stock scandal occurred around that time at a Philadelphia company with a similar name, leading the company's treasurer to commit

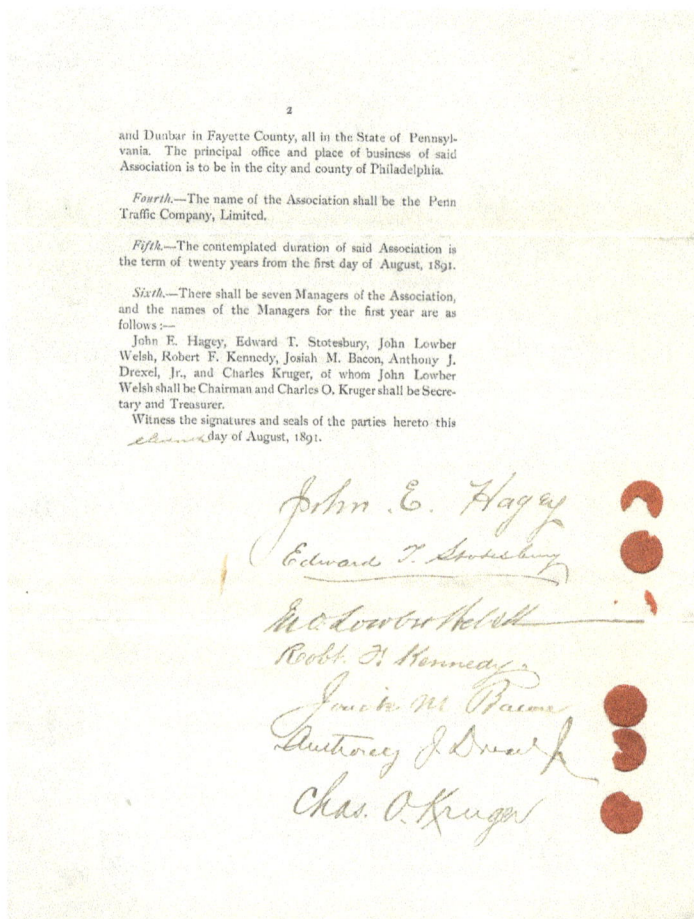

Documents courtesy of Darrel Holsopple

suicide. Since the new incarnation of Wood, Morrell & Co. had ties to Philadelphia, the owners worried that people might think there was a connection to the company involved in the scandal.

But what could they do with all the materials they'd already bought sporting the initials "PT?" The answer: come up with another name that fit those initials.

And that's exactly what they did, according to Kohler. Someone suggested "Penn Traffic," perhaps for the reasons described in the 100th anniversary theory, and the rest is history.

A similar theory documented in a Library of Congress history of the Penn Traffic Building includes many of the same details, but claims that the company involved in the stock scandal was actually Penn Trading itself, the parent company of the store. As Penn Trading took a hit, the investors of the Johnstown operation needed to distance their new venture from the rest of the company.

More Penn Traffic to Love

At the time of the change to Penn Traffic, general manager James McMillen left the store and took a job as resident manager of Cambria Iron Co. He was replaced by J.E. Hagey, who came to Johnstown from Vulcan, Michigan for the position.

Meanwhile, the store's owners finished construction of a new Penn Traffic Building in 1892. This building might have been designed by Addison Hutton, the architect credited with several notable local buildings as well as several department stores in Philadelphia. Hutton designed offices for the Gautier Works of Cambria Iron (1883), the Carnegie Library (1891), and a home for Powell Stackhouse (1882), among other buildings...though his role in designing the 1892 Penn Traffic store is unconfirmed.

GRAND OPENING

Three Departments---Johnstown's Greatest Store:

MILLINERY DEPARTMENT, NEW GROCERY DEPARTMENT, CRYSTAL CAFE.

THURSDAY, FRIDAY, and SATURDAY.

Orchestra Concert
THIS EVENING
7 to 9 o'clock.

JOHNSTOWN'S GREATEST STORE
PENN TRAFFIC CO. LTD.

Lorentz's Local Weather Forecast.
For Friday: Fair and cool.
For Saturday: Fair, warmer.
Frost is indicated for Friday and Saturday mornings.

The new structure featured solid oak paneling, carpeted floors, beveled glass mirrors, lots of Italian marble, and an open lattice elevator. It was the beginning of Penn Traffic's image of class, quality, and elegance...and the upgrades didn't end there.

Over the next two years, Penn Traffic Limited bought more ground along Washington Street, expanding its property to within a few feet of the adjacent fire station, and put up a three-story addition on the site. The brick and iron addition, designed to function as a warehouse, had 100 feet of frontage and 75 feet of depth. It was finished in 1894, marking the completion of the brand new Penn Traffic retail complex, setting the stage for a bold future of merchandising in Johnstown.

A future that included still more additions and improvements.

Photo from The Story of a Store, *courtesy of Dick Corbin*

Philada 9/23/92.

First Annual Report of the
Chairman of the
Penn Traffic Co. Limited.

The Capital of your Company was fully paid in by the subscribers amounting to $250.000 which was paid to the Cambria Iron Company for the following—

Stone buildings in Johnstown
        Hollidaysburg
        Mineral
        Bennington
        Birmingham $70.000.00
        Springfield Mines
        Dunlar

Merchandise on hand & accounts   180.000.00
Wheeler Store Building — In all $250.000.00

The business was immediately taken up under the direction of your manager Mr. John E. Hagey. Each department was carefully investigated and today is believed to be thoroughly organized.

The results of the years business is under the circumstances very satisfactory and

and has resulted in a net profit of $73.862.68 from which has been paid a dividend of 10% amounting to   25.000.00
    and the balance of $48.862.68—
has been carried to the credit of Surplus a/c and will it is hoped enable your Company to conduct its business in the future without borrowing large sums of money which it was forced to do this year.

Philada Aug 21st 1893.

Second Annual Report of the
Chairman of the
Penn Traffic Co. Limited.

The business during the year ending July 31st amounted to $731.592.00   while the expenses of conducting it foot up $84.078.00 (in which is included the state taxes of $1975.00, and bad debts of $11.000) equal to 11 40/100 %.
The net profit is $60.633.17
(or 8 28/100 % on the business done)
Two dividends of 5% each have been paid which have taken $25.000.00
Leaving a surplus for the
year of   35.633.17 $60.633.17
The Surplus a/c has now to the
credit $78.696.25 after charging out $572.65 cost of furniture
It has been found necessary to buy a piece of ground next to your store to give greater room for conducting the business. The price paid was $74.000 and work has been commenced upon the building which has been put under contract at a cost of $29.700.

With the great depression at Johnstown the outlook for business during the coming year is not encouraging.

PENN TRAFFIC CO.
Johnstown, Pa.

Documents courtesy of Darrel Holsopple

Chapter Four

Penn Traffic in 1897

Three years after the 1894 expansion, in 1897, Joseph Berlin--the same Joseph Berlin who had saved vital documents and financial books from the store safe in the Great Flood of '89--stepped into the post of General Manager.

At about the same time, the store completed its transition from a workingmen's supply store to a department store with a focus on the general public and no connection to the Cambria Iron Co.

Photo from The Story of a Store

These changes coincided with extensive remodeling that transformed the store from end to end. The results, completed at a cost of $12,000 by general contractors Saly & Lucas, were described as follows in a Penn Traffic newsletter from December 18, 1897:

Photo from Penn Traffic Co., 1854-1907,
courtesy of Dick Corbin

Beginning with the eastern end, the part rebuilt or restored and extended after the flood, first comes the dry goods department, 48 feet wide by 120 feet deep and as light as the outside day. Great lengths of counters and shelves range the sides. There is a beautiful oval counter near the

Photo from The Story of a Store,
courtesy of Dick Corbin

middle of the room, and hard by a half-circular counter of solid, heavily paneled oak, devoted solely to the tying up of packages. Back of this again, and the whole scene reminding the visitor of a fair in active progress, is a space of 10 feet by 10 on a raised platform, surrounded with an elaborate railing and balustrade of hard wood, the floor beautifully

carpeted and the enclosed space provided with easy-chairs and rockers, where ladies may sit to rest or while waiting to be served. But this is not all; for yet a little further back is another railing, partially enclosing the entrance to the ladies' toilet room. In the rear of all is the desk of the foreman.

On the western side of this room is a commodious stairway, and on the eastern side is a counter for checking parcels and packages and a large passenger elevator with a handsome open lattice cage or car and enclosures in copper and bronze. The car is furnished with mirrors and leather cushioned seats, and an annunciator puts it at the service

of the people without other call. But the smooth and pleasant journey to the upper floors must not yet be taken.

The visitor will naturally first inspect the lower floors, and adjoining the dry goods department on the west he will find the grocery store - spacious, sweet-smelling and airy as the morning; swift and obliging clerks serving or ready to serve patrons and having the assistance of many labor-saving devices in their work, among them a large freight elevator. In the rear on this floor, the green groceries are kept.

Through another door to the west, the visitor will enter the shoe department, which is neatly fitted up with the latest improved shoe store furnishings. Another beautiful passenger elevator starts from the rear portion of this store.

The hardware store comes next, filled with the newest in drawers and cases to the ceiling, easily accessible by means of carrying ladders. In the same room are kept tobacco and cigars.

And now the Visitor again finds himself among things good to eat - in the meat market. This room is divided by a handsome solid oak panel partition, having in it two oak doors set with beveled plate glass and a divided plate mirror. Also in this partition is built the beautiful open front of the huge refrigerator itself. The market is furnished with quartered oak marble top counters, and the walls are covered to a height of eight feet on each side with lengths of Italian marble, in which are set five large beveled plate mirrors framed in dark Tennessee stone. The walls

Photos from The Story of a Store, *courtesy of Dick Corbin*

22

above the marble are covered with heavy tiling paper, and above all is a beveled ceiling. The same partition and ceiling are the work of Saly & Lucas of Johnstown. The other decorations were put in by Bernard Gloekler of Pittsburgh.

The visitor now goes to the second floor by one of the two passenger elevators mentioned, handy in either end of the building. If the elevator from the dry goods store be taken, a great and beautiful room, the same size as the one below, is found. This is the clothing department. Here also is splendid light. The furnishings are hard wood tables and cases and a paneled tying-up counter.

Through a door to the west, the millinery department is entered, everything fairly shimmering in the rays of the sun if it be shining. This room is finely equipped with show, ribbon and cloak cases, including a large showpiece in walnut.

On the third floor above the clothing department, in a room the same size as those below, are kept great stocks of carpets, oil cloths, wall paper, and furniture.

In the great warehouse, reserve stocks of everything are kept in large quantities. An Otis freight elevator connects the different floors.

All of the four elevators in the stores are operated by water power, in order to secure which, in the quantity desired, it was found necessary to tap the Washington Street main and also to run a six inch pipe from the Main Street main.

The delivery department must not be forgotten. The stables are located between the warehouse and the Assistance fire engine house. Her four two-horse and three one-horse teams are kept here when not busy on the streets.

The delivery of goods to the homes of purchasers has recently been attended with great improvements, having been reduced to an exact system, so that deliveries are not only

Photos from The Story of a Store, *courtesy of Dick Corbin*

prompt but expeditious. The bicycle delivery has proved a great success, and will be extended as required.

An entirely new department is a room immediately in back of the credit or "skylight" office, handsomely and at the same time conveniently fitted up for the purpose of facilitating the settlement of accounts with customers.

Photos from The Story of a Store, *courtesy of Dick Corbin*

Chapter Five

Down in Flames

1900-1905

Courtesy of Darrel Holsopple

Things were looking up for Penn Traffic around the turn of the century. The renovations of 1897 had raised the store's profile, fueling a steady rise in customers and sales. Another round of renovations followed a few years later, culminating in a big grand opening celebration on October 3, 1901.

The Penn Traffic name was becoming well-known throughout the Johnstown area and beyond, synonymous with quality merchandise and service.

What had started as a humble general store in an unassuming wood building had become a thriving department store, a success story that seemed poised to grow even more as Johnstown's steel industry continued to boom.

From Penn Traffic Company 1854-1907

Photo from Penn Topics

25

Incorporation application letter to the state of Pennsylvania

To help assure that success, and take advantage of Pennsylvania's new corporation law, Penn Traffic's executives incorporated the business in 1903, changing it forever after from Penn Traffic Limited to the Penn Traffic Company, Inc.

Things were looking up, and the biggest plans yet were still on the horizon.

Then, the whole store burned to the ground.

Up in Smoke

Around 11 o'clock on the night of Monday, August 28, 1905, something caught fire in the Penn Traffic store.

The blaze spread quickly, and a crowd of hundreds of onlookers gathered outside. Firefighters arrived soon; after all, the local fire station was just next-door on Washington Street. Equipment problems negated their head start, however, as they were unable to pump sufficient water to the site of the fire.

Meanwhile, Chief Fire Marshal Horrocks and several firemen made their way to the part of the building where the blaze appeared to have originated. When they forced their way into the basement in the rear of the meat department, they saw something that seemed to confirm their suspicions. According to Horrocks, there were "five or six wagon loads of excelsior, old boxes, and paper burning fiercely, igniting the surrounding beams and timbers."

At first, the fire was confined to the basement. Before long, though, the elevator shafts and hallways acted as flues and drew the flames up through the building's three floors.

Realizing the situation was quickly deteriorating, Horrocks turned in a general alarm to summon other nearby fire companies. When no one showed up promptly, he repeated the alarm, and every fire company in the city rushed to the scene. Volunteers also poured in from Conemaugh, Dale Borough, and Franklin Borough.

By that time, the downtown fire crew had managed to get their hoses running at full capacity...but the blaze had gotten ahead of them. They fought valiantly alongside the other crews and volunteers who'd answered Horrocks' alarm, though it was becoming increasingly clear that the cause was lost.

Photo by Fletcher Photography, courtesy of Johnstown Area Heritage Association

Photo courtesy of Johnstown Area Heritage Association

Fiery Darts and Explosions

According to *The Daily Tribune*, "The flames needed no fanning, but quickly ate their way from the Walnut Street end of the big structure toward Market Street. The old portion of the building, below the jewelry store, was soon a veritable mass of flames.

"The fiery darts shot high into the heavens; to the ears of the assembled people came the sound of falling floors and timbers, and--as the flames reached the hardware department and the storage room where the extra stock of ammunition was kept--three loud reports, at intervals, which told of the finding of quantities of explosives by the flames."

One of those explosions blew out the front of the hardware department and injured bystanders with flying glass. Loose ammo cartridges continued to pop in the flames, spraying lead pellets indiscriminately into the street.

Luckily, Fire Marshal Horrocks had earlier thought to remove the stock of dynamite and gunpowder that had been stored in a shanty next to the rear of the building. Otherwise, the whole place would have become a giant bomb, exploding with enough force to wipe out numerous firefighters and onlookers alike.

Photo courtesy of Johnstown Area Heritage Association

Blackened, Smoking Ruins

Photo courtesy of Darrel Holsopple

The fire crews fought long into the night, but couldn't turn the tide. "Time after time, plucky firemen went into the building, which was now blazing in many places, only to be driven back by the heavy black smoke," recounted the *Tribune*.

"All night long, the flames roared, and at no time were they under control." Eventually, the firefighters gave up on Penn Traffic and instead worked to keep nearby structures from being caught in the conflagration.

By late morning, when the worst was over, Penn Traffic and its out-buildings were "a mass of blackened, smoking ruins, with gaunt, bare, brick walls outlined against the sky, threatening to topple down as each high wind blew and as the flames still burning at their bases devoured their support."

Only the main building of the Crystal Café was mostly intact, though the exterior suffered smoke and water damage.

At the time, it was the biggest fire in Johnstown history. Damage was estimated at half a million dollars, with $392,000 of that covered by the store's insurance. At least the store's accounting books and important documents were preserved in vaults and safes; some of them crashed through the burning building and ended up in the basement, but their contents weren't harmed.

As for the surrounding area, flying debris carried by the wind started small fires up the hill in Prospect, but they were all put out before they could cause any damage.

Best of all, in spite of the magnitude of the disaster, there were no major casualties. No

human lives were lost, though numerous firefighters had been injured, and several hospitalized, including a fireman hurled into the street by one of the explosions.

The fire did leave 328 Penn Traffic employees out of work...but not for long. The biggest disaster to strike the store since the Great Flood of 1889 would not keep Penn Traffic out of business for even a day.

Penn Traffic Phoenix

The fire was extinguished the morning of August 29, 1905; by the afternoon of that same day, employees had already set up temporary locations across the street.

A temporary meat market opened in the Quirk building at 328 Washington Street, supplied by Penn Traffic's own slaughterhouse. "While you will not find the elaborate marble and mahogany stalls of the old store, you WILL find all the choice cuts of meat you have been accustomed to—and the same force of salesmen to supply your needs," said the ad in the August 29 edition of the *Tribune*.

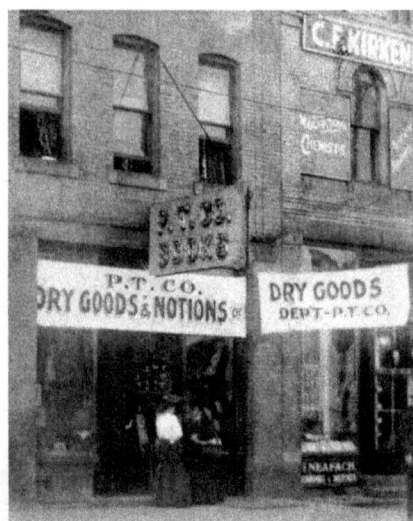

Photos courtesy of Johnstown Area Heritage Association

Penn Traffic also bought out Field Bros. & Schwing, produce wholesalers in the Ellis building at 322 Washington, and started selling groceries and produce out of their former home.

A temporary Crystal Café was also set up on the second floor of a nearby hotel, serving 23 breakfasts while the ashes of the big store were still smoldering.

Meanwhile, a general order department was organized in the Penn Traffic bookstore across the street from the main building. Customers were able to order out-of-stock merchandise from this department for delivery by mail, express, or freight.

According to Penn Traffic's newspaper ad the day after the blaze, "The stability of this vast establishment (already having overcome the disastrous effects of the Great Flood of '89) will, like the ancient Phoenix, rise above its ashes—a greater and more complete organization than ever." As the ad predicted, over the next three days, the dry goods, shoes, hardware, men's and women's clothing, furniture, and carpet departments also reopened across the street. Meanwhile, construction started on a full-blown Temporary Store on the site of the burned-down store to house all departments until a new permanent facility could be erected.

Six weeks after the fire, the Temporary Store was completed, stocked, and opened for business. The two-story frame building contained 22,680 feet--or half an acre--of floor space, and spanned 150 feet of frontage along Washington Street. At the time, it was the largest building that had ever been constructed so quickly in the city of Johnstown.

Not bad for a Temporary Store...but the permanent store that came after it would be the best one yet. It would replace the Temporary Store three years after the fire, in 1908, and would survive more disasters still to come...survive even the closing of the store itself and the end of the great company that conceived it.

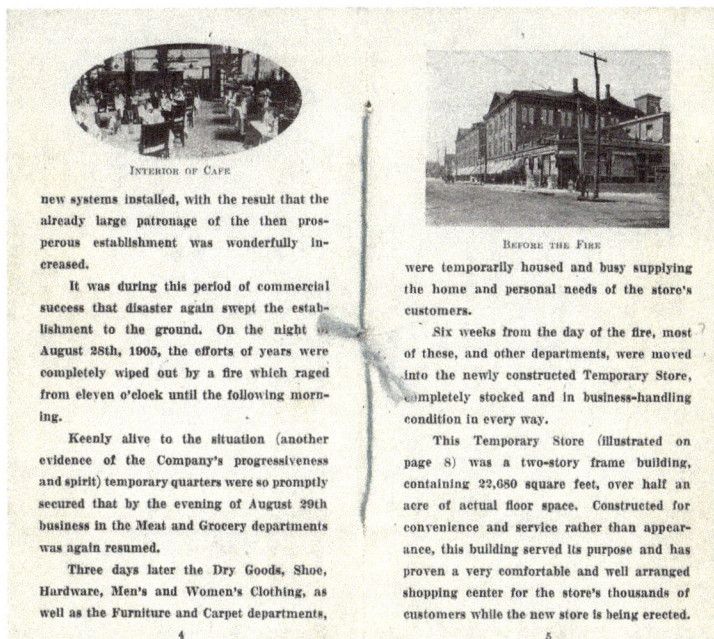

INTERIOR OF CAFÉ

new systems installed, with the result that the already large patronage of the then prosperous establishment was wonderfully increased.

It was during this period of commercial success that disaster again swept the establishment to the ground. On the night of August 28th, 1905, the efforts of years were completely wiped out by a fire which raged from eleven o'clock until the following morning.

Keenly alive to the situation (another evidence of the Company's progressiveness and spirit) temporary quarters were so promptly secured that by the evening of August 29th business in the Meat and Grocery departments was again resumed.

Three days later the Dry Goods, Shoe, Hardware, Men's and Women's Clothing, as well as the Furniture and Carpet departments,

4

BEFORE THE FIRE

were temporarily housed and busy supplying the home and personal needs of the store's customers.

Six weeks from the day of the fire, most of these, and other departments, were moved into the newly constructed Temporary Store, completely stocked and in business-handling condition in every way.

This Temporary Store (illustrated on page 8) was a two-story frame building, containing 22,680 square feet, over half an acre of actual floor space. Constructed for convenience and service rather than appearance, this building served its purpose and has proven a very comfortable and well arranged shopping center for the store's thousands of customers while the new store is being erected.

5

Photo and pages from Penn Traffic Company 1854-1907, *courtesy of Dick Corbin*

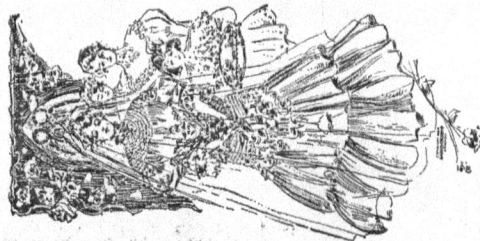

Ads from Jednota Slovak-language newspaper

Chapter Six
New Building, New Boss
1908-1909

On March 5, 1908, the future opened for business in downtown Johnstown. The new Penn Traffic Building, in the works since the fire of 1905, finally opened its doors to the public.

A spectacular three-day reception marked the occasion, attended by more than 5,000 guests from near and far. They came to tour the palatial new $500,000 store which so many of them would soon be visiting on a regular basis.

The crowd enjoyed refreshments and entertainment, plus a free exhibition of the famous $40,000 painting "In the Shadow of the Cross" by Henry Hammond Ahl. Amid the festivities, folks scoped out the new departments and familiarized themselves with the layout of the massive new edifice.

It was the same building that still stands along Washington Street today, the one that so many of us came to know and love as Penn Traffic. Big display windows spanned the front of the place, welcoming visitors to the spacious ground floor. A wide, grand staircase led to a gleaming mezzanine that provided a bird's eye view of the main level. Elevators carried passengers to see the abundant new merchandise on the second and third floors above, or in the basement below. And the fourth and fifth floors housed offices and ample room to grow.

Of all the stores that had stood on that site since 1854, it was the biggest by far. And it was *solid*, from its giant steel bones to its vast brick walls. It gave the impression of permanence, of being big and strong and stable enough to resist any disaster that might strike.

It was the kind of place that could anchor a town, reliably supply its citizens with whatever they needed, weather the storms of time and change...

And tower like a mountain or a church in the thoughts and dreams of people for decades to come, an institution helping to define and justify their lives.

A Visionary Rises

Shortly after the grand opening, in 1909, another change--just as important, though initially of a smaller, human scale--also helped lay the groundwork for Penn Traffic's future. This change started when Joseph Berlin decided to retire as General Manager of the store, clearing the way for a successor to take over.

The man who got the job, Samuel H. Heckman, had been with the company since 1901.

Courtesy of Linda Fritz Goble

A former resident of Lock Haven, Pennsylvania, Heckman had started his career as manager of the hardware department, which in those days sold everything from sporting goods to builders' supplies to major appliances. Now, with Berlin's departure, Heckman became a top executive with the power to help steer the store's destiny.

It was a role he took to heart in every possible way. In years to come, he would bring his personal vision to life in all aspects of the store, guiding it through major changes. He would help the store survive hard times and crises, and continue to thrive in the face of all challenges. And he would eventually become president of the entire company, helping to set the table for its biggest successes yet.

Courtesy of Dick Corbin

He would dominate Penn Traffic--and have a huge impact on Johnstown--for 49 years, all the way to 1958. Until then, he would be the best known face of the company, the one responsible for shepherding it during its brightest and darkest times.

Sincerely yours,

S H Heckman

President

Penn Traffic VIP

SAMUEL H. HECKMAN
PRESIDENT AND GENERAL MANAGER
YEARS OF SERVICE 57
1901–1958

They don't make them like Samuel H. Heckman anymore.

Here was a guy who worked 57 years at Penn Traffic, 35 of those as general manager and 25 as president. He steered the company through a major flood and the Great Depression. He built it into a giant success story, a consistently profitable retailer with a reputation for excellence.

And then he died in office, *at* the office. Because what else could someone who was synonymous with Penn Traffic do? Retire while he could still make a difference at the company he'd turned into a major player?

Might as well tell Johnstown not to flood anymore.

Strictly Business

Born in Lamar, Pennsylvania in 1872, Heckman was hired at Penn Traffic as a hardware buyer in 1901. By 1909, he was general manager; by 1933, he was company president.

Though he left the general manager role in 1944, he never quit the presidency. Along the way, he just kept building his legacy, making Penn Traffic a bigger and better company.

Even as he kept setting a good example for his grandson, Dick Corbin. "He was generous, lovable, cooperative, informative, and always available," remembers Dick.

Photos courtesy of Dick Corbin

"He was very religious, too. He had a daily prayer book and grace was said prior to every meal."

"I remember he was a nice man," says Betty Ghantous, who worked as a cashier supervisor at Penn Traffic from 1945 until 1957. "He would come and check everything out and talk to you like a friend, which was very nice. You don't often get that from a big boss."

On the job, Heckman was "strictly business and very concerned that his business was always as proper and presentable as it could possibly be," says Dick.

"He was very fair and understanding, but the rules were set, and they had to be followed."

In later years, Dick remembers him coming to the store almost every day, though by then he was in 80s and had to use a cane to get around. "He'd walk through the store and up into the stockrooms and make sure everything was lined up and in order. You knew he was there."

Giving as a Way of Life

But Sam had another side, too. He was always a big supporter of community activism and philanthropic works, doing his part to give back to the town and people who'd made his store such a big success.

He founded the Greater Johnstown Community Chest, supported the Cambria County Chapter of the American Red Cross, and served on the board of managers of Memorial Hospital and the Johnstown YMCA.

Throughout his life, he contributed time and money to many worthy causes. "If he saw somebody who needed help, there was never any question," says Dick. "If they needed help, he gave it to them out of his own pocket."

According to Dick, Sam helped many local young people, especially the children of store employees, to cover the costs of higher education. "I think he put more kids through college in his day than anyone in Johnstown did. He might not have paid every expense related to college, but he contributed enough to keep them going."

Sam also encouraged giving and volunteerism among Penn Traffic employees. In 1930, for example, when he was general manager of the store, he came up with a plan to raise money through employee donations for relief of the needy during the Great Depression. He thought it was the right thing to do, since the Penn Traffic staff had steady jobs with no pay cuts, though so many people were suffering and doing without.

The Glosser Alliance

Sam's work to improve the community often led him to team up with other local business leaders.

Dave Glosser, for example, was happy to work on local initiatives with Sam. Dave, a co-founder of the Glosser Bros. Department Store in Johnstown, was always on good terms with Penn Traffic's top executive.

"Dave and Sam were good friends," recalls Dick. "They were both retailers, but their competition was always friendly.

"They were local trailblazers. They were both very active locally to promote the city."

Still Tapping?

Away from work, when he wasn't using his time or money to improve the community or help those in need, Sam liked playing golf and spending time with his family. But his heart was always in Penn Traffic.

He could never stay away from the store for long. Even now, it hardly seems possible that he's been away since his death in 1958.

Or *has* he?

Next time you're in the Penn Traffic Building on Washington Street, listen carefully. Hear that tap-tap-tapping, ever so faint, around the corner of the hallway?

It might just be Sam Heckman with his cane, keeping watch, even now, over the place he loved best in all the world.

---

2   PENTRACO BULLETIN

Mr. Heckman's Appreciation of Your Holiday Business-Getting

Editor's Note: At the first meeting of the Welfare Club in 1917, Mr. Heckman expressed his pleasure at the way every one got up and dusted. The result was the biggest holiday business in the history of the store. This Temple of Spontaneity apologizes to its readers for holding up the message until four months after date of delivering.

His Address follows:

I have not been asked to take part in the program for the evening but I do not want in any way to crowd myself in or consume time that might otherwise be taken for better advantage, but I feel that this might be an opportune time to convey to you a few appreciative thoughts that have been in my mind since the closing of our very successful holiday season. From the very beginning of the holiday trade and with the excessive amount of money invested in merchandise and the increasing demand for superior service became more apparent each day and many other problems I must confess all of them weighed rather heavily on your management as the season advanced, but I want to say at this time that cannot be measured by increased sales and profits and that was the real spirit of willingness with which every employe was endeavoring to do their part and their very best.

The year which will close with the close of the present month will be the largest from point of sales in the history of the store. Not a single department excepted. All showing substantial increase marked conditions were never so favorable to increased sales and earnings as in the year 1916. The spirit of loyalty on the part of our employes has been all we could expect. The ideals we had in mind seven years ago have been hard to accomplish. While we have lived up to our slogan, Quality, we owe from perfection. We have accomplished just enough to make it obligatory on our part to accomplish even greater things. Looking to the future is problematical at the best. I would say the future holds out for us a greater world and a better condition. European problems are going to be settled in a manner that will draw humanity closer together. Both as nations and individuals will be able to see the wrong on our own part as quickly as we can see the wrong in others. If we once learn to realize that each of us can be sometimes wrong, sometimes right on a subject that in itself will enable us to meet each other in a spirit of co-operation. Let us practice and set as example of the spirit of friendship to all regardless of where they come from or who they may be. Let us try to be the big brother to those who are less fortunate than we are and we then may realize a future that is much happier than the past.

We have with your help and advice been able to evolve many things that aid in making our workers happy and contented. With the earnest co-operation of all our people with their faith in us and our faith in them let us hope to live it said that the Penn Traffic organization is the best and happiest in the community in which we serve and live.

A Big Drive for Increased April Business With Rewards for Big Efforts

Show the biggest percentage of gain over April 1916, and your Department, big or little, is a prize winner to the tune of $15 per member—Salespeople, manager, and assistant manager.

Two Departments can win a bonus. Yours is Class A if last April's business was $5,000 or over; Class B, if under that figure. The prize money is the same amount for both classes.

The individual that shows the biggest percentage of gain over last April's business wins a $25 bonus. This is a separate prize and all sales-people have the same chance of winning. In case the winner of the individual prize belongs to a winning Department, the effort is worth $40.

Here's best wishes for a big percentage of gain!

Cutting Prices
(With Apologies to "Hamlet.")

To cut or not to cut. That is the question:
Whether it is not better in the end
To let the chap who knows not the worth
Have the business at cut-throat prices, or
To take up arms against his competition,
And by opposing cut for cut, end it.
To cut—and by cutting put the other cutter
Out of business—'tis a consummation
Devoutly to be wished. To cut—
slash—
Perchance myself to get it in the neck—
Aye—there's the rub; for when one starts to meet
The other fellow's prices, 'tis like as not
He's up against it good and hard,
To cut and lsash is not to end the confusion
And the many evils the trade is pestered with.
Nay, nay, Pauline; 'tis but the forerunner
Of debt and mortgage such a course portends.
'Tis well to get the price the goods are worth
And not be bluffed into selling them for what
So-and-So will sell his goods for.
Price cutting doth appear unseemly
And fit only for the man who knows not
What his goods are worth, and, who ere long,
By stress of making vain comparison
'Twixt bank account and liabilities,
Will make his exit from the business.
—Anonymous
—L. S. Plaut's Honey Comb Brief

Sells Space to Employes Who Want to Buy and Sell Merchandise

The Hallegram, Halle Bros. Co., Cleveland, O., is conducting a "Want Ad" department, listing employes' offers to buy and sell at the rate of one cent per word.

"We consider that this department has justified itself for its first month's existence," says the Hallegram, "as it has sold about $50 worth of goods for individuals in the store, to other individuals in the store.

"We are having a great many articles of genuine value brought in for sale, and can guarantee real bargains to those who are looking for them.

"Advertising rates one cent per word in advance. Goods sold by this department without advertising, 15 cents flat rate.

"Among the things sold this month are the following: A rug, a corduroy skirt (new), a Geo'gette blouse (new), an ivory hair brush and comb (new), a bracelet, a pair of hockey skates and shoes, two gas stoves, a hat and coat, and electric fixtures."

Editor's Note: The Bulletin will carry a list of For Sale and Exchange articles, at the rate of one cent per word (money thus received to be applied to the expense fund for this publication) or 15c per exchange if not advertised, if the readers so desire. Let us know your wishes before the next issue, in June, 1917.

Mere Man's Version of It

Embroidery—A game played on porches of summer hotels; something you start but are not supposed to finish; when children do it they roll the hoop.

Quilting—Cloth checkers; a way to cut up otherwise valuable pieces of merchandise into small, irregular fragments; sometimes known as "crazy" and with reason.

Guest towel—A piece of very expensive linen with fussy stuff on the edges of it, seen only when there is company in the house; Christmas heirloom; something that's as sacred as a prayer-rug.

Boudoir cap—Another excuse for wearing a hat; "Isle of Safety" for disheveled hair; substitute for hairbrush when unexpected company arrives; garage for refractory curls.

Lingerie—Affectation of speech; slang for underclothes; why that monthly bill at the department store is so large; clothes worn inside and under.

Tatting—Queer sound, issuing from mouths of womenfolk while in sewing

---

PENTRACO BULLETIN   **3**

room; foreign language stuff; a swear-name for so emsort of sewing or something.

Doily—Patch for hole in tablecloth; linen postage stamp; what makes the pitcher always turn over; miniature wedding present.

Centerpiece—Fancy cloth, always on one side of table; where stains invariably happen; Aunt Susan's peace offering; blotter for fernery.

Piano scarf—Prevents turning of music sheets; the thing Bill burns with his cigar, while you are all singing "Annie Laurie;" lap robe for a Steinway.

Editor's Note: There's about 'steen columns of this stuff but—s'nuf, s'nuf, go on to the next article. Maybe, sometime, we'll print the balance to fill space. Or, if some one wants the complete folio, it's on sale at this office at the current rates of vegetable exchange—one potato per inch.

A Proposal a'la Mode
By Hamilton Fish Armstrong.

Scene: Sherry's.   Time: After Supper.
Don't speak those words you burn to say
And know I won't permit:
Suppress that ancient stereotype—
It really doesn't fit—
And just for fear your heart is set
On aping silly beaux
Pray listen why you must conceal
Your sentimental woes.
Supposing that you did (you won't!)
Put forth your useless plea,
In what gilt ball-room could you then
Enjoy a whirl with me?
Remembrance of the stupid mess
You've made of our affair
Would be recalled by every nudge
And every matron's store.
Who can find so gracefully
To wield my ostrich fan?
Who rescue my lace handkerchief?
Who snub the boresome man?
Who send me orchids?   Who suggest
A quiet dance and tea?
Who beg I count the pearls upon
My plaintive "Rosary?"
Thenceforth diverging paths we'd tread,
And if they were to meet
We'd stutter, blush, then cut and run
With awkward, scurrying feet.
Descend from your Venutian heights,
Forget your ill-timed woes,
And if you love me much you want—
You simply CAN'T—propose!

Courtesy of Dick Corbin

Photo by Fletcher Photography, courtesy of Darrel Holsopple

Photo from Penn Topics

Photo from Penn Topics

Photo from Penn Topics

Photo from Penn Topics

Chapter Seven

The Horses Must Go

1909-1924

THIRD ANNUAL
PICNIC
OF THE
PENN TRAFFIC CO.
EMPLOYEES

IDLEWILD PARK
AUGUST TENTH
1916

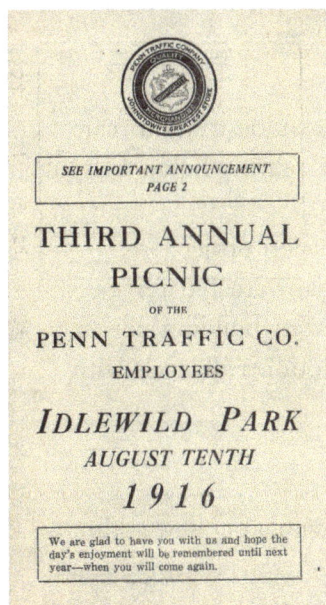

Courtesy of Dick Corbin

Modernization and steady sales growth characterized the fifteen years after the opening of the new Penn Traffic store.

By 1915, the company had installed electric lights and new elevators in the store. In the next year, 1916, the Budget Store opened in the basement. It remained a Penn Traffic institution for decades to come, providing lower-priced quality merchandise as an alternative to the higher-end goods sold on the upper floors.

Layout Circa 1917

The arrangement of the store's departments, circa 1917, went like this:

• Basement: budget store, appliances, and house furnishings
• Main floor: meat market, hardware, ladies' and men's shoes, dry goods, soda fountain, and candy
• Balcony: accounting office, cashier's office, employment department, and post office
• Second floor: grocery, men's clothing and furnishings, women's clothing and accessories
• Third floor: furniture and executive offices
• Fourth floor: carpets
• Annex: books, tobacco, and clock room

Photo courtesy of Dick Corbin

Roaring into the 20s

As the second decade of the 20th century drew to a close, Penn Traffic was riding a wave of rising success. Sales of more than four million dollars were reported for the fiscal year ending January 31, 1919, with posted net earnings of $340,575.

Photo courtesy of William Glosser

The influx of earnings helped spark a series of updates and initiatives in the store. In 1922, for example, Penn Traffic obtained a license for the first radio station in Johnstown. WTAC operated on 150 watt power and broadcast from studios on the fourth floor of the Penn Traffic Building.

Technology also impacted the company's home delivery system, as horse-drawn wagons were replaced by gasoline-powered automobiles. The transition to motorcars was complete by 1926; the last delivery horse was put out to pasture in 1927.

Meanwhile, another expansion project concluded in 1924. The company erected a five-story addition on the Public Safety building side of the store, enlarging the sales floor on all levels with much-needed square footage.

Photo courtesy of Dick Corbin

An Electrifying Future

Penn Traffic had come a long way by 1924. The store was bigger now, with a big new addition and a Budget Store in the basement. It had a delivery fleet of automobiles instead of horses and wagons. And the building was equipped with electricity and elevators...just in time, as it turned out, for those very conveniences to play a role in one of the most notorious events in the store's history.

Thieves were about to strike, turning Penn Traffic's own modern technology against it.

Photo courtesy of Johnstown Area Heritage Association

Fourth
Annual
Picnic

AUG
9TH

At
Idlewild
Park

PENTRACO BULLETIN

a MAGAZINE for KEEPING in TOUCH

VOL. III   AUGUST, 1917   NO. 4

A Word to All

Penn Traffic is more than a market. It's an institution. In the Public's eye, it towers above ordinary selling-places in size, integrity and age. The day of the Picnic Penn Traffic will be in the lime-light. While looked upon as an institution, any individual of the store can shatter the impression so indelibly stamped on outsider's minds. We must put our best foot forward, be helpful, courteous, obliging and pleasant. The picnic is our advertisement—an advertisement worth more than reams and bundles of printed matter. No one on store property would think of being rude to a patron. It must be the same on the picnic grounds. With the strong glare of the spot light on us, little defects loom up large. More reason to be extra careful. Penn Traffic was regarded as a "different kind of store" long before the most of us were born. The burden of sustaining that reputation rests upon the shoulders of to-day.

Published by PENN TRAFFIC CO. Johnstown, Pa.

BUILD NOT FOR TODAY'S VOLUME ONLY, BUT FOR STABILITY IN THE YEARS TO COME, PERMANENCY DEPENDS ONLY ON THE DEGREE OF SATISFACTION CONVEYED THROUGH THE HIGH QUALITY, SUPERIOR SERVICE AND A BROAD BUSINESS POLICY. IT IS FOR THESE THINGS WE STRIVE

PENN TRAFFIC CO.

PENTRACO BULLETIN

a MAGAZINE for KEEPING in TOUCH

VOL. III   NOVEMBER, 1917   NO. 7

THANKSGIVING Day will soon be here,
But it has ever been my way,
And one that's filled my soul with cheer,
To keep Thanksgiving every day.
It really helps a lot, you know,
To keep on paying as you go,
Not putting off till the account
Foots up to such a vast amount
That you're not certain if your store
Is quite sufficient for the score.

Published by PENN TRAFFIC CO. Johnstown, Pa.

Courtesy of Dick Corbin

SMILE

When you miss your train.
When you turn on the wrong faucet for your bath.
When you leave the light burning all night.
When the servant leaves when your friends arrive.
When the eggs aren't.
When you stub your toe or thump your finger.
When your wife gives you a box of cigars.
When the bill collector calls.
When your collar rubs or your button rolls.
When your shirt shrinks.
When you wager on the wrong one.
When you loan your umbrella.
When mother-in-law telegraphs.
When Thomas yowls at three.
When you set the alarm for five instead of eight.
When your razor becomes an axe in Mary's hands.
When somebody takes yours and leaves theirs.
When your lip is split.
Smile anyway and always and you're sure to have

A HAPPY NEW YEAR.

1918

PENTRACO BULLETIN

a MAGAZINE for KEEPING in TOUCH

VOL. III   FEBRUARY, 1918   NO. 10

SIXTY-FOURTH ANNIVERSARY EVENT NUMBER

THE Department Managers have gone on record to make this occasion greater than the last one. We of the selling branches must back them to the limit. Can it be done? The echo answers, yes!

Published by PENN TRAFFIC CO. Johnstown, Pa.

Good Advice

THIS little publication is published with a definite purpose—To help every one of the Penn Traffic family secure the best out of life. Each issue contains some exceedingly good advice in the form of different articles by people who know. These items are not clipped promiscuously but each article is selected because it fits into our store life and contains something of real worth.

In this modern day and time the old adage about following good advice is more or less out of date. Today we cannot merely be content with following good advice but it becomes necessary to catch up with it.

Hence the simplicity of the articles carried between these covers. May they be truly helpful.

PENTRACO BULLETIN

VOLUME THREE   APRIL 1918   NUMBER TWELVE

A Group of Penn Traffic Employees in the Early Days.

The above is a reproduction of a rather ancient photograph unearthed from some of Mr. Taney's belongings. Standing from left to right are: Charles C. Teeter, Thomas Kerby, Thomas Moses and Samuel Young. Sitting: John M. Taney, William Masterton, Samuel Weaver and Edward Thomas. Mr. Weaver was in charge of the credit office and the rest were connected with that office also, with the exception of Mr. Masterton, who was then manager of the Dry Goods Department, which has long since been divided in two sections, the Dry Goods Department and the Women's Furnishing Department under the direction of Mr. Given and Mr. Schlesinger, respectively. Messrs. Teeter, Masterton, Weaver and Thomas are dead. Mr. Kerby was last heard of from Kansas and Mr. Moses from Chicago. Mr. Young is with the Johnstown Traction Co. and Mr. Taney is still with Penn Traffic, having just entered his fiftieth year of association with the establishment last November.

* * *

Many a man is carried out feet first because he rushed in headlong.

Applebutter Day

It was applebutter and more applebutter in the Grocery Department March 22nd. The day promised to be dull and Alex Heslop was trying to arrange a few applebutter jars in the form of a display. Some how the applebutter was contrary and didn't want to be arranged. So Mr. Heslop instructed telephone girls, salespeople, solicitors and everybody else in the Grocery Department to talk applebutter. And they did with the following result: One hundred and thirty-five quarts were sold by the phone girls. Miss Ringler taking first place with a total of thirty-seven quarts.

Miss Burnheimer of the same group, was a close second, selling thirty-five quarts. Mr. Gohn held first place among the solicitors, selling forty-three quarts. Mr. Barclay lead the salespeople with twenty-four quarts. The grand total was three hundred and eighty-five quarts. That it was a great success goes without saying.

Courtesy of Dick Corbin

Chapter Eight

The Great Penn Traffic Robbery

1924

A watchman bound and gagged by gun-toting thieves. A vault broken into with special drilling equipment. A daring getaway with $40,000 in cash, diamonds, and other jewelry.

It sounds like something out of a movie, but it happened at Penn Traffic in Johnstown. And the thieves were never caught...

Cracking the Vault

It all started at approximately 3:45 A.M. on Monday, May 12, 1924, when 69-year-old watchman James A. Shelly of Dale Borough was making his rounds of the store. As Shelly stepped out of the elevator near the shoe department on the main floor, two men confronted him with guns and told him to put up his hands. Shelly fought back until one of the men pistol-whipped him, then handcuffed him and threw a counter cover cloth over his head.

Next, the burglars took Shelly to the fourth floor and broke into the office where the vault was located. They strapped Shelly to a chair with wire, then pulled out an electric drill they'd brought with them and plugged it into an electrical outlet on an office chandelier.

41

After twenty minutes of drilling out the vault's lock, the crooks had gained access to the store's stockpile of cash, checks, and other valuables. They took everything, loading it into traveling bags stolen from the first floor luggage department.

But they weren't done yet.

Diamonds Are a Crook's Best Friend

When they'd finishing plundering the vault, the burglars interrogated Shelly, demanding to know when the day watchman, Harry Sharp, was due to arrive for his shift. The clock was ticking; they knew they had to finish the job and escape before Sharp hit the door.

Next, the thieves took Shelly's keys, taped his mouth shut, and left him alone in the office, telling him they'd be back to "brain" him if he tried to get free. Then they barricaded him inside by pushing desks against the door.

With Shelly out of the way, the burglars took the elevator back down to the main floor, where the diamond vault was located. They drilled out the lock on that one, too, and emptied the contents of the vault into their stolen bags.

By the time they were done, they had $25,000 worth of diamonds and other jewelry, added to the $15,000 in cash and valuables from the vault upstairs.

It added up to a cool $40,000...a heck of a haul, considering that $40K was worth a lot more back in those days.

Delay of Discovery

When their bags were full, the burglars slipped out of the middle door of the store's main entrance, using Shelly's key to unlock it. They threw their bags in a car parked in front of the place, then got in and drove away.

If they were in a hurry, they didn't need to be. The crime--and poor James Shelly--weren't discovered for many hours.

Harry Sharp showed up at the store at 8:00 A.M., but didn't realize that a crime had been committed. He passed by both vaults during his rounds, but saw the vault doors were closed and kept on walking.

Luckily, Shelly's wife was on the case. When Shelly didn't come home from work, she phoned the store and asked where he was. Thinking Shelly had collapsed during his rounds, Penn Traffic staffers set out to find him...and soon turned up his toupee, tortoise shell glasses, and night watchman's clock near the elevator entrance on the fourth floor. (The night watchman's clock was a device used to confirm that a watchman was making his rounds. Keys were mounted at various locations throughout the store; the watchman had to insert and turn each key in his clock at certain times to keep a record of his travels.)

The hunt for Shelly ended when General Manager Karl Eckel heard the sounds of furniture being moved outside the fourth floor office. Shelly, it turned out, had freed himself from his bonds and was trying to force his way through the desks that had been pushed against the office door to trap him inside.

No Help from C.S.I.

When Shelly told his story, the investigation got underway. Based on evidence and Shelly's account, city detectives pieced together the details of what had happened. Police launched a search for additional witnesses and information.

They also brought in a fingerprint expert from Pittsburgh to dust the vaults for prints...but in those pre-C.S.I. days, criminal science wasn't what it is now. The crooks must have worn gloves, because they left no fingerprints behind. Even if they had, without a computer database to search, the prints would have been of only limited use.

So police kept up the search, though they had precious little evidence to point the way. According to the *Tribune*, reports indicated that local police had been tipped off about the visit of two criminal types two weeks before the robbery...but that story was not confirmed. Pittsburgh police worked on a theory that the men who'd committed the robbery were well-known criminals, but that direction was a dead end, as well.

So the crime went unsolved, and continues to be that way today. The thieves got away with $40K and disappeared into America or beyond to spend their ill-gotten gains.

And Penn Traffic was left to clean up after them, replacing the items they'd stolen and calling local banks to stop payment on the checks they'd spirited away in their loot sacks.

Photo courtesy of Dick Corbin

First meeting of the Quarter Century Club, 1929
Photo by Ressler Studio, courtesy of Dick Corbin

Photo by Ressler Studio, courtesy of Darrel Holsopple

ELIT FELIX
CHIEF ACCOUNTANT
YEARS OF SERVICE 63
1903–1966

Elit's family didn't know any better. When he was born, they named him after the captain of the ship that had brought some of them to the U.S. from Europe...but they screwed up the spelling. They didn't know English well, so "Elliot" became "Elit."

For some kids, that could have been a hindrance in life, but not Elit. He wore his unique name like a badge of honor and proceeded to excel in all that he attempted.

His name might have been a mistake, but he went on to live his life with great purpose and precision. He went on to fight in World War I, raise a family, and have a long and successful career at Penn Traffic.

Photo courtesy of Katherine Moser

Over There

According to his eldest daughter, Paula Kellar, Elit was a very intelligent and self-educated person. Born in 1893, he started working at the store as an errand boy at the age of 10. "He worked his way up from there," says Paula. "Eventually, he went to work in the accounting office."

Elit did so well that he was promoted to Credit Manager...but then his climb up the ladder was interrupted when he went off to war in 1918. "He is leaving our employ in course of a few days to enter the service of our County, and his leaving represents a distinct loss to our organization," wrote General Manager Heckman in a letter he gave to Elit upon his departure. "We trust he may be returned to us and again take up the position he is now leaving."

Elit went to boot camp at Fort Dix, New Jersey. He then attended Graduate Clerk School at the 7th Regiment F.A.R.D. Camp in Jackson, South Carolina. After that, he finally shipped out, arriving in Europe on September 3, 1918.

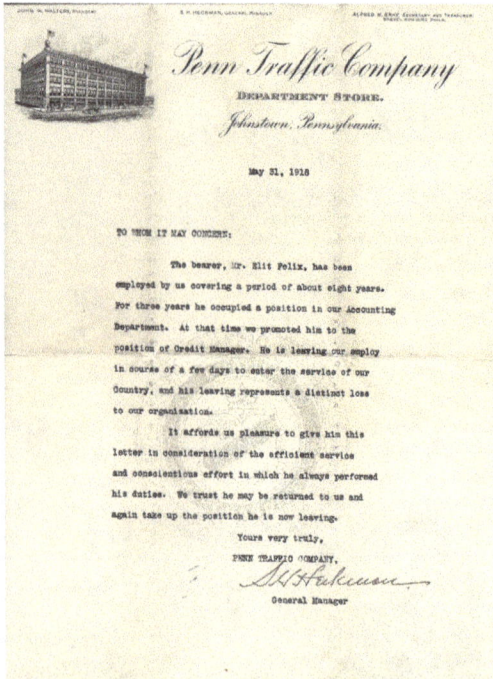

On October 22, 1918, Elit joined the Third Division, 18th U.S. Field Artillery. He fought with his unit in the Meuse-Argonne Offensive until November 11, when the armistice with Germany ended the war. As hostilities in Europe ceased, Elit had to be hospitalized with a severe case of trench foot. After his recovery, he went on to serve as a clerk in the Army of Occupation at regimental headquarters in Polch, Germany.

The Polch assignment ended on June 12, 1919. Elit remained in Germany a while longer, then returned to the U.S. and mustered out of the service in early September 1919. His next destination was Johnstown, of course, and the department store on Washington Street that he knew and loved so well.

Getting Hitched

After returning from the war, Elit resumed his career at Penn Traffic, rising to the position of head of the accounting department. With his dedication and attention to detail, he helped ensure that Penn Traffic's business was always conducted and tracked with rigorous accuracy, its financial obligations were met in a timely fashion, and its investors were always provided for and well-informed.

Meanwhile, he also got his personal life on the right track, dating and falling in love with a woman named Helen Krieger. Elit and Helen tied the knot on October 6, 1924...though the marriage ended tragically just 16 years later. Helen died of cancer on August 7, 1940, leaving Elit a grieving widower at the age of 47.

Would he ever meet someone new and start a family at that age? The answer turned out to be yes.

Mending a Broken Heart

Years after Helen's passing, Elit met a woman named Lucy Agró who worked at Penn Traffic. She was an independent contractor, a dress designer and seamstress who was paid by the company without being on the actual payroll.

Photos courtesy of Katherine Moser

"She used to see him going up and down in the elevator," says Elit's younger daughter, Kathy. "She saw that his buttons weren't always there, or his collar was frayed. He was a bachelor and didn't have someone to mend his clothes.

"So she took pity on him and started to help him with the mending. That led to a romance, which led to a marriage."

Elit and Lucy married in October, 1945. Their first child, Paula, was born in 1947, followed by a son, Elit, Jr., in 1948, and Kathy in 1952. At the time of Paula's birth, Elit, Sr. was 59 years old.

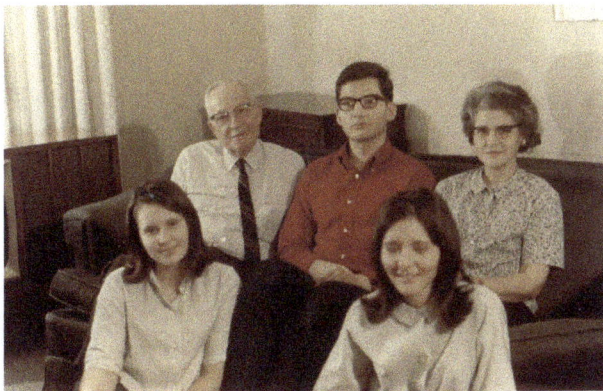

Singing Up A Storm

While the kids were growing up, the demands of Elit's job sometimes kept him away from them. "He worked a lot of late hours," remembers Paula. "He worked until the books were done right. He was the person responsible for those books, and they had to come out to the penny.

"The worst time was in the spring, around income tax time. Sometimes, he wouldn't get home until one or two in the morning."

That isn't to say he didn't find time to have fun with his kids. "He was a very fun person," says Paula. "He used to do crazy things."

Like the time she and Elit, Jr. were walking home across Westmont with Dad in a snowstorm on Christmas Eve. "We'd been at the store, and rode the Inclined Plane back to Westmont. Then we had to walk to our home in Upper Yoder.

"On the way, we came to the Westwood Shopping Center, and Dad decided we should go do some caroling for the shops that were still open. It was the middle of a huge snowstorm, but that's what we did.

"Here's this man and these two little children covered in snow, singing in these shops. They must have thought we were nuts.

"He would do fun things like that. Even though he was older when we were born, it wasn't like we had an old dad. He'd play ball with us. He taught us to ride bikes. He was really fun," says Paula.

Photos courtesy of Katherine Moser

47

The 24-Hour Retirement

As the years passed, Elit became increasingly important to the company. As the third largest stockholder, he had a certain amount of influence, though he chose not to join the Board of Directors. He did serve on the Board of Directors of Sani-Dairy, however, which was eventually acquired by Penn Traffic.

He finally retired at age 73 in 1966...only to go back to work 24 hours later. "Dad knew people all over town, and he was in demand," explains Paula. "As soon as he retired, Dale Bank called and asked if he would come work for them, which he did."

But by then, Elit was sick with cancer, and the new job didn't last. He died on December 28, 1970.

Until then, in spite of his illness, he did manage to visit his beloved Penn Traffic and the friends who still worked there.

"He went back to the office about once a week," says Kathy. "He grew jade plants and gave them to various people in the office to say thank you for all they'd done."

He was always welcomed with open arms, according to Paula. "When he worked, he was very serious and businesslike, but he was a very personable person. Everybody loved him. He had a way of making them smile."

Photos courtesy of Katherine Moser

Chapter Nine

Hard Times and High Waters

1933-1936

The 1930s weren't exactly the best of times for Penn Traffic. The Great Depression had knocked the national economy flat, and the local retail giant was no exception.

The company was down from $4 million in sales in 1919 to just $2 million in fiscal 1933. Penn Traffic posted a loss of $74,670 that year and failed to pay a dividend for the first time since 1910.

So business was not exactly booming. At least Samuel Heckman was still running the show, and had a track record of effective leadership. In fact, he became more active than ever in '33, stepping up to become president as well as general manager.

If anyone could help the company ride out the Depression, it was Heckman. He always seemed to know what to do in any given situation, and he had the ability to inspire those around him to get it done.

Under his leadership, Penn Traffic indeed managed to stay afloat through the next few years. Earnings were lower in 1934, but the company did post a small profit...and that trend continued in '35. Maybe things would keep picking up in '36; maybe there was a light at the end of the tunnel, after all.

Or there would have been, if the tunnel hadn't flooded.

Being Prepared

When the St. Patrick's Day flood struck on March 17, 1936, Penn Traffic was more prepared than most of its neighbors. The response of the store's employees to the rising waters was the picture of clearheadedness, discipline, and

49

teamwork. As a result, large quantities of merchandise were saved, and no lives were lost.

Mr. Heckman, it turns out, had been watching local weather conditions for quite some time. He'd taken note of the heavy snowfall that winter and the recent rise in temperatures. He'd been very aware of the heavy rains over the past few days, and the fact that the higher temperatures had been rapidly thawing the snow pack.

That was why, in the months leading up to St. Patrick's Day, Heckman had organized a High Water Crew to salvage as much of the store as possible in the event of a deluge.

The High Water Crew consisted of seven captains, each of whom led a team of ten men. In the event of flooding during the night, a watchman would notify each captain; the captains would then summon their teams, and everyone would rush to the store to carry out their tasks according to plan.

Fortunately, the flood of '36 happened during the day, so many personnel were already at the store. And thanks to Heckman's foresight, they were well-prepared to do their part to save what they could.

The Basement Brigade

Around noon on March 17, when it looked like flooding might be imminent, Penn Traffic staff moved all electrical appliances from the basement stock rooms to the fourth floor.

Later, around one o'clock, the rivers started to rise more quickly, and the flood threat became much more real. Urgently, the High Water Crew pressed all workers in the store into service.

Soon, every available man and woman in Penn Traffic--some 250 of them in all--was hard at work barricading the store and hauling merchandise from the basement to the first floor.

By 1:45 P.M., all sand bags and barricades were in place around the store entrances. Not a drop of water had gotten inside, at that point.

But the water was rising fast outside. As the workers kept emptying the basement, the river wall between the store's west end and the Bethlehem dispensary building gave way. Suddenly, river water was gushing across Washington Street, smashing the display windows of stores over there and carrying away merchandise.

According to a detailed eyewitness account by Penn Traffic's assistant general manager, Harry D. Corbin, the water in the street was three feet deep by 2:30 P.M. "About this time something crashed against the window used for men's displays," wrote Harry, "permitting mater to rush in--almost trapping several men who were carrying merchandise from this section. Two-by-four boards were then used to barricade the corner window to save it from breaking further under the terrible water pressure."

Chaos swirled beyond the walls of the store, but the Penn Traffic team kept clear heads and followed their plan. As the last of the basement

Photo from Penn Topics, *1954*

merchandise was moved to the first floor, personnel shut down the boilers to prevent a possible explosion.

For a precious few moments, it seemed that everything was under control. The members of the High Water Crew took a break, surveying what they had accomplished.

Then, at 3:00, the big corner window shattered, and cold, muddy water rushed onto the first floor.

The Race to the Second Floor

Quickly, team leaders decided to remove all barricades from the basement entrance, letting the water rush freely downstairs instead of backing up across the floor. That gave the staff a little extra time to move as much merchandise as they could from the first floor to the balcony.

"Over 300 people were now rushing through the main floor with anything they could carry," wrote Harry. "Brigade lines were formed from the bottom of the balcony steps to the second floor and passed merchandise all the way up. Girls, small in stature, lifted loads that stalwart men would have ordinarily considered heavy. Every worker displayed extreme strength and speed."

Unfortunately, the rain kept pouring outside, and the water kept rising. At 4:00, telephone service went out. At 5:00, the electricity shut off. And at 5:30, the water was so high, the staff had to abandon the first floor.

By then, a great deal of merchandise had been moved up to the balcony, including jewelry, linens, towels, stationery, notions, books, toiletries, drugs, men's shoes, and a small quantity of men's furnishings, neckwear, and underwear. Equipment from the restaurant had also been rescued.

Everyone paused to shovel in a quick meal in the fourth floor auditorium, sharing coffee, cold meats, baked goods, and food items salvaged from the restaurant.

Returning downstairs at 7:00, they saw that the main floor was still filling up, and the steps to the balcony were half underwater. Now, the race was on to move everything from the balcony to the second floor.

"None Knew What Had Happened to Loved Ones"

As the staff hauled merchandise up yet another level, the water kept climbing. By the time team members had finished with the merchandise and hauled up equipment and supplies from the beauty shop, optometrist's office, and superintendent's office located there, the water had risen high enough to touch the balcony floor.

At that point, everyone abandoned the balcony. From 8:00 P.M. until midnight, they stayed on the second floor, trapped by the water and deprived of power, gas, and phone service.

Photos courtesy of Dick Corbin

All they could do was watch the disaster continue to unfold outside. "A very swift current was now flowing westward down Washington Street," wrote Harry. "We could plainly distinguish electric refrigerators, crates of fruit from the wholesale district, furniture and all manner of home and store things moving downstream at a very rapid rate. All first floors across the street were completely under water at nine o'clock and remained submerged in the same depth or slightly higher until after 12:00.

"During this period, the 400 people who were in our store gathered in groups. Some played cards, some sang and others just talked--anything to keep their minds off the terrible disaster that was upon us. Many of these same people knew their own homes had been destroyed; none knew what had happed to loved ones. But, as the early morning hours came, and there was nothing to do but sit waiting until the many street-rivers of water had subsided, they began to worry and wonder."

The Morning After

Finally, around 12:15 A.M., the water began to recede. "A cheer went up and everyone seemed to take on a new lease on life," wrote Harry. Then, "After all had satisfied themselves that the water was really going down, many fell asleep and quiet was ordered."

But many members of the High Water Crew stayed awake, meeting over the next several hours

to plan for the cleanup and recovery. They organized divisions to take on various tasks, including Salvage, Cleaning, First Aid, Police, Construction, Mechanical, Commissary, Registration, and Emergency.

At 5:00 A.M., all sleeping personnel were awakened and summoned to a 6:00 breakfast. Daylight finally broke around 6:30, after which an all-hands meeting was held to explain the cleanup and recovery plan.

Photos courtesy of Dick Corbin

Around 8:00 A.M., State Police and State Militia arrived on the first trains to enter the city since the flood. Later that morning, when the water was finally low enough for trucks to approach the store, Penn Traffic staff who wanted to get home to loved ones were driven out. Streetcar service was down, so staff members were taken to dropoff points from which they could walk home.

The cleanup slowly began across Johnstown, though it was soon interrupted by frightening news. Around 4:00, as another downpour drenched the city, radio reports said that the Quemahoning Dam had burst, and a massive new flood surge was headed for the valley.

According Harry, "The water had receded and the streets in most sections of the city were crowded with refugees, soldiers, police, and sight-seers. The mad scramble they all made for their lives was a sight never to be forgotten. It is believed that more people died from the effects of that scare than drowned in the waters of the night before."

Photos courtesy of Dick Corbin

As fear gripped Johnstown, people rushed into Penn Traffic to seek refuge. Everyone crowded the upper floors, waiting for the next phase of the disaster...only to learn it was all a false alarm.

$300,000 in Losses

The next day, with the initial shock of the disaster behind them, Penn Traffic personnel assessed the damage to the store.

Photo courtesy of Dick Corbin

It was bad, though it could have been much worse if the staff hadn't worked so hard to move merchandise out of harm's way.

"The water had reached a height of 10 feet 7 inches on the first floor," wrote Harry. "All display windows were washed out and glass broken with the exception of three. The first floor and everything which had not been carried to the upper floors were a total loss."

Photo courtesy of Katherine Moser

Cash registers and credit machines were ruined. All meat cases and metal fixtures in the grocery would have to be replaced, as would all cables and electrical wiring below the first floor.

When the numbers were added up, losses totaled $300,000. That broke down to $125,000 in lost merchandise, $150,000 in equipment, and $25,000 in damage to the building.

Photo courtesy of Dick Corbin

Getting the Money Flowing Again

In the days that followed, store employees and hired contractors from Berkebile Brothers worked to clear debris from the store. Fire companies from Barnesboro and Boswell pumped water out of the basement, which took several days.

Photo courtesy of Katherine Moser

54

The main focus was on repairing the big front windows, setting up temporary tables, counters, and shelves, and reopening for business as soon as possible. That happened two weeks after the flood, on April 1.

By then, the entire first floor had been converted to a temporary store housing men's and boys' furnishings, shoes, dresses, girls' apparel, coats, and all basement departments. Fitting rooms were set up in the store's east end. All first floor departments were stocked with brand new merchandise ordered soon after the flood by Penn Traffic buyers.

Meanwhile, plans were set in motion to make more permanent repairs. A new men's store opened months later, on June 8. By July,

Courtesy of Katherine Moser

other departments had been restored and reopened, as well. By August, the rebuilt Fountain Room restaurant was also back in business, returned to the first floor from its temporary home in the fourth floor auditorium.

Penn Traffic also made arrangements to help its employees rebuild their own lives, too. The company's directors, prompted by Mr. Heckman, set up a $10,000 fund to help staff members return their homes to pre-flood condition. When all was said and done, payments were actually closer to $12,000. Of the store's 450 employees at the time, approximately 25% had been in need of relief after the disaster.

© The Tribune-Democrat, courtesy of Johnstown Area Heritage Association

Photos by James DuPont, courtesy of Johnstown Area Heritage Association

Photos by James DuPont, courtesy of Johnstown Area Heritage Association

Photo by James DuPont, courtesy of Darrel Holsopple

Photo by James DuPont, courtesy of Johnstown Area Heritage Association

Photo by James DuPont, courtesy of Darrel Holsopple

Photos by James DuPont, courtesy of Johnstown Area Heritage Association

Photo by James DuPont, courtesy of Johnstown Area Heritage Association

Photo by James DuPont, courtesy of Johnstown Area Heritage Association

Photo by James DuPont, courtesy of Darrel Holsopple

Photo by James DuPont, courtesy of Darrel Holsopple

Memory Department

Penn Traffic was the ooh-la-la store of Johnstown. My Aunt Helen bought my birthday gift there every year. My parents took my two brothers and my sister and I there every year to gaze at the spectacular Christmas window. We stood there, faces pressed against the window in awe and wonder. Then, we got in line to sit on Santa's lap to ask for our Christmas wishes. I still have my pictures with Santa. In the summertime, Mom took me down during "Old-Fashioned Bargain Days." What a treat. What memories.

Lorrie Sracic Pavcik

Photo courtesy of Johnstown Area Heritage Association

I shopped at Penn Traffic all the time. I just loved it. I bought all my clothes there, plus lots of other things. I bought the furniture for my home there, and I still have it to this day! I moved it from my house to my current apartment, and I still use it. What a wonderful store that was! I miss it so very much.

Eileen Heinrich

I always loved going to Penn Traffic to shop. My very favorite purchases were feathery hats made from ostrich feathers. I bought one in black and one in pink. I've searched for years to find them since then, but never succeeded. Sure do miss that store. Many wonderful memories!
Linda Pritt

I remember going with my mom as a very young girl, and my Grandma worked in the alterations department. She worked on wedding gowns and fur coats. I think it was on the third floor, but I'm not positive about that now. She was the best at her job. I would go visit with her while Mom was shopping. I remember watching her work with the lace, ever so careful not to put any snags in it, and the furs. She told me they were very expensive. I was amazed at how she handled the fur and the machine.

My grandma's name is Inez Roberts. She taught me how to sew and make different things. She is gone now, but I will always remember going there, even if I don't remember much else these days.
Donna Logue

Meeting of the Quarter Century Club, 1937

Chapter Ten

The War and What Came After

1941-1953

If people were looking for less stress after the Great Depression, they didn't find it in the 1940s. World War II was the opposite of a return to normal, as much of the planet erupted in brutal conflict.

Factory orders rose to support the war effort, bringing a degree of economic recovery...but shortages and rationing made it more challenging to conduct business as usual.

Still, as local steel production boomed during the war, bringing new wealth to the local economy, Penn Traffic continued to thrive. Customers employed by Bethlehem alone were enough to keep the cash registers ringing through the 1940s.

Meanwhile, personnel changes at the store were helping keep a solid core leadership in place and point the way to postwar prosperity.

Photo courtesy of Darrel Holsopple

L. to R.: Karl V. Eckel, E.L. Hoffman, G. Fesler Edwards, S.H. Heckman
Photo ccourtesy of Dick Corbin

The Heckman-Eckel Team

In 1941, Assistant General Manager Harry D. Corbin died from a heart condition at age 47, making way for Comptroller Karl V. Eckel to assume his position. Eckel had been with the company since 1911, starting as a part-time "cash boy" and going full-time after graduating high school in 1918.

Just three years after his promotion to assistant G.M., Eckel became the first person in 35 years other than Samuel Heckman to fill the post of general manager. The move came about in 1944, when Heckman stepped down as general manager; he decided to stay in place as company president, but he handed over the G.M. reins to Eckel.

The Heckman-Eckel team would remain prominent for years to come, guiding Penn Traffic as it grew its downtown business...and looked toward expansion beyond the downtown area.

Improvements Aplenty

The first fruits of this realigned top management team came to pass in the later years of the 1940s.

Improvements and renovations had been put off during the war because of the scarcity of building materials. Once the war ended, however, and restrictions on construction were lifted, Penn Traffic was able to bring some major plans for its headquarters to life.

Six new elevators were installed in the store

Photo by Hesselbein Studio, courtesy of Johnstown Area Heritage Association

in 1946, providing improved access to all floors of the building. A new supermarket was added in 1947, expanding the size of the grocery department and the product choices available to shoppers.

Then, in 1949, a new five-story addition was constructed at the rear of the building. One of the first occupants of this new space was the Penn Traffic beauty salon.

Photo by Hesselbein Studio, courtesy of Johnstown Area Heritage Association

Cooling Off in a Big Way

More improvements occurred in 1953, including a 100-foot extension of the mezzanine and the installation of a storewide all-electric air conditioning system.

The new system was designed by the H.F. Lenz Company to cool 200,000 square feet of floor space, counteracting the heat from up to 5,000 occupants, 600,000 watts of lighting, and 40,000 cubic feet of 95-degree outside air introduced into the building per minute. The combined heat generated by all these sources was enough to melt 1,100 tons of ice every 24 hours.

Building superintendent Ralph Hammett and Carl V. Eckel

To house the massive equipment needed for this system, the installation crew from Berkebile Brothers built a special structure on the roof of the store. This structure enclosed a 75,000-pound induced draft water tower, the key component of a water cooling system capable of chilling 1,800 gallons of water per minute. To support the added weight of the enclosure and its contents, Berkebile Brothers had to reinforce 12 support columns from the roof all the way down to the footings under the basement floor.

To install ductwork for the air conditioning system throughout the building, the contractors had to use more than 50 tons of sheet metal.

They also installed a high-voltage electrostatic air purifier as part of the system. The purifier removed dust and other impurities from the air by giving them a static charge, then trapping them with collection screens that had an opposite charge.

$250,000 Worth of Comfort

When the huge new air conditioning system was finished, the bill topped $250,000. It was a hefty price tag, but Penn Traffic executives knew it would pay off down the road. The more comfortable shoppers were, the more likely they'd be to linger in the store and buy more merchandise.

"The entire program is in line with our policy of keeping our plant and facilities in first-class condition for the benefit and convenience of our many customers," said General Manager Karl Eckel.

Photos from Today in Penelec, *May-June 1955*

Air conditioning would help Penn Traffic stay competitive. It would also give the company something to brag about when it reached its next milestone.

That milestone, coming the very next year, would be a big one. A *giant* one. And the company was going to pull out all the stops to celebrate it in style.

After all, it wasn't every day that Penn Traffic had a hundredth birthday party.

Photo courtesy of Darrel Holsopple

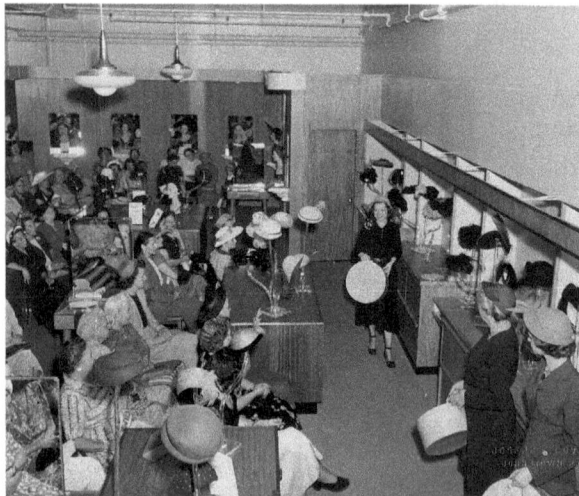

Photo by Joseph E. Cover, courtesy of Johnstown Area Heritage Association

Photo courtesy of Johnstown Area Heritage Association

BETTY GHANTOUS
HEAD CASHIER
YEARS OF SERVICE 12
1945–1957

Betty Ghantous was lucky. Unlike most mothers-to-be, she didn't lose her job at Penn Traffic as soon as she got pregnant.

The personnel manager, Mr. Goddard, let her stay another three months because she wasn't showing yet. But when the three months were up, home she went.

And when she tried to come back to work part-time after having her daughter, Mr. Goddard turned her away. Betty remembers he said he was going to let her go on unemployment. "'You go home and raise your daughter.' That's what he told me," says Betty. "So I did."

It was just the way things were in 1957.

Photo courtesy of Betty Ghantous

All Through the Store

Betty first applied at Penn Traffic in 1945, the day after graduating from high school. She was hired on the spot as a full-time gift wrapper and started the following day.

Soon, she became a floating cashier, working as needed in all departments of the store. Eventually, this led to a fixed assignment at the cashier desk in the men's and boys' department on the second floor.

That, in turn, brought bigger and better things. Betty was promoted to a secretarial position in the personnel office, a job that required her to supervise all cashiers and wrappers in the store.

"That job took me throughout the whole store," recalls Betty. "From the fifth floor down to the basement. I had to walk all over and check on all the cashiers and gift wrappers. I didn't just sit at a desk, I was all over."

While traveling the store, she got to know every inch of the place and made plenty of friends. "I got to know everybody that way," she says. "Everyone in the store knew me well."

But her many duties limited the time she had to socialize. Every morning, for example, she had to schedule each cashier's and gift wrapper's breaks, ensuring their stations were covered during their absence. "Everyone got a 15-minute break in the morning," says Betty. "Then a lunch hour. Then another 15-minute break in the afternoon. I was in charge of all that for the whole store."

The Penn Traffic Singers

Betty loved her job right up till the end, when she was three months pregnant and had to leave. She enjoyed her duties, her rounds through the building, the people she got to know...and the singing.

"Every Christmas season, we had a choral group that was always fun and sang in different places. I was in that group, and I loved it.

"The day after Thanksgiving, on Black Friday, we'd sing carols on the central stairs going up from the first floor to the mezzanine. We'd stand on those middle steps, and the clerks would gather around, and we'd all sing Christmas carols.

"It was wonderful. It really put me in the holiday spirit," says Betty.

Friends Remembered

She went on to help her husband establish his business, Elias Painting, which is still a thriving concern. Her son, Albert, who also worked for Penn Traffic at one time, runs the company these days.

And Betty, who is 87, has a little more time to think back on her favorite parts of Penn Traffic...the people, especially.

"I had lots of friends there," she remembers. "We'd get together outside work sometimes and have a ball. On nights when the store was open late, we'd walk up to an Italian restaurant at the top of the Prospect viaduct and have dinner there.

"My best friend in the store was probably Theresa Resoneck, though," says Betty. "She worked with me in the personnel office. We got along really well and had so much fun together.

"Then there was the girl who worked in the photo studio on the mezzanine. I went to lunch with her in the Penn Traffic restaurant a lot. My favorite meal there was hot dogs and sauerkraut.

Photos from Penn Topics Christmas Edition, *1954*

"There were just so many nice people," remembers Betty. "Like the little Italian guy who sold furs. He wanted to sell me a fur so badly, and I kept saying no. I was too short to wear a fur, I told him."

She saw President Samuel Heckman and his grandsons, Dick and Bill Corbin, around the store a lot, too. But one of her fondest memories is courtesy of Lester Leidy, who worked in the display department.

"Mr. Leidy always did a beautiful job on the Christmas windows," says Betty. "I just loved them. Like everyone, I looked forward to them every year.

"When I got married, he gave me a pair of cherubs from that year's Christmas window. He said, 'Here, Betty. Decorate your home with these.' So I used them to decorate our living room.

"And I still have them to this day," says Betty.

Penn Traffic
Our 100th Christmas

and a
Merry, Merry Christmas
to all!

PENN TOPICS

A Christmas Message From Management

We find ourselves again at that season which marks the year's ending and the new year's beginning and are shocked into an awareness that time moves quickly and relentlessly on its endless way.

It seems such a short time ago that we entered our 100th year and now as we approach its end, we think retrospectively of the many unforgettable events that have been shared and enjoyed together.

We express our sincere appreciation for your interest and loyalty. With such splendid cooperation we can enter our second century with high hopes and confidence that we will successfully meet the challenge of serving the community.

Christmas marks the time of year when faith, hope and charity seem to fill the hearts of men and when tolerance and brotherly kindness become more than abstract principles.

As we welcome the coming of the New Year and the beginning of our second century, we earnestly hope that the phenomenal advances made in material progress are matched by men collectively in learning to live at peace with their neighbors and that the spirit of "Peace on Earth, Good Will toward Men," shall prevail.

That you and your families may have a Merry Christmas and a Happy New Year is our sincere wish.

For Shopping Service,
dial 535-3581

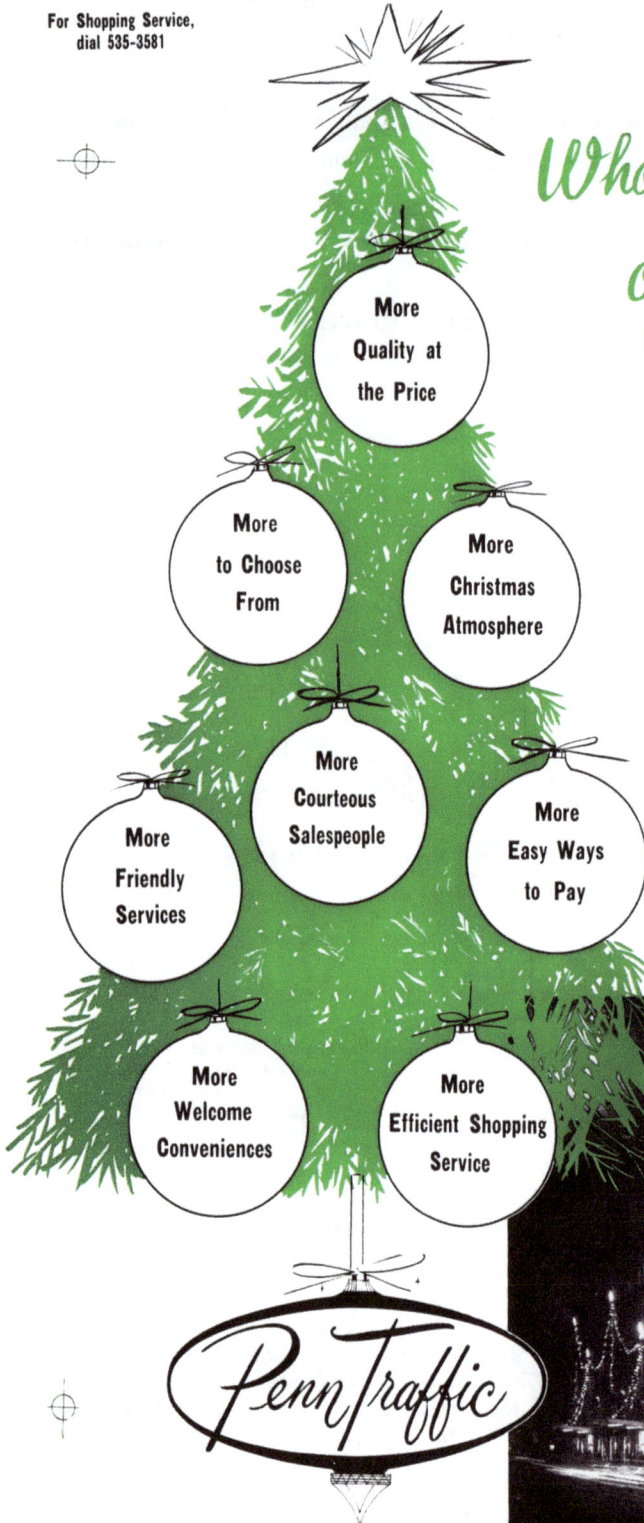

Who has more of what you want?

More Quality at the Price

More to Choose From

More Christmas Atmosphere

More Courteous Salespeople

More Friendly Services

More Easy Ways to Pay

More Welcome Conveniences

More Efficient Shopping Service

Penn Traffic

Penn Traffic has! More to choose from, more Christmas atmosphere, more friendly services, more courteous sales personnel, more of all the things you look for in a store at Christmas time or any time. Shop at the store that has more of what you want, and stands back of what you buy.

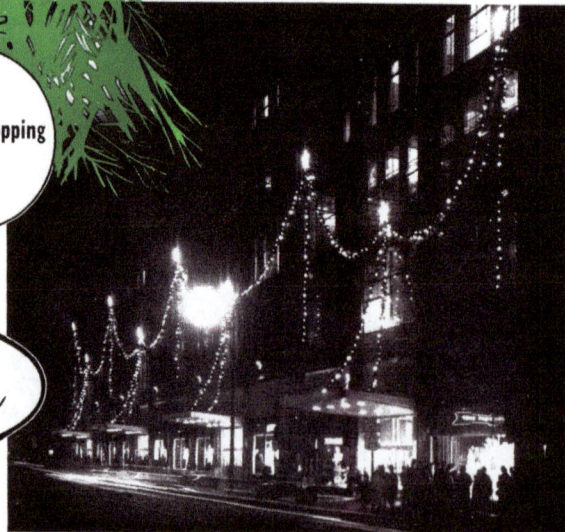

Christmas Shop 9:30 to 9 Friday   Bring the children to see Santa, Fourth Floor

Artwork courtesy of Deb Goldie-Rogers

MEMORY DEPARTMENT

I had lunch there often when I worked in town. I enjoyed everything, especially that delicious stuffing, which I would order with everything. My mom was a waitress there in the 1940s, and she learned how it was made and has passed it on to us. I still make it to this day.

Alicia Krape

How about buying groceries in the grocery department and having them delivered? This was during World War II, when gasoline was rationed.

Natalie Coleman

I worked at Penn Traffic during my last year in high school (1949-1950) making 35¢ an hour. It was a good place to work, and I always enjoyed eating there, also. I started there as a "dish girl," worked up to waitress, and also relieved the hostess and filled in for her when she was off. My boss was Mrs. Heubner, and the usual tip, which you were always glad to see, was 25¢. When we could have our lunch, we only had to pay half-price for it. (Working there was a lot better than when I had worked at Glossers for 25¢ an hour before that.)

Shirley Trautman Boerstler

My mother told me that her mother used to be a chocolate decorator at Penn Traffic. She taught me the meanings of all the designs on top of the chocolates that she had learned from her mother.

What I remember best about the store was going with my mom to all the departments while she taught my sister and I about fine linens and china, how to tell crystal from glass, linen from cotton, plate from silver...well, you get the picture. Afterwards, if we were good, we would go to lunch in the cafeteria. But my favorite part was the ladies' room. It had a lounge where the ladies would sit and compare their purchases. I thought that was the height of class!

Barbara Mainhart

Photo by Hesselbein Studio, courtesy of Johnstown Area Heritage Association

I was a down-in-the-dirt, bruised and scratched tomboy. My parents, grandmother and great-grandmother could not deal with it. They sent me to Penn Traffic etiquette classes. P.S., the classes didn't work!

Mary Elizabeth Clark Margerum

My mother was a waitress at PT back in 1951. Her girlfriend Peggy was also a waitress. Peggy introduced my mother to her brother, who was home on leave from the Marines. He proposed to my mother the night they met, they eloped that week, and are still married. My mother said she got hired at PT because she had experience as a car hop. Back then, it was hard getting a job at PT because everyone wanted in! Her experience gave her a little edge over the competition!

Kathleen Mack

Photo courtesy of Kathleen Mack

Penn Traffic VIP

DICK CORBIN
VICE PRESIDENT IN CHARGE OF
BRANCH STORES
YEARS OF SERVICE 34
1946-1980

The Corbin brothers always come up. Ask anyone who worked at Penn Traffic or its branch stores from the 50s through the 70s about the people they remember most, and they'll always mention the Corbins at some point.

Dick and Bill Corbin were celebrities in the store, with a touch of royalty for good measure. After all, they were the grandsons of Samuel Heckman, the legendary top executive who'd built and shaped the company from 1909 to the 1950s.

But more than that, Dick and Bill were respected and well-liked in the store. They were often seen making the rounds of the place, together or separately--dark-haired Dick and Bill the blond.

They worked their way up through the ranks and carried their weight throughout their careers. And they always made it a point to be friendly and helpful, no matter how high up the food chain they got.

From the Bulge to the Bottom

Dick came to work at Penn Traffic in 1946, after serving in Europe during World War II. As part of the 84th Infantry Division, he'd fought in one of the most famous battles of the war, the Battle of the Bulge.

Photos from Penn Traffic 1968 Annual Report

71

In spite of his connection to President Heckman, he started at the bottom, receiving and marking merchandise in the stockroom.

From there, Dick eventually moved to the merchandise division, supporting all departments of the store. It was the perfect opportunity to learn everything he could about all aspects of the operation.

Working under the merchandising manager, Dick got experience buying merchandise and developing sales. "The merchandise division would decide what inventory the departments should be aiming for, and allot the money they were allowed to spend to reach those goals," explains Dick. "Then we would set up the sales and work with the advertising department to promote them."

Business at the time was going strong. The postwar recovery was in full swing, and the economy in general was booming. There was more than enough work to keep Dick busy.

Photo from Penn Traffic 1976 Annual Report

PENN TRAFFIC— RICHLAND MALL HAS EXPANDED (AND MANY DEPTS. IN WESTWOOD, TOO)

We're expanding departments and services in our Richland Mall store and some departments in our Westwood store.

You'll discover our beautiful updated merchandise, helpful sales personnel, and our long-standing reputation for fashion leadership and value . . . all continuing the Penn Traffic tradition of serving you better. Shop Penn Traffic Richland Mall and Westwood.

. . . FOR YOUR SHOPPING CONVENIENCE! PENN TRAFFIC HAS EXPANDED MANY OF THE DEPARTMENTS IN RICHLAND MALL

- new furniture center
- expanded curtains-draperies
- expanded rugs and carpeting
- expanded china and silver
- expanded all fashion departments
- expanded men's clothing-suits

. . . FOR YOUR SHOPPING CONVENIENCE, PENN TRAFFIC HAS RELOCATED THESE DEPARTMENTS INTO RICHLAND MALL

- relocated bridal gowns and the bridal registry into Richland Mall
- relocated tailors and alterations departments into the Richland Mall
- relocated expert trained furniture, carpet, and drapery personnel from the downtown store to Richland Mall

Penn Traffic

• SHOP RICHLAND MALL AND WESTWOOD 10 TO 10 DAILY •

Branching Out

He stayed in merchandising until the early 1960s, when the company started opening branch stores. Penn Traffic needed someone to oversee those new stores, and Dick was in the right place at the right time (with the right experience, thanks to working his way up from the bottom) to do the job.

The company started with two new stores (in Indiana, PA and Westmont) in 1962, then rolled out more every few years after that. Dick helped develop, open, and manage all of them.

"I was in charge of everything from directing the installation of fixtures to putting in the proper merchandise," says Dick. "I also worked with Penn Traffic's personnel director to hire all the managers and area supervisors."

Thanks in part to his efforts, the branch stores were a success for the company...at least until they were sold to Hess's in 1982. But by then, Dick was already gone.

He retired in 1980 after 35 years with Penn Traffic and moved to Sanibel Island, Florida, where he went into business with his son.

BROTHERS PROMOTED

Richard Corbin of 812 Luzerne Street *(left)* and William Corbin of 900 Luzerne Street, brothers, have been promoted by Penn Traffic Company. They are sons of Mrs. Harry D. Corbin of Menoher Boulevard and the late Mr. Corbin and grandsons of the late S. H. Heckman, who for many years was president and general manager of Penn Traffic. Richard Corbin, who joined the downtown store in 1946, has been named director of research and development, a newly created division. A graduate of Washington & Lee University and an Army veteran, he served in the store's merchandise office before becoming assistant general merchandise manager in 1955. He is married to the former Dorothy Faverty and is the father of two sons and a daughter. William Corbin is married to the former Carolyn Griffith and is the father of two sons. Also a graduate of Washington & Lee, he was with the Federal Bureau of Investigation in New York before joining Penn Traffic in 1953. He had been assistant divisional manager of women's fashions since 1955 and now becomes assistant general merchandise manager, filling the position vacated by his brother.

Bill Corbin, F.B.I.

Brother Bill's career at Penn Traffic took a different tack. Three years younger than Dick, he also served in World War II, followed by a stint in the F.B.I. After transferring to Alabama, then Georgia, then New York City, he decided he'd rather return to Johnstown to raise his family.

So he quit the F.B.I. and got a job at Penn Traffic. Dick, who'd already been working there for some time, encouraged and supported him from the start.

"We got along really well," says Dick. "He was outgoing and had a nice personality, and we worked well together.

"Did I mention he was also a heck of a lot better-looking than I was?" Dick laughs.

With his eagerness to learn and strong work ethic, Bill succeeded at Penn Traffic. Like Dick, he found a place in the merchandising division--but where Dick moved on to the branch stores, Bill stayed in merchandising. Eventually, he was put in charge

of that division and became Vice President of the Johnstown Department Store.

He spent more than 30 years at Penn Traffic before retiring to Florida, like his brother. He died in 2000.

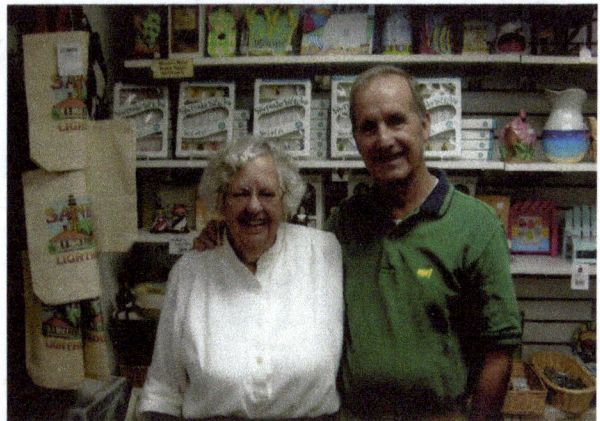

Full Circle

Today, at age 92, Dick has come full circle.

After starting at the bottom at Penn Traffic in 1946, he's at the bottom again...in a way. These days, he works as a sales clerk at Sand Castle Gifts & Gourmet in Sanibel, Florida, the store he started years ago with his son, Steve.

New owners run the store now, but Dick still enjoys going in and keeping busy. "I urge everyone to stay active physically and mentally," he says. "It's too easy to just get on the couch and waste away."

The work reminds him of his past retail career at Penn Traffic. "It was a great place to work. We had no internal problems. Everybody got along well.

"We had a quarter-century club that had a whole bunch of people in it. There were people who'd worked there 30 or 40 years, because it such a good place to work. Not just for executives, but for everyone.

"It was a wonderful store, and it gave those of us who worked there a very pleasant life," says Dick.

Photos courtesy of Dick Corbin

Photo courtesy of Darrel Holsopple

Chapter Eleven

Blowing Out 100 Candles

1954

Penn Traffic knew how to throw a party. When its hundredth anniversary year arrived in 1954, the company milked it for all it was worth.

The first quarter of that year, from January through March, was all about the anniversary. There were banquets, parties, fashion shows, contests, special window displays...and, of course, a heck of a sale. This was retail, after all.

Advertising, including a host of newspaper ads, home mailers, and 73 billboards, spread the message far and wide. You couldn't miss it, and why would you want to?

Penn Traffic was having a 100th birthday party, and everyone was invited.

All Prizes Are Hats

Thanks to extensive planning and arrangements the year before, the Penn Traffic staff was able to roll out its series of first quarter events in quick succession, all while completing yet another facilities upgrade and ramping up for the sale of the century.

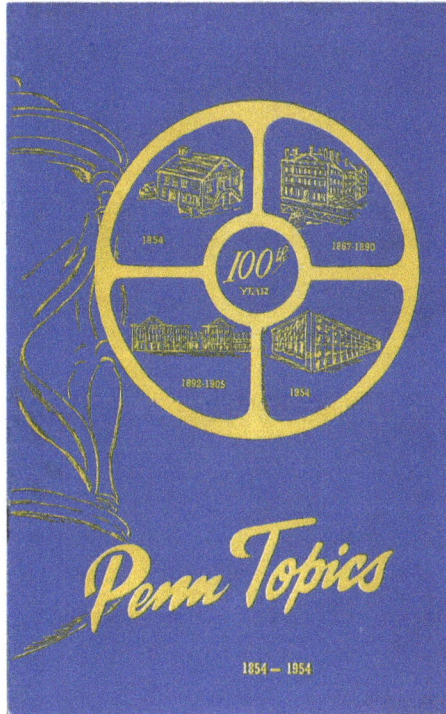

The upgrade resulted in the modernization of the first floor, plus the acquisition and renovation of the Swope Building on Main Street for use as a warehouse, TV and appliance service center, and a shop for drapery making, carpet cutting, and furniture refinishing.

As for the sale, Penn Traffic personnel worked diligently, starting in the previous quarter, to complete all planning, ordering, and preparations. Even in the midst of all that, they were able to consider other important parts of the anniversary...like hats and dioramas.

An Old Time Hat Contest ran January 15-30, attracting 231 contestants. The winners received new hats from the store millinery--a $25 hat for first prize, a $13.95 hat for second, and an $8.95 hat for third.

Photo from Penn Topics

Meanwhile, new anniversary-related displays were unveiled in the windows on January 17. Six windows featured dioramas depicting historical scenes: the exterior of the Stiles, Allen & Co. store in 1854; the interior of the same store; the exterior of the third store in 1891; the Pennsylvania Canal basin in Johnstown; an aqueduct across the Little Conemaugh River in 1845; and one of the ten inclined planes used by the Portage Railroad. The three Penn Traffic-related dioramas were created by the store's display department, led by Mr. Montgomery. The other three were designed and constructed by Evan Parcell of Washington, PA.

In addition to the dioramas, historical displays were installed in other windows. The "Father Time Window" housed an exhibit of old shoes dating from 1906. The big corner window included authentic old costumes, an old bicycle, a baby carriage, and other antiques, set up in front of a backdrop of an old Washington Street scene painted on velvet.

Even as the anniversary window displays were unveiled, the slate of events continued to move forward. The Quarter Century Club banquet was held on January 20, honoring employees who'd been with the company at least 25 years. A total of 170 members and guests attended, including eight new members admitted to the club that night.

Photos courtesy of Darrel Holsopple

76

A Dinner to Remember

Next came the biggest event of all: the official 100th anniversary dinner on Wednesday, February 10 at 7 P.M. The gala affair at the War Memorial Arena was open only to employees--no families or other guests. According to the final tally, 750 of them attended, coming together to celebrate the company's first century in business.

"I was there," says Marie Neff, who worked at Penn Traffic from 1945 to 1982. "All the bosses and their wives were there, too. It was a beautiful time, and it was so much fun to be there."

As the Penn Traffic family dined on baked steak, "Potatoes Conemaugh," "G.M. Peas" (a play on the store's "G.M.P." layaway program, or "Group Merchandise Plan"), and "Cold Slaw Joseph Johns" (with "Century Ice Cream" for dessert), they were entertained by Tommy Piro and his orchestra. The diners joined in group singalongs, too, crooning standards with special lyrics adapted for the occasion, like this one, sung to the tune of "I've Been Working on the Railroad":

I've been working at the Pee-Tee
All the live-long day.
I've been working at the Pee-Tee
That's where I get my pay
I can see the century going
In-to His-to-ry this year
But I guess I won't be help-ing
The next hund-redth cheer!

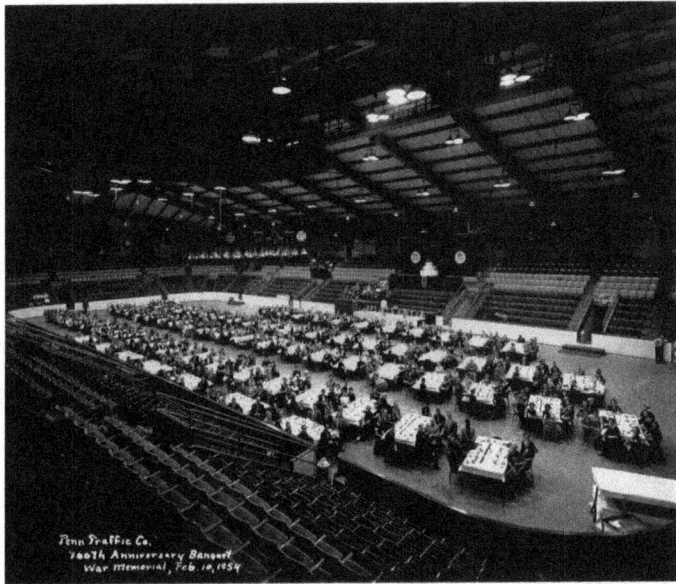

Photo courtesy of Darrel Holsopple

Honoring Heckman

After dinner, there were speeches, toasts, and a performance by the 35-voice Kiwanis Chorus of Altoona, directed by Howard Lindaman. General Manager Karl Eckel delivered the anniversary message, praising the employees for their part in the store's progress.

Photo from Penn Topics

"Management is proud of the store family--a wonderful group of people," said Eckel. "We want to express our sincere appreciation for your past cooperation. With your continued interest and loyalty we can approach the future with high hopes and confidence – with a determination through the common endeavor all of us to keep Penn Traffic moving ever forward."

Eckel spoke optimistically about future prospects for the company and the country it called home. "America has never been more prosperous. Never have so many fruits of our labors been available to make life easier and happier for all. Never have the new frontiers created by science, technology and business been more exciting.

"Thank God for America, our wonderful country of limitless opportunity, where the rights of an individual are considered important and where under a system of free enterprise an institution can grow and prosper."

Eckel also singled out Samuel Heckman for his contributions. The company president, who was 81 years old at the time, was at the head table with the other VIPs.

"As we think of steps in our development, it naturally directs our thoughts to our beloved president, Mr. Heckman," said Eckel. "With over 50 years of service, he has had a hand in most of the important steps the company has taken.

"A man of sound judgment and great modesty, whose only desire throughout his long period of service, has been not to gain fame or personal glory but to build an institution which would merit the confidence of the entire community. To a high degree the Penn Traffic as it is known today is a living testimonial to his splendid leadership."

Eckel's comments were the perfect lead-in to the night's final highlight. As the crowd sang "God Bless America," a bronze plaque was presented to Mr. Heckman, commemorating his work with the company.

The plaque read: "A tribute to Samuel H. Heckman, president of Penn Traffic Company, from his associates, in appreciation of his kindness and inspiration and his constant regard for our welfare. Presented on the occasion of Penn Traffic Company's 100th anniversary, February 1954."

"I was so happy for my grandfather to be receiving this special honor," says Dick Corbin, who was at the dinner that night. "I was so proud of him."

After the plaque presentation, there was dancing to the music of the orchestra. "Everybody danced," remembers Betty Ghantous, who attended the dinner. "At the time, formal dancing was at its peak. I just loved it."

Drag Time!

How could Penn Traffic top that historic dinner at the War Memorial? With a drag show, of course!

Actually, men in drag were just one part of the next event, a special edition of the annual store party held at the Johnstown Masonic Temple. It happened on February 25, 1954, and brought in a whopping 1,000 employees and guests.

Photos courtesy of Darrel Holsopple

There was food, bingo, and dancing, but the highlight was an entertainment program put together by the organizers. Introduced by commentator Margaret Schultz, employees performed a variety of musical numbers and comedy skits, plus a "fashion show" starring male co-workers dressed in drag. One after another, men in women's clothing and wigs trotted across the stage, clowning around and even dancing in a chorus line.

The Masonic Temple roared with laughter as the Penn Traffic family celebrated the 100th anniversary in their own raucous, rowdy way, a contrast from the elegant decorum of the dinner at the War Memorial.

"Dagmar" Dittmar

Photo from Penn Topics

Lee   Lou   Sam
Renz   Mazlo   Mosholder

Photos from Penn Topics

"Zsa Zsa"
Gunter

Photo from Penn Topics

Photo courtesy of Darrel Holsopple

Photo courtesy of Darrel Holsopple

New York Models Turn Heads

The next big event of the anniversary was a fashion show--a *real* one, not a drag revue.

The show, with the theme "Then and Now," took place at the War Memorial on March 12. Tickets were priced at $1.50 and sold by local hospital auxiliary volunteers.

Some 4,000 people showed up to watch a presentation of cutting edge fashions, plus vintage outfits (rented from Helen Virginia Meyers in New York) honoring Penn Traffic's birth in 1854. Bridal attire and swimwear were also featured.

Fifteen models from the store walked the runway, along with five "nationally famous professional models" and commentator Susan Trowbridge from the John Robert Powers Agency in New York City. The Powers Agency models included Teddy Ayer, Glendora Donaldson, Ruth Parkes Keller, Stasia Linder, and Rita Tennant.

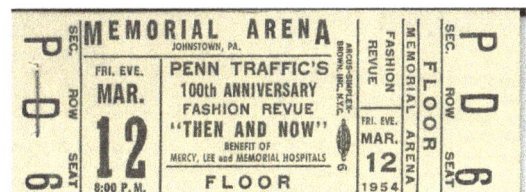

Showing off fashions was only part of the show, however. Door prizes were also handed out, including a $100 Penn Traffic gift certificate, a bottle of Shalimar perfume, and a bottle of Chanel No. 5.

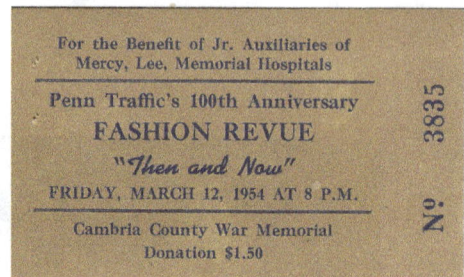

For the Benefit of Jr. Auxiliaries of
Mercy, Lee, Memorial Hospitals
Penn Traffic's 100th Anniversary
FASHION REVUE
"Then and Now"
FRIDAY, MARCH 12, 1954 AT 8 P.M.
Cambria County War Memorial
Donation $1.50

Nº 3835

Local hospital auxiliaries were big winners, too, as the proceeds of the fashion show were donated to benefit their activities. Penn Traffic Secretary-Treasurer G. Fesler Edwards handed out checks to the presidents of three local auxiliaries: Memorial received $3,175; Mercy got $1,429; and Lee got $1,360.

Sale of the Century

As all these events were held, from the hat contest to the fashion show, a huge 100th Anniversary Sale was underway at the store. The sale, which ran from February 16 through March 13, was comprehensive, heavily promoted...and came with high expectations from management.

"A review of the merchandise to be presented reveals values the like of which we have never before offered," said Karl Eckel in his remarks at the anniversary dinner. "From every indication, our customers are anxiously awaiting the opening day--so let's turn loose that friendly PT selling charm you are capable of and make this the greatest sale ever."

Photos from Penn Topics

The big investment in advertising paid off, as shoppers turned out in droves. Sales figures were strong, and goals were met, due in part, no doubt, to the company's philosophy as practiced by its sales force.

"An alert attitude toward our work is necessary," said Karl Eckel, "as we try our level best by our customer contacts, personal interest, knowledge of merchandise, intelligent selling, and courteous service to convince customers that Penn Traffic is the place to come for their every need."

Photo courtesy of Darrel Holsopple

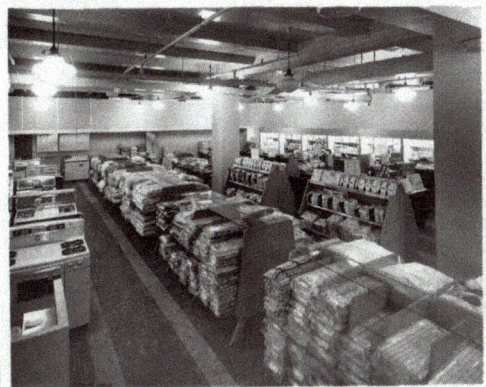
Photo courtesy of Darrel Holsopple

Photo by Russell Heffley, courtesy of Darrel Holsopple

Photo courtesy of Darrel Holsopple

Photo courtesy of Darrel Holsopple

MEMORY DEPARTMENT

I remember trips to Penn Traffic with my Aunt Ethel the week before Easter to shop for a new dress, hat, gloves, and a purse. We would have such fun walking through every inch of the store, oohing and aahing about all the beautiful things we saw. Then the most special thing, eating in the restaurant--a club sandwich and a chocolate milkshake--so delicious! Wonderful memories (circa 1951).

Gretchen Redick Rogers

My husband, Jerry Langer, saw Howdy Doody, Buffalo Bob Smith, and Clara Bell at Penn Traffic in 1953. He got squirted with seltzer water by Clara Bell! Great memories!

Suzanne Klucik Langer

I remember going shopping with my mother and Aunt Ann and stopping in the restaurant for a piece of pie as a treat. I also remember Penn Traffic delivering things directly to our house. I still have my Aunt's Penn Traffic charge plate somewhere, in a pretty case with a keychain from Hallman's Chevrolet! An oh-so-feminine touch from the 1950s!

Beth Paczolt Weiner

My Dad, Dick Walsh, leased space in Penn Traffic from 1956 until the closing of the store. He sold sewing machines on the mezzanine. I grew up in that store, going up and down the back stairways and working for my dad, first at his workshop in our house helping him repair machines... then in the warehouse getting new machines ready for delivery...and in high school and college on the floor selling machines and accessories to customers.

I have many great memories of the store, the people who worked there, the restaurant (hot turkey sandwiches with gravy), and the candy counter with the Penn Way candy made on the fifth floor by Harry Steele and his staff. Now I go into the building to the courtrooms, and in breaks between cases, fondly remember where each department was located.

What memories!

Jim Walsh

In the late '50s, if we carried a heavy schedule in high school at Westmont, we could get permission to take swimming at the "Y" on Friday afternoons when we had early dismissal. Too many times I skipped swimming and joined my friends at the Penn Traffic restaurant for their Chocolate Mint Parfait. Irresistible!

Linda Goble

Penn Traffic had the best Santa Claus in the late 1950s. My parents took my sister and me each Christmas to have our picture taken with him. He was a sweet, kind, and very authentic-looking Santa.

Diane Rooney Bennett

I worked in ladies' clothing at Penn Traffic while in college. I also modeled some, at the store's bridal shows. At size 8/10, I represented the chubby bride. In the late '50s, I bought glassware (bowls, berry dishes, and more for 10¢ and 25¢). It was from one of the Ohio glass makers who was going out of business; best bargain ever at Penn Traffic. It even impressed my mom.

I still have an Easter candy egg box. Loved the coconut. Mom got fruit and nut, too.

I also remember being mesmerized by the Christmas windows. My aunt, Geri Jurasek, also worked there and modeled. She was beautiful.

Eleanor Kisha Donovan

Penn Traffic VIP

MARIE NEFF
ACCOUNTS PAYABLE (AND MODELING)
YEARS OF SERVICE 37
1945-1982

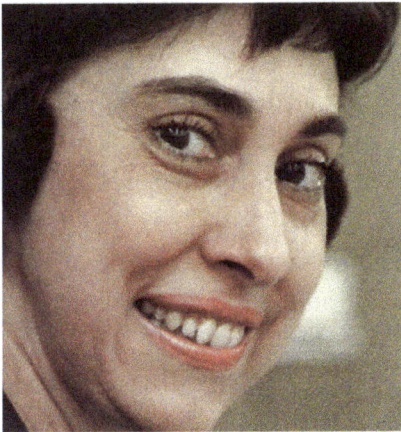

Photo from Penn Traffic 1974 Annual Report

Marie Neff was walking down the runway at the Penn Traffic bridal show, modeling a bridesmaid's outfit, when her headpiece flew up in the air.

"It just went *zingo*, right off my head!" she remembers. "But I took it in stride. I reached right up and caught it and pulled it back down, and everyone clapped."

It made for a memorable bridal show, though it was just one moment of a long and memorable career. Marie is a 37-year veteran of Penn Traffic, one of the few people you can talk to who worked under both Samuel Heckman and Larry Rosen--the president most responsible for building the company and the last president of the department store division.

Pasta Under Pressure

Marie has seen, and heard, an extraordinary amount of the company's history... some momentous...and some hilarious, like the story of the pasta and the pressure cooker.

"I remember Mr. George Sudcop was the manager of the housewares department when pressure cookers first came out," says Marie. "This is when I was working in the accounts payable office.

"George came up to accounts payable and told us about this lady who came in and was all upset. It turns out she was cooking spaghetti in her pressure cooker and the lid let go and she had it all over her ceiling.

"Let me tell you, we laughed our heads off at that! I said you know what, George, that wasn't fair. I'm sure that poor soul had a terrible time getting all that spaghetti and sauce off her ceiling."

Something Terrifically Horrible

Even with plenty to laugh about, 37 years seems like a long time to work in one place. How then did Marie manage to sustain such a lengthy career?

"Penn Traffic really held on to you. They tried to help you," says Marie. "They didn't just fire you for any little thing. They really were very lenient, and it was just a good place to work. You felt very confident when you went to work in the morning. I loved it.

"We always used to say, the only way you would leave Penn Traffic is if you did something terrifically horrible, and they fired you, or if you got another job and left on your own, or if you died and they carried you out," says Marie.

It didn't turn out quite that way in the end. Marie lost her job in 1982, when Hess's bought the department store division, and her work in the accounts payable office dried up.

But until then, it was a heck of a ride. And it all started with going to church at the tail end of the Second World War.

Pew-to-Pew Networking

After graduating from Johnstown High in June 1945, Marie was determined to find a job. Penn Traffic came to mind, since the store's vice president, Karl Eckel, went to the same church she attended. So one Sunday morning at Zion Lutheran, she asked Mr. Eckel if he knew of a job for her at Penn Traffic.

Marie's pew-to-pew networking paid off. Mr. Eckel told her parents to bring her in for an interview, and she was hired in August (right around the time of another historic event, when the Japanese surrendered to the Allies, effectively ending World War II).

In her first days at Penn Traffic, Marie worked as a clerk on the first floor, selling umbrellas and gloves. She enjoyed the work, especially events like the annual Men's Night.

"Every Christmas season, the guys would have a whole night at Penn Traffic by themselves to buy gifts for their wives, girlfriends, mothers, sisters, or daughters," says Marie. "It was a hoot, it really was.

"We used to have a ball, joking around and helping the men find the right gifts. Some of those poor guys needed all the help they could get!"

Though working on the sales floor was fun, it wasn't long until Marie left for an office job upstairs. She went to work in the accounts payable office on the fifth floor, starting at the order desk.

"When department managers ordered something, we got invoices that we had to check against their orders," recalls Marie. "The managers would come up to the order desk, and we'd look up the status of their orders in our files. Then we'd tell them what had come in, what hadn't, and what they needed to reorder."

Because You're a Penn Traffic Girl

Eventually, Marie left the order desk and went to work on the bookkeeping machines. After that, she became a full-fledged bookkeeper, tracking and reporting on the company's finances.

"Every day, we got all the receipts from the downtown Penn Traffic store," remembers Marie.

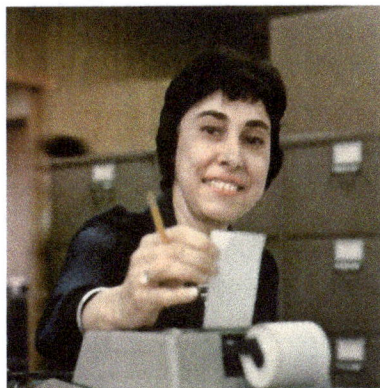
Photo from Penn Traffic 1974 Annual Report

"Later, when we expanded with the PT stores, all their receipts came in, too.

"I worked with the cashier's office, the accounting office, and the controller to pull in and process all the numbers. Then, we issued our daily reports on sales, what we had in the bank, and our overall finances."

The controller, John Gunter, was Marie's boss and oversaw her efforts. "He was very nice, a real gentleman. All the bosses were. I really liked all of them, and I loved my job.

"I was proud to work there. I knew it meant something. The store had so much prestige.

"Once, I was told by a businessman in Johnstown, if you ever get tired of working there, come and see me for a job. You won't even need a resume. I asked him why, and he just said, because you're a Penn Traffic girl."

Life on the Runway

The demand for Penn Traffic girls didn't end with offers of full-time employment, however. Local companies also came calling when Marie started her modeling career.

"I modeled for the bridal shows at Penn Traffic, and that was a lot of fun," says Marie. "They were held on the second floor, and we always had nice crowds for them. The organizers picked different girls from around the store, and I was one of them.

From Penn Topics

"People from other stores liked what they saw and tried to recruit me to model for them. For example, a local furrier wanted me to model his company's furs. I had to ask Mr. Gunter, because Penn Traffic sold furs, too, but he didn't mind. He said Penn Traffic wanted to stay on friendly terms with other Johnstown merchants, so it was perfectly okay."

Modeling for Penn Traffic was still Marie's favorite, though, even if the fashion shows sometimes got a little crazy. "Once, they put me in a bridal gown that had buttons all the way up the back of the neck. Naturally, I was in a big hurry between outfits and had to get back on stage really fast.

"Two helpers were behind me, frantically buttoning me up at the last minute. Then, the announcer gave my cue, and I had to start walking. They barely got the last button closed as I stepped out on the runway. It was all I could do to keep a straight face."

As fun and crazy as modeling could be, it also helped Marie make a difference in the community. Through the years, it became an important part of the volunteer work she did as a member of the Lee Hospital Auxiliary.

Bedpans for Presidents

Penn Traffic encouraged its employees to volunteer for organizations that helped the community. Marie answered the call by joining the Lee Hospital Auxiliary as a Red Cross nurse's aide in 1952.

She liked it so much that she was still there when Lee was sold to Conemaugh Health System in 2005. "I was heartbroken when it was sold. When I went to work as a volunteer there, everybody was just wonderful. When we left at night, the doctors would even come out and thank us."

Not to mention, there were plenty of opportunities for comedy.

"I remember once I was carrying two empty bedpans, one in each hand," says Marie. "I was coming out of a room, and I ran right into Mr. Edwards, president of Penn Traffic! I said to him, oops! He just looked at me and laughed. I said, well, now you know what I do in my spare time! From then on, he kind'a grinned every time he saw me at the store."

Then there was the time she got over her fear of blood. "I couldn't stand the sight of blood. It made me sick.

"Then, one night, I had to work in the emergency room. Wouldn't you know it, we had a real run of blood and guts.

"The longer I was there, the worse the patients we got, everything from a little kid to football players. I swear, they must've had a rock fight somewhere, because all I got done doing was helping clean out holes in the head and cleaning bloody instruments.

"When it was all over, I came home and said to Mother, well, I'm over the blood thing."

Aside from her duties as a nurse's aide, Marie also modeled in benefit style shows that raised money for the hospital. But fashion shows weren't the only benefits they had.

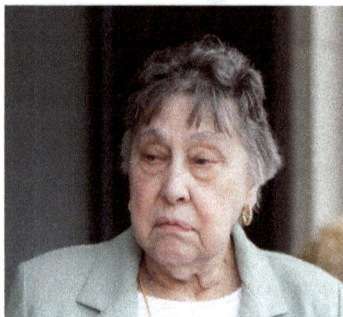

"We had a horse show down at Point Stadium once, and I had to go out and give trophies to the winners. I'll tell you what, I never felt so humble as when I had to give somebody a trophy and walk off the field with a horse's behind staring me in the face.

"Then they found a copperhead snake in one of the hay bales. I'd been sitting on those bales, waiting to give out the trophies! I could've been bitten!"

The Unforgettable Flavor

After losing her job at Penn Traffic after the department store sale to Hess's in 1982, Marie went to work for a local ophthalmologist, Dr. Robert Winstanley. When he retired, she accepted a job with Dr. Dan Carusi.

Now retired herself, she still thinks about her Penn Traffic days...the people, especially.

"I liked everybody who worked there. They were all friendly and ready to help you. You knew if they told you something, you could believe them."

She misses the quality merchandise, too. "You could buy anything in Penn Traffic. You could walk in there and get anything.

"And the merchandise was always beautiful and very, very good.

Photos by Philip Balko

88

"Then they had the budget store down in the basement, and that was still very nice. I'd go down there and buy things, because that was good quality, too, and a little bit less expensive than upstairs."

Photo by Russell Heffley, courtesy of Darrel Holsopple

Photo by Russell Heffley, courtesy of Darrel Holsopple

But what does she miss most? It might just be a baked good.

"My mother would call me at work and say we were having spaghetti, go down and get some rolls. I knew exactly what she wanted.

"They made rolls at the Penn Traffic bakery with sesame seeds on them, and they were *soooo* good. You had to get there in time, as soon as they came out of the oven, because they always sold out. Everybody wanted those fresh, warm rolls with the sesame seeds on top.

"I swear, I can still taste them."

Bakery photo by Hesselbein Studio, courtesy of Johnstown Area Heritage Association

Soon the doorway opens to a New Year

but one by one our own doorways will
close until each has had a face lifting

Penn Traffic is continuing its long-range program of modernization. You've probably seen signs of it already. This time it's NEW ENTRANCES. One by one the old ones will be converted to doorways of such modern beauty as the architect's sketch you see here, and Penn Traffic hopes that as many of you will pass through these new portals (and as often), in 1957 and the years to come, as through the old ones in 1956.

In spite of barricades and obstacles outside, there will be as warm a welcome as ever awaiting you inside, and we hope that in the coming months you will regard our face-lifting operation not as an inconvenience, but as evidence of our faith in the future of Johnstown and of Penn Traffic, and particularly our interest in you as customers, who welcome attractive entrances to the store you shop in just as much as you do attractive doorways in the homes you visit.

Open 9 to 5 today and MONDAY

Closed Tuesday, January 1

Chapter Twelve

The Tapping Stops

1956-1958

Karl Eckel had a thing for sprucing the place up. Two years after the 100th anniversary, he embarked on another improvement plan for the store at a cost of $100,000.

This one was all about the front doors. The four entrances along Washington Street would be remodeled and modernized, and new marquees would be installed over the doorways.

"This is a further indication of our faith in the downtown area as a shopping center," Karl Eckel told the *Tribune-Democrat* at the start of the project, just after Christmas in 1956.

The work was finished the following summer. It doubled the size of the entrance leading into the men's store, which was probably the most widely used door in the store at the time. Gleaming new aluminum and glass fittings were installed at all four entrances. The store looked better and more modern than ever.

Photos courtesy of Darrel Holsopple

91

The improvements came just in time for big changes at Penn Traffic--the beginning of the biggest growth spurt in company history. But first, what was perhaps the biggest change of all was about to occur...the equivalent, at Penn Traffic, of an earthquake measuring 9.0 on the Richter scale.

The grand old man of the store was on his last legs.

Samuel H. Heckman, R.I.P.

Had anyone at Penn Traffic been there as long as Mr. Heckman? Had anyone does as much as he'd done to grow the business? Had anyone else at the store done as much to improve the local community and the lives of those in need who lived there?

Would anyone leave as big a hole in the world when he died?

The answers to these questions seemed obvious on August 26, 1958, when Sam died at the age of 86. He collapsed at home from what was thought to be a stroke and was taken to Memorial Hospital, where he died later that day.

In spite of his advanced age, his death stunned the Penn Traffic family. Everyone was so used to seeing him at the store, walking the floors to review the state of the business, that it was inconceivable to think he was gone. It was impossible to imagine the store without the tapping of his cane.

He had been a guiding force and more since long before most of the employees had been working there. He had become so identified with the place, that the two had become inextricably linked. For as long as he lived, he never left it for long; he never resigned as president, never stopped being protector.

Yet, suddenly, he was gone. The bronze plaque with his face on it, presented at the 100th anniversary dinner, still hung in the store's lobby, but the flesh and bone features on which it had been modeled were never coming back.

Could Penn Traffic thrive without him? Could the company stay on track without his guidance?

These questions were about to be answered the hard way, the only way they could be. The future was coming on strong, and Samuel Heckman would not be a part of it.

A TRIBUTE TO
SAMUEL H. HECKMAN
PRESIDENT OF PENN TRAFFIC COMPANY
FROM HIS ASSOCIATES

From Penn Topics

Penn Traffic VIP

PAULA & KATHY FELIX
THE PENN TRAFFIC BRATS
YEARS OF FUN 1950S-1960S

Imagine, as a child, having the run of the downtown Penn Traffic store when it was closed on Sundays.

Imagine getting to sit on the laps of the switchboard operators when they were taking calls in their hidden niche.

Imagine getting to watch the annual Christmas parade from the best seat in the house--the windows on the fifth floor of the Penn Traffic Building.

Perhaps best of all, imagine getting a private preview of the top secret new Christmas window displays before anyone else in Johnstown.

Permission to feel jealous, *granted*. Because Paula and Kathy Felix experienced all this wonderfulness and more.

The Boss's Daughters

Kathy and Paula practically grew up in the downtown store, which in those days was like growing up in Walt Disney Land. They got to experience life behind the scenes of Penn Traffic like few other people, because their father, Elit Felix, was the store's chief accountant.

"We grew up as the Penn Traffic brats," remembers Paula, whose last name is Kellar these days. "We had the run of the place, though we were never allowed to behave badly because our father worked there."

Photos courtesy of Katherine Moser

93

"It was like a home to us," says Kathy, whose last name is now Moser. "It was very, very special. I loved it."

The Felix girls were born five years apart--Paula in 1947 and Kathy in 1952. Their Penn Traffic adventures happened mostly in the mid-to-late 50s, during the time many consider to be the golden age of the store.

Today, they both treasure their memories of those years and realize how lucky they were to grow up in such a magical place.

Scary Hair Dryers

One of the privileges they enjoyed was spending time at Penn Traffic when it was closed to the general public. "The store was closed on Sundays because of the blue laws," remembers Kathy. "Often, that was when my father took us with him to the store...I think because my mother wanted to get us out of her hair for a while.

"While Dad worked on the books or whatever he did, I would play. I would also take tours of the store with the watchman, who was an old friend of my father and mother's. He would take me with him on his rounds. He had a little machine with him, and he turned the key in certain locations. Every once in a while, he would let me turn it instead."

Kathy loved exploring the deserted store on Sundays, when everything seemed so different and strange and magical. But sometimes, it seemed a little scary to her, as well.

"There were two places that frightened me when I was little," she recalls. "First, there was the beauty salon,

because the hair dryers were scary-looking. Then, in the men's department, there was one stairway that always terrified me, because I got locked inside it one time. My father was in the accounting office on the fifth floor, and he called down to me, but I got confused and didn't know which way to go."

Photos courtesy of Darrel Holsopple

Second Family

As much fun as it was to explore Penn Traffic after hours, the girls also loved visiting when the store was open for business. It was then that they got to take advantage of various attractions and spend time with the employees, who were like a second family to them.

"The employees all knew us and would watch out for us," says Paula. "We would ride down on the bus and get off at the corner, and one of them would meet us.

"If Kathy and I were visiting Dad in his office, and we needed to go somewhere, Dad or someone who worked with him would phone ahead and ask an employee to watch out for us."

The Felix sisters still remember many of the staffers who befriended them back in the day. The female elevator operator, for instance, was friendly and always looked out for the girls (and their brother, Elit, who sometimes joined their adventures).

Kathy loved going to see the women in the candy kitchen. "I got to see how they did the pretty designs on top of the pieces of candy. This one candy had a certain design, and this other candy had another design, and I remember them

Photo courtesy of Darrel Holsopple

doing that, and they were very patient and explained it all to me. I was not allowed to do it myself, of course, but they explained it to me."

"I remember there was a maintenance person named Sam," says Paula. "He would say to us, 'Do you children want to take a walk with me?' And we would say, sure, why not? He'd take us all over the building."

Some of the girls' other favorite people worked at the switchboard, which was located on an upper floor, away from the prying eyes of customers. "They had a space like a narrow hallway, and there were maybe 20 phone operators in there, lined up against the wall," explains Paula.

"They worked with a massive phone switchboard. Each of them wore a headset with a microphone attached. They spent the day connecting calls by hand using colored cords with bullet-shaped plugs on the end.

"They would let us sit on their laps when it wasn't busy and connect calls. It was pretty cool. I liked doing that," says Paula.

The Marble Bathroom

The switchboard was one of the sisters' favorite places in the store. So was the restaurant.

"I remember the restaurant being all red," says Kathy. "It was very plush. We went there on special occasions with the whole family."

Paula still remembers her favorite foods from the menu. "On Thursday, they would have mashed potatoes, gravy, and stuffing...the best stuffing on God's Earth. And of course they had all kinds of desserts made in my beloved bakery."

Kathy also loved the bakery, especially the Spanish bar cake. They also made Paula's favorite, raisin-filled cookies.

Paula liked spending time in the music department. "They had sound booths where you could play records and see if you wanted to buy them. The booths were wood up to your waist, then glass above that so people could see you weren't throwing the records around or anything like that."

Then there was the ladies' room on the mezzanine, which both girls loved. "It was all marble, and it was beautiful in there," remembers Paula. "There must have been ten seats, and all these marble stalls and a marble floor and walls. When someone flushed the toilet or ran water in a sink, the noise echoed and was almost deafening. It really echoed in that space."

"The ladies' room doorway had a kind of half-shell partition protecting it," says Kathy. "It kept you from just walking in like you do in store bathrooms today."

The girls' most favorite places of all, however, were only extra-special at a certain time of the year--Christmas.

Backstage Passes

When Penn Traffic held its annual Christmas parade, the accounting office on the fifth floor, where the girls' father worked, became their special reviewing stand.

"In those days, you could open the windows," remembers Kathy. "They would open the windows, and we'd gather around to watch the whole parade from there.

"It was freezing cold, but we had the best seats in the house. I always wanted to see more, though. I remember

Dad yanking me back constantly because I kept leaning farther out the window."

The Christmas season was also when the store unveiled its famous holiday display window, which changed every year. The unveiling was a big event, attracting people from all over to see the new display for the first time.

But the Penn Traffic brats got to see the latest Christmas display before anyone else. "The decorators pulled curtains across the window so no one could see the display before the public unveiling," remembers Paula. "But my brother and sister and I got a special backstage preview.

"There was a back door in the window area for the window dressers to come and go. When the display was done, they would open the door and let us go in and look at it.

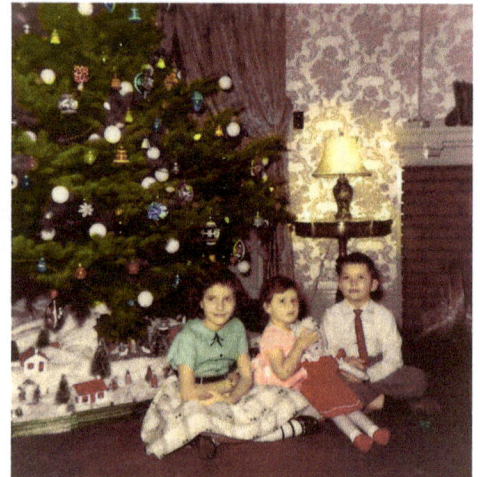

Photos courtesy of Katherine Moser

"It was just so magical, walking in and seeing the decorations and mechanical figures from that angle. It was the best Christmas gift ever--our own secret preview that no one else could share."

Afterward, the kids also attended the great unveiling, seeing the window display from the street with a huge crowd of people. "Someone would always save us a place on the street, up close to the window," says Paula. "It was always a cold night, not long before Christmas. I

Photo by Brian Krise

remember there was often snow falling. Back then, they didn't do things like have Christmastime events before Thanksgiving.

Photo courtesy of Katherine Moser

"Everybody was buzzing. Then, when they opened the curtain and switched on the lights in the window, everyone gasped and cheered. People clapped and pushed in closer, taking in all the details.

"My sister and brother and I just loved it, because we got to see the display from a different angle on the street. And we all shared the secret of our special behind-the-scenes visit, which was all the more magical because it was just between us," says Paula.

From Brats to Grown-Ups

Years later, when the girls had grown, they continued to be connected to Penn Traffic. They both worked there during summers and holidays when they were home from college.

"I worked in the accounting office during inventory," says Kathy. "I would help go over the figures after employees had counted up all the merchandise."

"I was a waitress in the restaurant, and happy to be one," says Paula. "It wasn't easy work, but it was a fascinating experience because I got to see how everything was done.

"And I loved the elegance of the place, the way we treated our customers. Penn Traffic taught us to treat everyone with kindness and respect."

When Kathy got married, she ordered her wedding cake from the Penn Traffic bakery. She had her reception at the Dairy Dell restaurant in Westmont.

She moved to New Jersey, where she lives to this day, but she never got over her love affair with Penn Traffic. "It was such a welcoming place to me. It was always such a joy to go into. I miss it terribly."

Paula, who now lives in Schellsburg, PA, seconds that emotion. "I think about it a lot. It was absolutely fascinating for us as kids.

"I mean, having the entire building as our haven, our home away from home? Are you kidding? Can you imagine?

"It was really something."

Photo courtesy of Katherine Moser

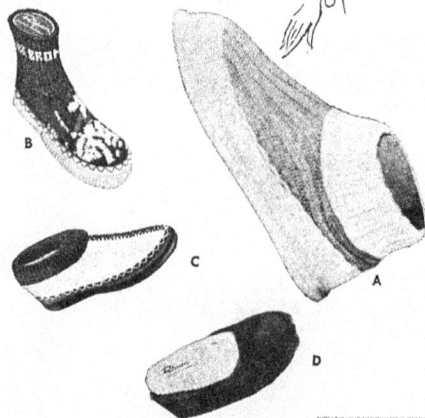

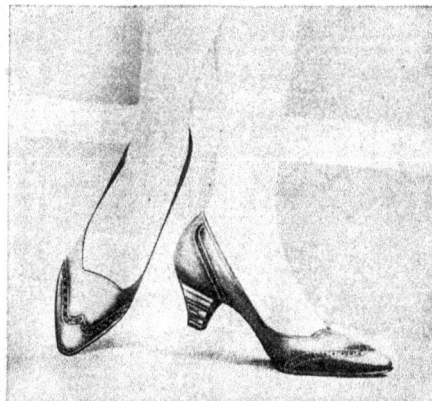

MEMORY DEPARTMENT

I remember so many things about Penn Traffic. It was our Marshall Field's. I remember taking my little brother there to get his picture taken, then going to the lunch room to get ice cream. I loved Christmas shopping there. Each window had a Christmas scene...so festive. My mom ordered from Penn Traffic often, and a delivery truck would bring her orders to the house. They would just automatically charge you. I can still see the charge card, which measured about 1 inch by 2½ inches. I always felt good walking through that store.

Trudy Cassidy Hanley

Photo by Philip Balko

I have very fond memories of Penn Traffic as a child. We would walk there with my grandmother and have dinner. They sold everything. I loved to see the windows at Christmas. When we were in our teens, my sisters and friends would go there for ice cream sodas. My grandmother would take all her grandchildren there for a special treat. We loved going there.

Kim Barnhill

My father, Ron Krause, was the head of maintenance for the store. His shop was on the top floor, near the candy kitchen. He built many of the displays in the store, as well as in the windows. I believe he also helped with the Christmas displays in Central Park.

Betty Ann Krause

I remember my mother taking me to Cosmetics to buy Estee Lauder makeup when I was in high school. I loved it! Mrs. Pavlik waited on us. She was from our Moxham neighborhood. Nice memories from back in the day. Penn Traffic was a classy store!

Suzanne Klucik Langer

Photo by Hesselbein Studio, courtesy of Johnstown Area Heritage Association

When my sister and I were little girls, our family did not have much, so we were on a closely watched budget. Nevertheless, every now and then my mother would take us to the Penn Traffic tearoom, where we would always order the club sandwich salad plate. This consisted of four thick sandwich quarters neatly stacked on end, with fresh fruits and salads in between, with a nice big scoop of orange sherbet in the center of the plate. As we were just little, this was enough for all three of us to eat, accompanied by one large chocolate milkshake that we also shared. It was delectable, but the relaxed and somewhat elegant environment there was what we craved, too.

Penn Traffic made you feel special. So special that after college, I worked there as the Special Events Director out of the Advertising Department, doing fashion shows, trunk shows, and even the big Seventeen Fashion Show as well as the Bridal Show. That was a great job, and Penn Traffic was a great and progressive place to work.

It was truly a wonderful store with lots of great memories for everyone who passed through the doors.

Linda Harris Mihaly

Photos courtesy of Darrel Holsopple

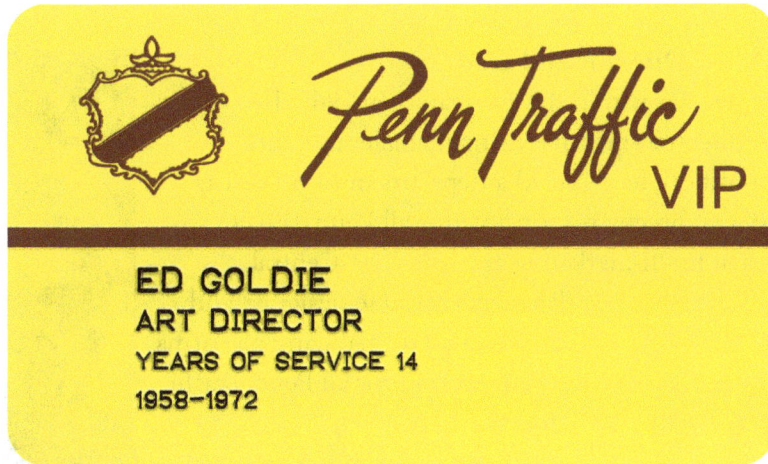

ED GOLDIE
ART DIRECTOR
YEARS OF SERVICE 14
1958-1972

He was the man who drew Penn Traffic.

Many artists worked in the company's advertising department through the years, drawing images for newspaper ads and billboards. But Ed had a singular talent that shone brightly during his 14 years in the game.

His layouts were unique, his figures lifelike yet stylized. He had a way of making shoppers want to buy merchandise based on nothing more than a pen-and-ink drawing on a newspaper page.

Looking back now at the work he did then, it's easy to see why he was such an integral part of the store's success during a time many consider to be its heyday.

Photo courtesy of Deb Goldie-Rogers

A Pedigree Fit for Penn Traffic

Ed studied drawing and design at the Margaret Morrison School of Fine Art at Carnegie-Mellon University. He followed that by attending the Pittsburgh Art Institute, further enhancing and perfecting his craft.

By the time he graduated in 1958, he was ready to apply his skills in a professional setting...and his artistic pedigree made him a strong candidate for a job at Penn Traffic. That same year, he found work as a commercial artist and illustrator at the store.

"He was a fantastic artist," remembers Glenn Falk, who worked in the display department at the time. "He was very, very talented."

He was also destined to make a love connection at the store. He met his future wife, Jean Thomas, at Penn Traffic, where she was working as a salesperson in the juniors department. They married in 1961 and stayed together for 28 years.

Director and Dad

Ed's talent took him far within the company. In 1965, Ed was promoted to art director and advertising manager at Penn Traffic. In his new position, he directed a department of 12 artists and copywriters and was directly responsible for all Penn Traffic advertising for stores in multi-marketing areas in West-Central Pennsylvania. He designed and coordinated displays and all forms of advertising for all Penn Traffic stores.

Even as he built his career at Penn Traffic, Ed was building a family at home. Between 1967 and 1973, he and Jean had four children--Christine, David, Deb, and Diana.

According to Deb, Ed was a loving father, though he wasn't home much. "Dad worked a lot, so I didn't see him until later in the evening most nights," says Deb. "He traveled sometimes for work, too.

"But when he was home, he was patient with us. He was there when we needed him."

Deb remembers going to the Alcove for pizza with Ed and her brother and sisters on Friday nights. "He used to give us change to put in the jukebox."

She also recalls spending time with her family at Bethco Pines and the Bethlehem Management Club. Ed's father, George Goldie, was a member of both thanks to his job as a boss at Bethlehem Steel.

A Passion for Art

Meanwhile, Ed's passion for art in his work and personal life never diminished. He didn't have a home studio--the house was too small for that--but he found opportunities to practice his passion wherever he could.

"Dad made signs for cheerleading events and the church we attended," says Deb.

"I remember we had to create 6-8 signs on poster paper for high school football games," remembers Deb's sister, Diana. "Some would be displayed on the walls of Point Stadium, and others would be run through by the players at the start of the games.

"Dad took time out of his workday and made the best-looking signs for us," says Diana. "He drafted all the words in block format and colored everything with paint markers. They were amazing!"

Though Ed always tried to bring art to life for his kids, none of them picked up the baton and made it a career. But his talent influenced them in other ways.

"I think my sisters and I inherited his artistic tendencies in ways other than drawing," says Christine. "I think we all have his flair for décor and fashion."

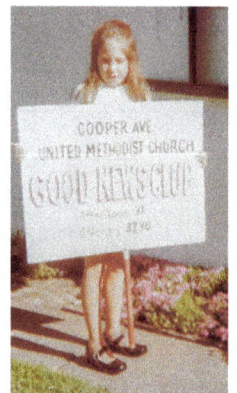

Photos courtesy of Deb Goldie-Rogers

A New Page

Through the years, Ed kept the quality work flowing at Penn Traffic. He continued crafting his unique brand of commercial illustrations, bringing a flair to Penn Traffic's advertising that helped sustain its classy, stylish image in the eyes of the public.

His run as advertising director ended in 1972, however, when he left Penn Traffic for a job at Kane & Company Advertising in Johnstown. He joined Kane as a commercial artist and designer, a role that led him to apply his talents to a multitude of new challenges.

At Kane, Ed worked on major accounts, including industrial, banking, tourism, and commercial projects. He designed brochures, exhibit displays, civic and political campaign materials...and newspaper advertising, of course.

Ed worked at Kane & Company until business dried up in 1990. "Once, Dad did an ad for a sewing machine company," remembers Deb. "Kane didn't have the money to pay him for his work, so they paid him with a new sewing machine."

Just Do Your Best

Ed finally left Kane in 1990. He died of throat cancer a few short years later, in 1997, at the age of 60.

But he left a lasting impression on his children. "He was mild-mannered and always taught us good manners," says Christine. "And he always dressed impeccably."

"He coached little league baseball at St. Theresa's," says David. "I remember he always told the kids, 'Do your best, don't worry, it's all fun.'"

"He said that about everything in life," says Deb. "Just do your best."

And he made a mark on many lives with his work. His illustrations are landmarks of an era when hand-drawn pictures on a page, not photos or digital graphics, were enough to stoke our imaginations and make us run, not walk, to buy something we hadn't thought of until then.

Today, his talent survives in the images that illustrate this chapter, and other drawings throughout this book. He couldn't have known it when he first drew them in the 1960s and 70s. He probably had no idea that his work was good for anything but selling products on a newspaper page.

But here it is, reaching across the decades to bring back memories and tell us what the artist himself can no longer say. His pictures speak volumes about his talent, his heart, and his life, just as Penn Traffic itself continues to speak to us though it is also no longer with us in a physical sense.

Artwork courtesy of Deb Goldie-Rogers

Johnstown Tribune-Democrat, Thursday, March 2, 1967   3

BOLD
BRIGHTS

The message comes through loud and clear . . . bright bold colors for a spring with zing! Fashion designers bypass the pales and pretties for the drama of apple green, bright orange, lemon yellow. Look for these bright bolds in head to toe fashions.

A. Evan Piccone acetate knit wonderful weekend wardrobe. Jacket, $30; slacks, $15; turtle neck striped shell, $13; matching skirt, $13.
Sport Shop, 2nd Floor of Fashion

B. Costume Suit with back-belted coat over a matching shift dress -- 89% rayon, 11% acetate, in apple green or orange, $70.
Coats, 2nd Floor of Fashion
Silk Turban and matching scarf from our millinery department, 18.98.

C. Junior Baby Tent in a colorburst of paisley . . . in zephyrlight Orlon® acrylic challis, $18.
Junior Colony, 2nd Floor of Fashion

D. Adelaar skirt and blouse of Bahama cloth . . . 84% rayon, 16% flax, custom loomed for Adelaar by Crown Fabrics. Blouse, $12; skirt, $10.
Sport Shop, 2nd Floor of Fashion

E. Susan Thomas op-check skirt and jacket, with striped shell for pattern contrast. 55% cotton, 45% Arnel® triacetate, $46.
Better Dresses, 2nd Floor of Fashion

Penn Traffic

Artwork courtesy of Deb Goldie-Rogers

This
Spring,
Go-Go

Pink

Pale pink, bright pink,
soft pink, glowing pink,
any pink...great for Spring
and great for YOU! All on
our "new look" Second
Floor of Fashion.

Left to Right:
Rayon linen A-line step-in by
Jonathan Logan. Sizes 7 to 13.
Also in yellow.
                    14.98
                  Junior Colony
Pure silk sheath with sunburst
tucking at neck and waistline,
inverted side pleats. Sizes 10
to 20. $25
                  Dresses
Rayon and silk coordinates by
Adelaar, sizes 10 to 18. Also in
green and pecan.
Skirt...7.98   Top...8.98
                  Sportswear
Slightly-shaped nubby wool
boucle coat, sizes 6 to 16. Also
in celery and toast. 49.95
                  Coats and Suits

Penn Traffic   2ND FLOOR OF FASHION

Shop Wednesday 9:30 to 5 -- Thursday 9:30 to 9

Artwork courtesy of Deb Goldie-Rogers

Subtle, Flattering and New ... the romantic color suggesting the mystery of the East!

PERSIAN BLUE

An excitingly new and different shade
of blue that is wonderfully compatible
with other colors in accessories.

A--Carol Craig double knit wool sheath with the most marvelous shaping to give it the high-waisted look. Sizes 10 to 18.
$25
Dresses, Second Floor

B--Anglo Monotone Coat . . . suave new shape . . . slender, but eased with low placed back belt. Beautifully detailed in textured wool. Petite sizes 6 to 14.
89.95
Coats, Second Floor

C--Three-Piece Suit Costume . . . smart longer length jacket and slim skirt in mohair loop wool and nylon . . . plus the softest printed wool blouse. Sizes 10 to 16.
79.95
Suits, Second Floor

D--The Costume is lovely in Persian Blue wool with 10% cashmere . . . the one-piece dress topped with soft rayon crepe. Misses' sizes.
59.95
Fashion Salon, Second Floor

E--sweater and skirt with the very new sportive look. Shadow plaid skirt with hip-stitched pleats in wool. Sizes 8 to 16 . . . . **12.98** Bulky knit mohair and wool pullover sweater with V-neckline news. Sizes 34 to 40.
10.98
Sportswear, Second Floor

F--Roberta Bernay fedora with the sportive look (13.98) is one of many new hats in Persian Blue, priced from **$5** to **13.98**.
Millinery, Second Floor

Penn Traffic

SHOP UNTIL 9 TONIGHT
DIAL 535-3581 FOR PERSONAL SHOPPING SERVICE

Artwork courtesy of Deb Goldie-Rogers

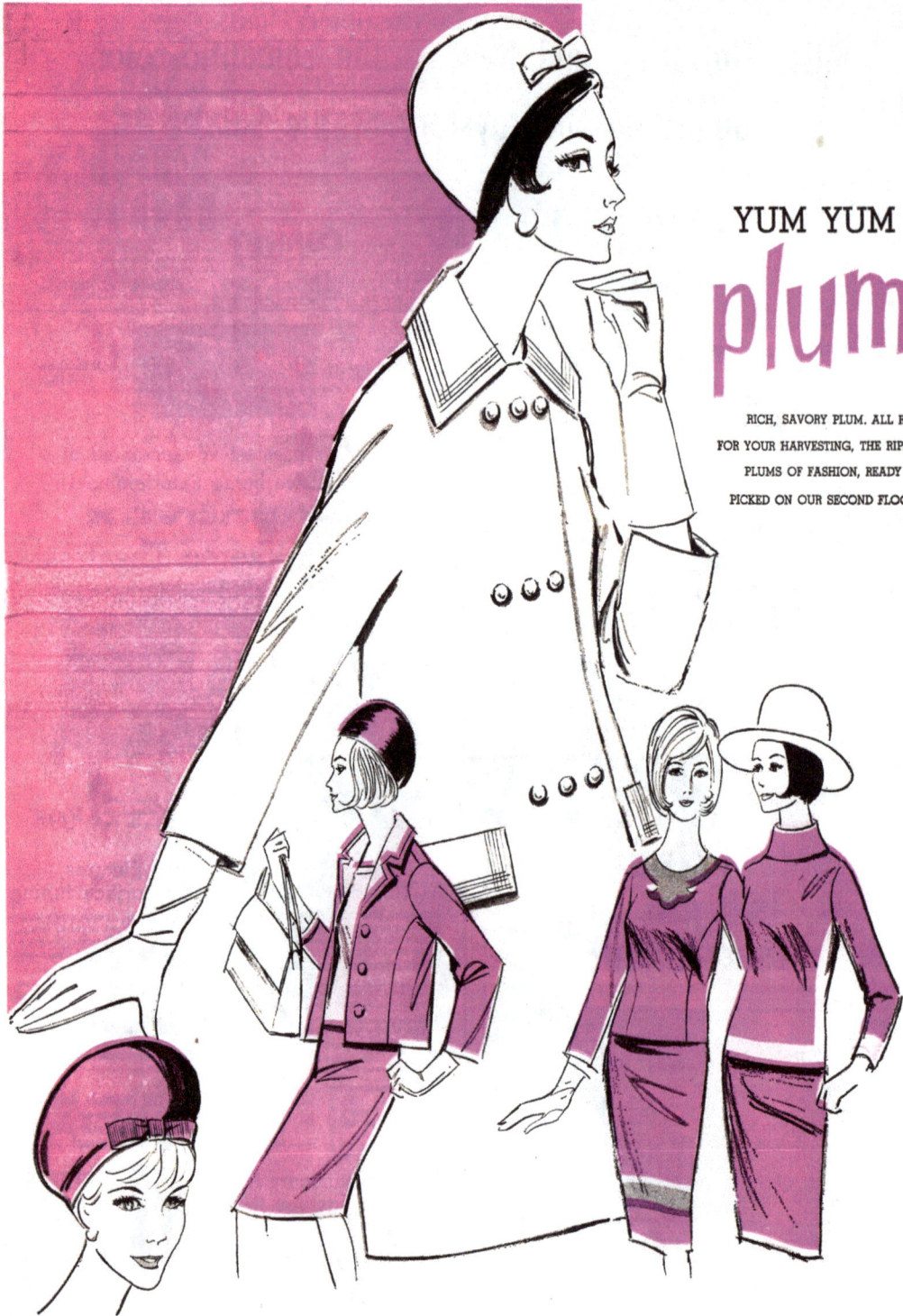

YUM YUM
plum

RICH, SAVORY PLUM. ALL READY
FOR YOUR HARVESTING, THE RIPEST
PLUMS OF FASHION, READY TO BE
PICKED ON OUR SECOND FLOOR

PLUM BEAUTIFUL, THE PICK OF THE FALL CROP!

Growing wild at Penn Traffic . . . the color, new and tantilizing; the textures, rich and exciting; the silhou- PLUM ettes will flatter every size. Here, a modified tent coat in sizes 6 to 18, $65. The hat is from a great array. The Men'del double knit wool costume, in half sizes, $65. Green suede accents the neckline and skirt of this double knit, in misses' sizes, $39. Colebrook separates of wool, the sweater, $13; the skirt, $12.

2nd Floor of Fashion

PennTraffic

SHOP TODAY 9:30 TO 5

Artwork courtesy of Deb Goldie-Rogers

MEMORY DEPARTMENT

I loved shopping at Penn Traffic as a child and then as a teen. The restaurant was a favorite place, always so good with homemade food that never disappointed. But my favorite memory is being a young mom and taking my two daughters, Christy and Sara, to have breakfast with Santa at that restaurant. A delicious meal of scrambled eggs, bacon, toast, juice, and hot chocolate with marshmallows was served, and then Santa came around and visited each child and gave each one a real toy (not just a candy cane!).

My oldest daughter received a small camera one year. It was the highlight of their childhood to go to that event at Penn Traffic until, sadly, we moved away. Now it is a wonderful memory they've both shared with their own children.

Beverly Longo Henry

I remember standing in line to see Santa Claus.....the line was long, but we were ushered to him on a lush carpet with velvety, burgundy ropes with gold on each side, making an aisle worthy of standing in line waiting to meet royalty! Which, of course, we were! After all, it was Santa Claus!

Patricia Bowers

I remember going to lunch when I was a preteen with my friend Kim and her mother. It made us feel all grown-up!

Susan Costlow

As a little girl, I was invited to model coats in a small fashion show in the children's department. My mom bought the coat I modeled, a gray chinchilla. It was a beauty, and I wore it till I outgrew it. I loved that grownup experience of modeling, even though I was only six years old!

Beverly Longo Henry

"Old-Fashioned Bargain Days" was a community event in June. ALL retailers participated, and Penn Traffic pulled out all the stops. Every employee was required to wear appropriate "costumes": bowler hats and bow ties for the men, and little frilly sleep caps or pioneer-style hats for the women. Barber shop quartets sang both inside and outside the store. There were reduced prices in every department, including in the "lunchroom." The store was absolutely PACKED with bargain hunters, as was the city.

Paula Kellar

I worked at Penn Traffic for about a year and a half in the advertising department. We were right next to the candy kitchen. I got to watch how they made all the chocolates.

My aunt, Margaret Benson, was the assistant to the president for years and did all the training for all the new people. My grandmother and great aunt also worked there. Also, my cousin was in charge of the display department. That store was so wonderful. And I am proud that I got to work there!

Debra Heidingsfelder Knobel

Photo courtesy of Debra Heidingsfelder Knobel

110

Penn Traffic VIP

GLENN FALK
DISPLAY DEPARTMENT
YEARS OF SERVICE 7
1958–1965

When you ask people what they remember best about Penn Traffic, they almost always mention the Christmas window displays. Glenn Falk of Windber, Pennsylvania is one of the ace designers who helped make those windows a reality.

Though the truth is, Glenn brought the windows to life all year 'round. He and the rest of the display team cooked up elaborate scenes that drew customers every week, not just during the holidays.

"We changed our window displays pretty much every week," says Glenn. "They were important to the store, and the public really loved them.

"People would see the products in the windows and want to buy them. But there was more to it than that.

"It was an image, too. Even if people weren't interested in certain products, the displays created an image of the type of store Penn Traffic was and the kind of merchandise it had," explains Glenn.

Nine Windows Wide

The display team was always jumping in those days. Not only did they have to change the windows every week, but the changes had to be made to a total of nine windows arranged along the ground floor across the front of the building.

According to Glenn, the team was responsible for three windows dedicated to men's apparel, three for women's apparel, one for accessories, and one for the budget store. Another window, on the corner closest to the Johnstown public safety building, was set aside for furniture...except during the Christmas season, when it served as the main holiday display featuring mechanical figures.

In Glenn's time, the installation of displays took place during the day, with no curtain to block public view. That meant observation--and distractions--from passersby were common.

111

"People waved and knocked all the time," says Glenn. "Sometimes, we waved back. But mostly, we didn't pay any attention to onlookers. We had a job to do."

Creative Freedom Under Glass

Glenn and his teammates took a lot of pride in their work. He says they tried hard to make Penn Traffic's window displays more artistic and attention-getting than those of other stores.

Their success was due, in part, to the creative freedom the company gave them. Though buyers supplied the products that were scheduled to be featured, the display team had plenty of leeway in deciding how to showcase them.

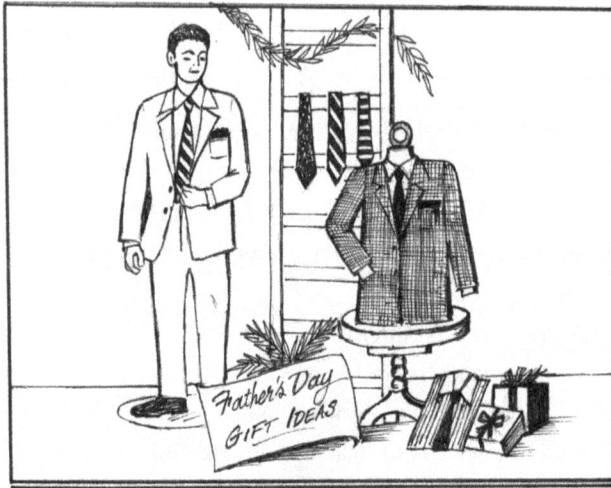

"The display designs were planned out by anyone who set up the windows," says Glenn. "We could use our own ideas and be as creative as we wanted, while staying true to the image of the store."

Display personnel could use whatever mannequins and trim they had available to enhance a scene. Trim could include floral arrangements, fencing, tables, or whatever props, decorations, or set pieces were stocked in the team's workshop.

According to Glenn, the display group's workshop was located on an upper floor of the store, looking out over Washington Street toward the Hendler Hotel (current location of the Social Security office). The shop was full of trim, tools, and drawing boards, and was also home to the sign shop.

The Advertising department was based nearby, up the hall. This was good, because Advertising and Display worked closely in those days. The copy (text) for all the signs, show cards, and window cards used in the displays was generated by Advertising, then sent to the Display department.

It was a busy place, but Glenn says there was plenty of staff to handle the work flow.

"We had some big crews operating out of that shop," remembers Glenn. "Each crew had a display manager and an assistant, plus extras who did the heavy lifting but weren't responsible for artwork or decorating.

Artwork by Glenn Falk

"We had lots of talented people. Sam Mosholder, for example, taught me a great deal. He was one of the window decorators I worked with," says Glenn.

Together, Glenn and his co-workers showed off their talent each and every week...but the windows always shined the brightest at Christmas time.

Holiday Masterpieces

"The holidays were a big thing for us," recalls Glenn. "We went all-out with decorations throughout the store...but especially in the big corner window."

Glenn says there was something new in the corner window every Christmas, always including some kind of mechanical figures.

Ironically, the most eagerly anticipated windows of the year involved the least creative input from the display team.

"The local team never designed the Christmas window. Management would go to the big display shows in New York City every year, where they would buy or rent an entire display as a complete package," says Glenn. "Then we would install them. But it wasn't easy. There was a lot to it."

The results were worth the effort. Every year, people drove in from all around the region and gathered for the big unveiling. The crowd in front of the store would gasp and cheer and clap, pointing out the many decorative touches put in place by the Display team.

Penn Traffic Satisfaction

Glenn left Penn Traffic in 1965 for a display job at Sears, but it wasn't the same. Most of the work at Sears involved interior displays on racks and walls instead of in windows.

And he never had as much creative freedom, he says. "The big chain stores like Sears have formats you have to follow. The displays are all designed for you.

"But the displays at Penn Traffic were all original ideas. Everything there was your own creation. It was much more satisfying in that regard," says Glenn.

Artwork by Glenn Falk

FREE MONOGRAMMING!

Now Thru November 30
On Any Van Heusen Shirt
You Buy At Penn Traffic

- Three Monogram Styles To Choose From
- 70 Brilliant Monogramming Colors

Now thru November 30 we will monogram any Van Heusen shirt you purchase in any of three monogramming styles shown below. Not only that, but you can select from 70 great monogramming colors! Come in today!

THREE MONOGRAMMING STYLES:

| SCRIPT | DIAMOND | BLOCK |

Van Heusen Shirts... Colors, Vibrant Stripes

A. The look of tomorrow's fashion ... the elegant taste of yesterday. Both are yours in this single shirt from the Hampshire House collection. Buttondown collar. French cuffs ... of Dacron polyester and cotton. In rich colors and bold stripes. Sizes 14½ to 17, sleeves 32 to 35.

Solids ...... $9   Stripes $10
Tie by Resilio $6

B. For the traditional man, our classic shirts ... from the Hampshire House collection, of course ... inspired. They have the kind of stripes that has become a world standard ... in fresh color combinations that complement the very newest suit shades. Tailored with button-down collars and long-pointed collars. 2-button cuffs ... in Dacron polyester and cotton. Sizes 14½ to 17, sleeves 32 to 35.   18
Tie by Damon 7.50

C & D. Century — the remarkable new shirt for the Seventies now showing vibrant colors amid new stripes for stripes ... gold ... new luster and fabric. Permanently pressed Vanopress Dacron polyester and cotton broadcloth with Bradley collar. Sizes 14½ to 17, sleeves 32 to 35.
Solids ......7.50   Stripes 7.50
C. Tie by Beau Brummel 4.50
D. Tie by Bronzini 6.50

VAN HEUSEN

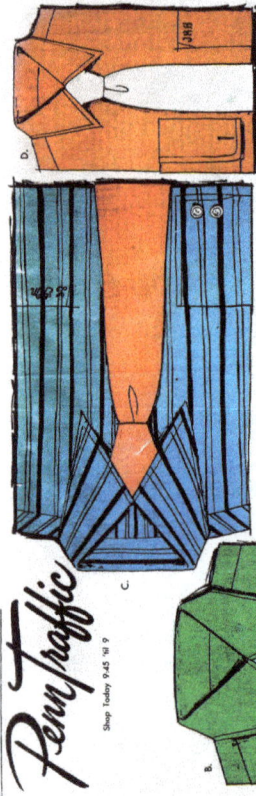

NOW THROUGH NOV. 30

Free Monogramming
On Any Arrow Shirt
You Buy At Penn Traffic

- Three Monogram Styles To Choose From
- 70 Brilliant Monogramming Colors

Now thru November 30 we will monogram any Arrow shirt you purchase in any of three monogramming styles shown below. Not only that, you can select from 70 great monogramming colors! Come in today!

THREE MONOGRAMMING STYLES:

| BLOCK | DIAMOND | SCRIPT |

Arrow Shirts... Colors And Stripes Forever!

A. Arrow Collar Man ... the boldest, all-scale skin fashion in menswear. Today's Arrow Collar Man has transposed the best of yesterday into today's great look. See the bright stripes and dramatic colors with the higher, longer-pointed collars. Wide 2-button cuffs ... in Permo-Iron fabric. Sizes 14½ to 17, sleeves 32 to 35.
Tie by Bronzini 6.50

B & C. See "Roaring Twenties" ... a special group of exciting styles from Arrow's Kent Collection of dress shirts. A bright, bold, all-man look in stripes and vibrant colors with ... far longer-pointed collar. 2-button cuffs ... tapered from shoulder to waist. Modern-day easy-care Permo-Iron fabric. Sizes 14½ to 17, sleeves 32 to 35. $11
B. Tie by Resilio $6
C. Tie by Beau Brummel 4.50

D. Choose Belmont Club ... the expensive looking everyday shirt ... in the newest, most-wanted colors and solids ... Permo-Iron in a Fortrel polyester and cotton blend that keeps its smooth freshness all day. Sizes 14½ to 17, sleeves 32 to 35. $6
Tie by Damon 6.50

Arrow

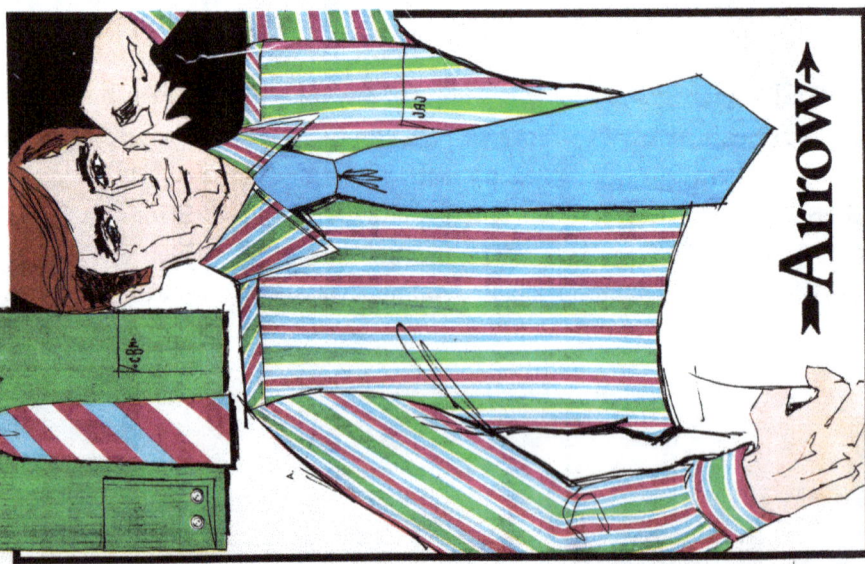

MEMORY DEPARTMENT

I started working as a waitress in the Penn Traffic dining room after I graduated. Donald Leventry was my boss. We had lunch and dinner specials for 60¢! Nobody could beat our cold fudge sundaes, rice pudding, and wonderful pies. The employees would eat there and leave a dime per person for a tip; of course it was back in 1961! I was there in the afternoon when we heard the news that JFK was shot. No one believed me when I told the guests. I really loved Penn Traffic and did all my shopping there with my 15% employee discount!

Evie Evanisko

I lived in Johnstown from 1950 to 1967. I delivered the morning *Tribune-Democrat* paper from 1961 to 1964. The little bit of money I made from delivering papers, I used to buy pants and shirts for school at the Penn Traffic department store. The store personnel were always great to talk to about what was the best style for me. I felt like a million dollars after shopping there. Thanks to all at Penn Traffic.

John Smith

We small town kids always considered Johnstown a big city. I remember our shopping trips to Penn Traffic. I got my senior prom gown there. When I worked in Johnstown in the '60s, it was a regular stop at lunchtime and after work.

Bernie Dillon

My Penn Traffic wedding gown was gorgeous and cost $55. The veil cost $25. And I bought them the morning of our wedding. That was 1966.
Jane Oleksak

I remember riding the trolley with my grandma into town every Saturday. We always stopped for lunch at Penn Traffic. I got the ham salad sandwich, and she got the chop suey. Afterwards, we would head to their bakery for maple rolls. I can still smell them!
Robin Hartnett Taylor

My Dad, Sam Castiglione, was the furrier for Penn Traffic until he went on disability in 1968. He actually left before that. He died at age 46, the day before he was to receive 100% disability. He used to do the Santa suit in the Christmas window each year.

My wedding gown and those of my bridal party all came from Penn Traffic's Bridal Shop. I have so many pleasant memories of such a wonderful store. No matter what is in the building, it will ALWAYS be Penn Traffic, the store where my dad worked for 23 years. Oh yeah, and I met my husband there, too. He was a friend of Dad's.
Patty Castiglione Devich

Photos courtesy of Patty Castiglione Devich

Chapter Thirteen

Growth Spurt

1962-1964

What if somebody asked you what the biggest year in Penn Traffic's history was? The turning point that changed everything for the company forever?

You might want to pick 1962. That's a pretty safe bet.

1962 was the year of Riverside and PT, the start of the biggest expansion that Penn Traffic had ever known. It was the year that a single-store company, limited to a base of operations in downtown Johnstown, became a company with multiple stores throughout the region and a hunger to develop and acquire even more.

Down by the Riverside

The first move in this new direction--though the planning behind it went on for quite a while before that--came in early 1962. It was then that the Penn Traffic Company merged with Supervalue Corp., owners of the Riverside supermarket chain based in DuBois, PA. The merger, to the tune of $2.4 million in Penn Traffic stock, added ten Riverside markets to the company.

Photo from Penn Traffic 1977 Annual Report

It was opposed by chief accountant Elit Felix, who insisted it was the worst thing Penn Traffic could ever do... but Felix couldn't stop it, though he was the company's third biggest shareholder. Like it or not, Penn Traffic was jumping into the supermarket game.

But gaining a foothold in the grocery business wasn't the only reason for the purchase. Penn Traffic executives had a more elaborate plan in mind, one that would give them a bigger stake in the retail marketplace.

With the Riverside chain in their pocket, Penn Traffic's planners moved forward with developing two new stores in Indiana, PA and Westwood, a Johnstown suburb. The stores would have familiar aspects, yet be very different from anything the company had attempted in the past. They would also be at the forefront of trends in the field, merging merchandising and grocery sales in a way that was fresh and forward-thinking.

When the first result of this plan opened in August of '62 in Indiana, PA, the public finally got a look at what Penn Traffic had in mind: a brand new one-stop shopping concept that bundled together the company's two divisions under one roof.

The Combination Stores

The Indiana, PA unit was the first of Penn Traffic's new "combination stores." Split down the middle, this "PT" store had a supermarket on one side (stocked and operated by the Riverside division) and a department store on the other. The two sides had separate checkouts and separate staffs, united only in that they were located in the same building.

Would this configuration, a novel approach in the area, succeed in Indiana? Penn Traffic's confidence was high...high enough that the company had a second store in the works before the Indiana PT opened its doors.

This second PT was located in the Westwood Shopping Center in Johnstown's Westmont Borough. Its layout would be almost identical to the Indiana unit, with a grocery store on one side and a department store on the other.

And, like the Indiana PT, the Westwood store would fall under the supervision of Dick Corbin, Vice President of Branch Stores for the company. It would also follow the same sales strategy as Indiana, a strategy Dick would carry forward into future expansions.

"We wanted to appeal to customers with a more moderate income," says Dick. "The same buyers did all the buying for the downtown Penn Traffic store, but they focused on less upscale merchandise for the combination stores.

"It proved to be a successful strategy."

Indeed, the Indiana store posted strong sales numbers, suggesting the same would be true in Westwood. When the second store opened two months later, in October 1962, it seemed the predictions had been accurate.

Photos from Penn Traffic 1967 Annual Report

Photo by Philip Balko

Crowds flocked to the Westwood PT, and the cash registers rang like crazy. It looked like the PT experiment would be a smash hit, beginning a bold new chapter in Penn Traffic's history.

Story of a PT Girl

Marge Jeschonek was there at the start, working on the department store side of the Westwood PT when it first opened.

"I worked at the service desk and office," says Marge. "That area was manned by four or five of us, including the office manager, Doris Yoder.

"It was a very busy place. We cashed checks, handled layaways, accepted utility bill and credit card payments, ran the post office, and balanced cash register drawers.

"The store was constantly busy, and so were we."

Marge remembers that the Westwood PT was managed by Ken Miller in those days, though other managers and executives also visited often. "G. Fesler Edwards and Dick and Bill Corbin came up a lot, especially when the store first opened. It was a big deal, since it was one of the first stores of its kind in the company.

"The buyers, like Lou Maslo, came up often, too. They came to see what was needed and make sure the merchandise was stocked."

Marge worked at the Westwood PT for 2 years, during which she got to know the place very well. "When you went in, there was a big entryway going all the way back. Riverside was on the left, a complete grocery store, and PT was on the right, with all the various departments.

"Each side had its own cash registers. Riverside's were all in one section, and PT's were in the departments. You paid for your purchases in the different departments."

According to Marge, on the department store side, the service desk was located to the right of the entrance. "The men's department was next. I think the boys' department was after that, then children's, then infants'.

Photo by Philip Balko

119

"The shoe department, which was leased by an outside company, was in the back of the store. Then, the other departments were arranged along the other side, starting with hardware, running all the way up to the service desk."

There was also a partial second level, with offices and an employee lunchroom. "They didn't serve food there. You brought your own.

"Sometimes, I'd eat lunch up there. Other times, I'd eat at the snack bar in Riverside."

Photo by Philip Balko

Overall, Marge says her experience at PT was a good one. "The management treated us really well. "Mr. Miller was very nice to work for. Dick and Bill Corbin were very nice, too."

She liked it so much that she went back in 1966 after leaving in '64 to get married and start a family.

The Pay Divide

As time passed, it became clear that the PT combination store concept worked well and was profitable. It wasn't necessarily perfect in every way, though.

RIVERSIDE DIVISION of PENN TRAFFIC CO.
OPERATIONS STAFF & MARKET MANAGERS (APRIL 1964)

From the start, a division existed when it came to employee pay. Since Riverside, which ran the grocery half of the store, was unionized, workers there made much more per hour than those on the department store side.

Years later, hard feelings over this issue led employees on the department store side to take steps toward unionization. They went as far as holding a National Labor Relations Board certification election, though union supporters didn't get the votes they needed to move forward.

DuBois Bound

As the combination stores in Indiana and Westwood continued to post strong numbers, Penn Traffic's leadership explored possibilities for further expansion. They did market research, crunched numbers, hashed it out, and finally decided to open a third new store in DuBois, PA.

The new store opened in October 1964. Located in the hometown of the Riverside division's administrative headquarters, it was well-positioned to receive strong customer support...and it did. The DuBois combination store was a hit.

It was also the last one ever opened by the Penn Traffic Company.

Penn Traffic VIP

JEAN JUCHA
WOMENSWEAR SALES CLERK
YEARS OF SERVICE 8
1958–1966

Photo by Philip Balko

Every once in a while, Jean Jucha just had to strip a mannequin in one of Penn Traffic's display windows.

"Sometimes, a customer would want a dress on display in one of the windows," remembers Jean. "But the only one in the size she needed was on the mannequin in the window.

"So down I'd go to the window and strip the dress right off the mannequin and sell it. Anything to keep a Penn Traffic customer happy," says Jean.

As a womenswear sales person at Penn Traffic for eight years, that was something Jean got very good at. Keeping customers happy was her bread and butter on a daily basis.

Seventeen Look-of-Knowledge

Jean's career at Penn Traffic started with a fashion show in 1958, when she was 17 years old. It was the "Seventeen Look-of-Knowledge" show, and it revolved around clothes featured in *Seventeen* magazine. Nineteen girls from local high schools served as models, including Jean, and the prize was a gift certificate.

Thursday, August 23rd, at 7 p. m.—Second Floor

Watch the show in air-conditioned comfort!

Open Till 9 Thursday

eventeen
"Look-of-Knowledge" Fashion Show

Thursday, August 23rd, at 7 p. m.—Second Floor

Commentators— Maxine Segal, Westmont
Barbara Jean Pensinger, Southmont

Hostesses— Leuanne Kane, Central
Mary Ann Wagner, Central

Cast of Models— (pictured here)

Producers—our high school fashion staff
Models—nineteen local high school girls
Fashions—from the pages of Seventeen
Commentators—two of our fashion staff

Fay Ashman, Central
Carole Block, Westmont
Helen Caras, Franklin-East Taylor
Carole Furnary, Garfield
Dorothy Gantos, Cochran
Helene Guttilla, Joseph Johns
Mary Lou Hastings, Ferndale
Lynn Hendler, Westmont
Kay Hippler, Catholic High
Janet Keiper, Richland Township
Barbara Kunkle, Central
Beverly Ling, Dale
Valeria Marina, Conemaugh Township
Geraldine Perry, Catholic High
Jo Ann Pestis, Conemaugh Township
Barbara Pristas, Conemaugh Joint
Nina Teitelbaum, Southmont
Jean Thomas, Central
Doreen Wagner, Central

Courtesy of Jean Jucha

"Everyone got a Penn Traffic gift certificate just for being in the show. I was excited, because that meant I would be able to get some clothes from the store. I didn't usually get to shop there, since the prices were on the high side, and my parents didn't have a lot of money," says Jean.

Soon, Jean was able to shop at Penn Traffic much more often, because she had an employee discount. After graduating from Johnstown Central High School, she applied for a job at the store, and got one by September of 1958.

"I started as a stock girl, putting clothes into bins on the sales floor according to sizes," says Jean. "Then I became a salesperson in the juniors' sportswear department on the second floor.

"As you came up the steps from the mezzanine, it was to the left. Later, they moved it to the opposite side of the store."

Jean liked her job so much, she kept it for eight years. She was still working in the juniors' department, in fact, when she left Penn Traffic in 1966.

The Pin Money Shop

"I sold clothes in sizes 3 to 15," says Jean. "And I sold clothes from a lot of different manufacturers, like Jonathan Logan, Mr. Mort, and Jean D'Arc."

At first, she could only sell items in her own department. But the store soon changed its policy. "By then, you were allowed to sell in all the departments. If you had a customer who wanted a coat or suit, you could go to the coat or suit department and sell them what they wanted," says Jean.

As a result of that policy, Jean got to learn more about other departments, especially those in her vicinity on the second floor.

"The second floor of Penn Traffic was all ladies' apparel," recalls Jean. "What we call ready-to-wear.

"As you came up the stairs from the first floor, the millinery department was to the right. Shoes were next to them.

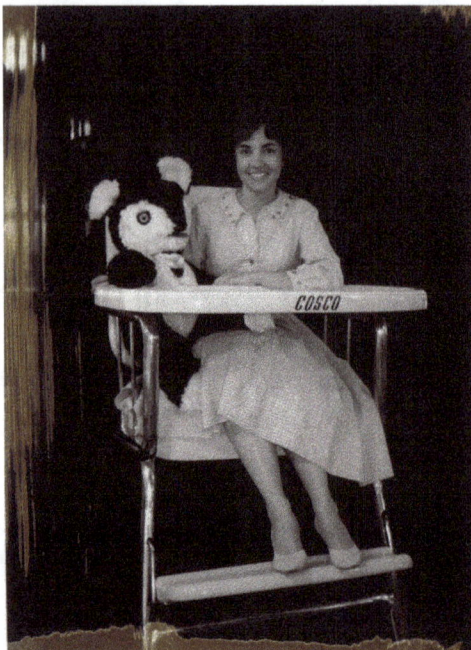

"Juniors' dresses were to the left, then better dresses. Then, wedding and prom gowns were back in the corner. Then there was the sportswear department.

"Next, there was what we used to call the pin money shop, which might also have been called the daytime dresses department. They sold housedresses, most made locally by Kay Artley, a Johnstown company."

Between the juniors' department and pin money shop, there was a small area with a cashier who rang up sales and wrapped gifts.

Jean also remembers a department called the Penn Shop. "It wasn't a big section, really. More like a big walk-in closet. They sold dresses for $39.95 and up, which was a lot of money for a dress in 1958. They were nice clothes, and they were expensive."

Photo courtesy of Jean Jucha

According to Jean, a man named Bob Todd managed the sportswear, dresses, and all the ready-to-wear in those days. The shoe and millinery departments were leased, however, and operated by outside companies.

A Work of Art

From one department to the next, one thing never changed at Penn Traffic. Jean says all the sales people shared a commitment to personalized customer service.

"We got to know our customers, and they got to know us. We had a comfortable feeling with each other.

"We knew what they wanted and tried to make sure we could get it for them. People appreciated the service and always came back," says Jean.

The courtesy and helpfulness extended not only to customers, but among Penn Traffic employees. "I worked with a lot of nice people, including the management," says Jean. "Everybody got along real well and did what they could to help each other."

It was true, though, that some employees got along better than others. Jean got along so well with one co-worker, in fact, that she ended up marrying him.

She met Ed Goldie, the store's art director, in 1959. "He worked in advertising, and I worked on the second floor," remembers Jean. "We married in 1961 and stayed together for 28 years."

The marriage ended in 1989. By then, Jean had been gone from the store for 23 years.

Mannequins of the Mezzanine

Jean married an artist, but he wasn't the only one in the family with a creative streak. As part of her job in the juniors' department, Jean got to try her hand at some in-store display work.

"As you went up the stairs to the mezzanine, on either side of the stairs facing the first floor, there was a platform with a mannequin on it," explains Jean. "Our department got to dress one of those mannequins, which were in a prime location to catch the eyes of customers.

"I'd put junior dresses on the mannequin and change them fairly often. That way, people got to see the different styles from our department.

Photos courtesy of Jean Jucha

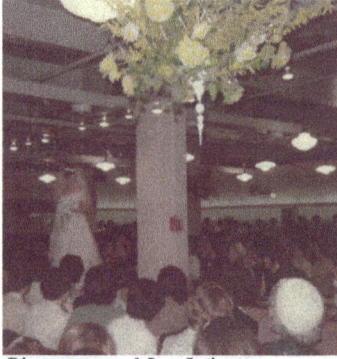

Photo courtesy of Jean Jucha

"It was fun dressing and posing that mannequin," says Jean. "I got to be a little creative, and I knew lots of people would see my work."

Jean also got to have fun modeling clothes in the store's fashion shows, which always drew a crowd. "The fashion shows were nice," she says. "We got to walk the runway in the latest sportswear, dresses, suits, or whatever.

"They went all out for the bridal shows, though. When you were in a bridal show, you wore a wedding dress or a bridesmaid's dress or something for the honeymoon.

"Then there was the show where they brought in the fashions from New York that would be in style for the following year. I think they called it the Vesta Shaffer show," says Jean.

Dancing the Penn Traffic

Nowadays, Jean has a busy life teaching ballroom dancing, but she remembers the magic of Penn Traffic and wishes it were still in full bloom. "A lot of times, when I drive past the Penn Traffic Building downtown, I see the windows aren't there, or the ones that are still there are all dark.

"I say to myself, 'Oh, I remember when the windows were all lit and decorated. I remember all the people coming and going.' It was really something to see.

"You could find anything you wanted in the floors of that building," Jean says with a smile. "They had everything. And the clothes were just gorgeous. They were beautiful.

"It was such a special place and time. I feel lucky that I was a part of it."

Photo courtesy of Darrel Holsopple

Memory Department

This goes back to when I was a youngster in the mid-1960s, when times were different. When we went shopping, and my mom was shopping for me or for other surprises, she would take me to the mezzanine seating, where I read a book. She reminded me not to talk to strangers. She has always taken good care of me, and perhaps was even too vigilant, so I get a kick out of telling her that if she did that today, she would be arrested for child abandonment!

We loved Penn Traffic and would usually eat in the restaurant when we were downtown for an appointment. I almost always had a hamburger, fries, and a Coca-Cola. Penn Traffic had the best hamburger buns and Coca-Cola fountain beverages.

All six of my pictures with Santa were taken there. My mom worked there also, including in the toy department. It was a grand old store.

Marianne Spampinato

125   *Photos courtesy of Marianne Spampinato*

I remember our mom taking us to Penn Traffic to buy our Buster Brown shoes for school and our PF Flyers for summer. We would sit on the carousel, and Howard Stark would measure our feet.

Ann Trexler

My mom and Mrs. LaPorta worked in the kitchen of the restaurant for years. My dad would stop by the bakery every payday and bring us cupcakes, a jelly roll, or some other special treat. The Easter candy was the best! Penn Traffic was probably our first "upscale" department store. I was in a fashion show there one year, too.

Helene Guarino

I remember going to Girl Scout Day at Penn Traffic. They made the most delicious crème de menthe ice cream sundaes on that day. My mom would take me and my sisters, dressed in our Girl Scout uniforms, for this special treat.

Arlene Carolus Bennett

I worked at Christmastime in the perfume department, wrapping perfumes for customers. Of course, most of the customers were men buying for their wives! It was the most wonderful time of the year and I have many fond memories!

Sharon Ortag

My sister, Donna Lambert, worked in the cafeteria. We spent a lot of time there while shopping in Penn Traffic. They made the best cold fudge sundaes in the world. I can still remember the layout of the store. My Mother also ordered a lot and had things delivered to the house.

Betty Lambert Krause

My friend Becky and I loved going to the furniture department, and we would pretend we were grown-up and they had different rooms decorated for us. We would pick out which rooms we wanted in our house. And, of course, I will never forget the beautiful window Christmas displays. I loved that store!

LaWana Manganello Duque

I remember the amazing fly fishing tackle department at the State College store.

Dick Crestood

They had a beauty shop in Penn Traffic that did everything. My sister and I were allowed to go in there, since we were the Penn Traffic brats.

To curl ladies' hair, they had machines that had pipes and hoses attached to them. It was crazy. The curler was on the end of the hose. These ladies looked like they were from outer space.

Paula Kellar

I remember the striped boxes with the purple lids and the purple Easter grass. A large fruit and nut egg came to our house every Easter. I remember the decorations around the egg, too. My sister liked the Penn Pigs, which were filled with coconut.

Katherine M Moser

Photo by Philip Balko

127

Penn Traffic

OPEN 9:30 to 5 Tuesdays, Wednesdays, Fridays!
9:30 to 9 Thursdays! 9 to 5 Saturdays! Noon to 9 Mondays!

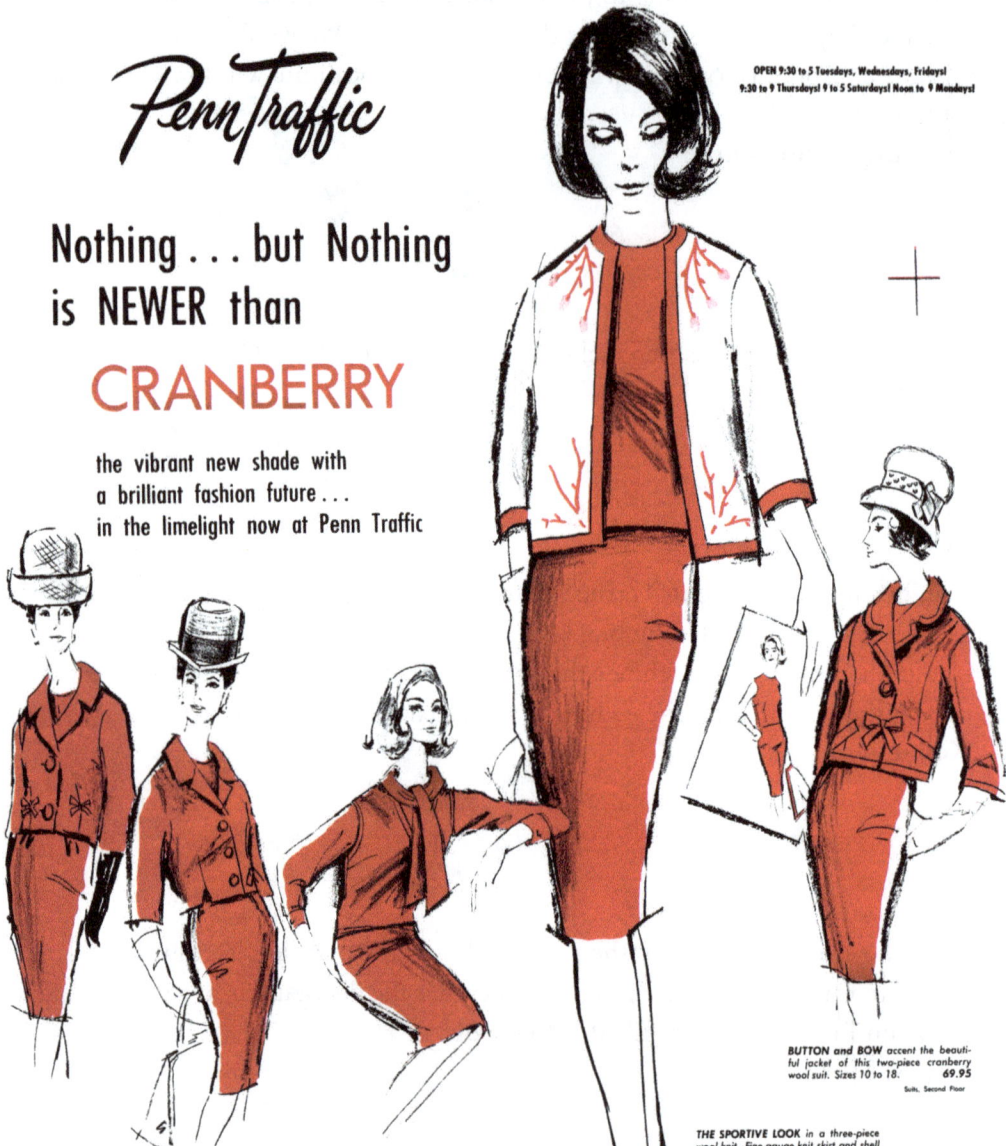

Nothing . . . but Nothing is NEWER than

CRANBERRY

the vibrant new shade with
a brilliant fashion future . . .
in the limelight now at Penn Traffic

BUTTON and BOW accent the beautiful jacket of this two-piece cranberry wool suit. Sizes 10 to 18.   69.95

Suits, Second Floor

THE COSTUME newer-than-new in cranberry wool and cashmere fabric. Slim dress with cap sleeves and waistline jacket. Misses' sizes.   69.95

Fashion Salon, Second Floor

CAROL CRAIG costume of cranberry rayan adds a 3-button jacket to a slim short-sleeve dress with bateau neckline. Sizes 10 to 18.   17.95

Dresses, Second Floor

JUNIOR fashion by Sue Brett. Three-part story . . . skirt and overblouse topped with V-neck, sleeveless vest zipped in back. Sizes 5 to 13. $25

Junior Dresses, Second Floor

THE SPORTIVE LOOK in a three-piece wool knit. Fine gauge knit skirt and shell top red as cranberries . . . topped with bulky white Chanel-type jacket trimmed in cranberry and pink. Sizes 8 to 16.   39.98

Sportswear, Second Floor

CRAZY OVER CRANBERRY HATS . . . sketched a cuff toque by Janquil ($5) from our collection   from $5 to 13.98.

Millinery, Second Floor

PINK GLOVES . . . perfect accent for a cranberry color costume. The soft nylon shortie $2. The shirred 4-button length $3. Sizes 6 to 8.

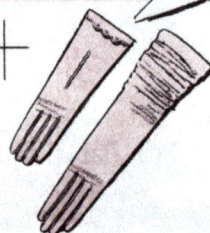

Gloves, Main Floor

BRILLIANCE of costume jewelry comes alive with cranberry color. Crystal neckline $8* and earrings $3*

*Plus 10% Fed. tax

Jewelry, Main Floor

Artwork courtesy of Deb Goldie-Rogers

Penn Traffic VIP

VIRGINIA O'HERRICK
UMBRELLA SALESPERSON
YEARS OF SERVICE 16
1961–1977

In a town known for floods, selling umbrellas turned out to be a steady way of making a living for Virginia O'Herrick.

After starting in 1961 in the budget basement at Penn Traffic and moving on to sportswear and hosiery, Virginia was promoted to head salesperson at the store's umbrella counter. When she took that job, she received a "steady clock number," meaning she was a full-time employee of the company.

She held that same job for years to come, until--ironically--she lost it because of a torrential downpour...the one that led to the Johnstown Flood of 1977.

Photo courtesy of Virginia O'Herrick

An Open and Shut Product

For most of her Penn Traffic career, Virginia sold umbrellas and gloves at a counter on the first floor of the store, near the sportswear and hosiery departments.

Virginia remembers her manager, Eddie Hoffman, as "one terrific boss," a good guy "who treated his help wonderfully."

She also got along well with Lois Robinson in sportswear and Pat Farwell and Audrey Miklos in hosiery. The employees and bosses at Penn Traffic were like one big, happy family and always went out of their way to be friendly and say hello.

But socializing took a back seat to the product Virginia sold. Umbrellas were always her bread and butter, and her days revolved around selling them.

Getting a Handle on the Day

Each morning, Virginia entered the store through the door leading to the first floor men's department, at the end of the store closest to the Johnstown public safety building. She went down a few more steps to the clock room, where she punched in to start her shift.

129

"I came in at nine o'clock every morning, unless it was Christmas," says Virginia. "That was our busiest time. During the holiday season, we opened at 8 A.M., closed at 9, and never stopped moving in between."

After punching in, Virginia walked to her area on the first floor and removed the big dust cloths from the umbrella counter. She spent some time cleaning and setting up, and then she was ready to greet her first customers.

Occasionally, she had to go to the stock area on the fifth floor and check incoming orders. "If a shipment of umbrellas came in, I had to make sure they were the ones I'd ordered," explains Virginia. "If they were the right ones, I marked them for delivery to the sales floor. Then someone else would tag them to sell and bring them to my counter."

From there, it was up to Virginia to help customers select the right umbrellas or gloves to meet their needs. Some longtime brands, like Totes, were steady sellers, promising tried-and-true quality and dependability. Other brands, like Isotoner gloves, were newer, but quickly established a good reputation.

Some products, however, turned out to be short-lived fads. "I remember the year the see-through domed umbrella came out, the one that came down over your head," says Virginia. "We sold them like crazy for a while.

"But a lot of them came back as returns. They weren't made in the U.S., and the quality just wasn't there."

Whatever her sales for the day, Virginia had to balance the cash drawer from her register at the end of her shift. "You took out what you made in sales," she explains. "The money that was left had to be the same amount as what you started with that morning.

"When you closed out at night, you took the cash drawer up to the treasurer's office on the fourth floor. Then you punched out and went home."

Fond Memories

Though Virginia lost her job when the store closed after the 1977 flood, she still remembers Penn Traffic fondly. Certain aspects of the store made a lasting impression on her, as they did so many other employees and shoppers.

"I loved Penn Way candy, of course," says Virginia. "It was the best candy going. I used to buy it and send it for Christmas gifts.

"Speaking of Christmas, I always loved the way they decorated the store for the holidays. There was always Christmas music playing over the speakers, and it really gave everyone the holiday spirit.

"I enjoyed Women's Day each year," says Virginia. "People who worked at the store elected different women to take the place of the male executives for a day.

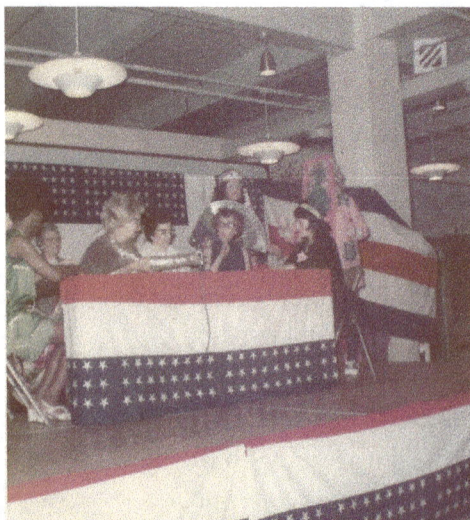

Photo courtesy of Virginia O'Herrick

"One year, I got to be controller John Gunter, which was a lot of fun.

"And I loved the restaurant, too, and the employee cafeteria on the third floor. I ate in both often and always enjoyed the food. The same ladies worked in the cafeteria from the time I started till the day I quit.

"Penn Traffic was just a wonderful place to work. I liked the whole atmosphere, everything about it," says Virginia.

Chapter Fourteen

Penn Traffic's Milk Mustache

1966-1968

After the opening of the DuBois PT, the Penn Traffic Company backed away from the combination store concept. Instead, resources were diverted to the acquisition and development of more supermarkets.

In the third quarter of 1966, for example, the company bought supermarkets in Oil City, Meadville, and Titusville, PA, and converted them to Riversides. Construction also started on another Riverside store in the Shenango Valley Mall in Sharon, PA.

That isn't to say the company was giving up on department stores. In early 1967, construction started on a new 82,500 square foot Penn Traffic store in the Nittany Mall in State College, PA. This new unit would be a straight-up department store, however, not a PT combination store. A new Riverside was planned for State College, but it wouldn't be part of Penn Traffic in the Nittany Mall.

Then there was PT Sports in the Westwood plaza. This standalone unit, opened in 1965, was separated from the PT combination store by the Hello Shop.

Albert Ghantous, owner and president of Elias Painting and Contracting in Johnstown, worked as a sales clerk at PT Sports from the fall of 1981 until early 1983. He says they sold all manner of sporting goods, including hunting apparel, fishing equipment, guns, ammunition, and hunting licenses.

"We also sold TVs and select electronics," explains Albert. "At one point, we even sold LaserDisc players and discs."

No More Combination Stores

PT Sports and Penn Traffic State College aside, the company continued to devote more attention to its supermarket division. The DuBois PT turned out to be the last new combination store ever opened by Penn Traffic.

Why did the company change its focus? Sales were up by 8.7% in '67, from $43,810,908 in '66 to $47,619,841. Earnings were up, too, from $1,781,960 to $1,946,084. Looking back even further, net sales had increased a whopping 64.54% since 1962, when the Indiana and Westmont stores had opened. The combination stores contributed to those increases, so why stop making new ones?

Maybe it was a nod to the changing retail landscape, in which shopping malls like Nittany were beginning to gain a foothold. In such a climate, mall-oriented full-line department stores might make more sense over the long run than combination stores that were better suited to a shopping center environment.

Whatever the rationale behind the shift, it wasn't the only change of direction for the company. Penn Traffic

continued to try new things to boost its bottom line.

Like cafeterias.

Photos from Penn Traffic 1971 Annual Report

134

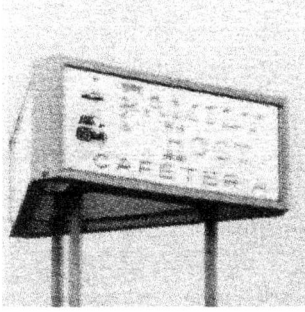

Grab Yourself a Tray

Did you know Penn Traffic once owned a restaurant in Altoona, PA called the Family Host Cafeteria? True story!

The free-standing 230 seat unit opened on January 25, 1967, at "the busiest intersection in the Altoona area, adjacent to a major shopping center," according to the company's 1966 annual report.

The cafeteria came about "after more than a year of research and development work." Penn Traffic planned to take advantage of rising demand from the public for cafeteria-style dining. According to the annual report, the number of cafeterias had more than doubled since 1962.

The economics of cafeterias were also appealing. Cafeterias could serve more customers faster than traditional sit-down restaurants. This led to higher sales volume at peak meal times, offsetting the costs of food, equipment, and personnel.

Penn Traffic President G. Fesler Edwards said response to the Family Host Cafeteria was promising. "Initial public reception of this attractive new establishment has been beyond our optimistic projects," he said, "and it is exceedingly gratifying to begin a new venture on this bright note."

The annual report said there might even be more Family Hosts on the way. "As we become more experienced in cafeteria operation, and as we build a record of success with this initial unit, we anticipate seeking out and researching possible sites for additional cafeteria units."

But a year later, the Family Host Cafeteria wasn't the big story. The people at Penn Traffic had milk on their minds by then.

Photos from Penn Traffic 1966 Annual Report

Dairies Are a Store's Best Friend

There was no need to cry over spilled milk on January 1, 1968. The coming of the New Year brought with it Penn Traffic's merger with Johnstown Sanitary Dairy Company, Inc., aka Sani-Dairy.

Founded in 1902, Sani-Dairy shipped milk, ice cream, dairy specialties, and ice cream novelties from plants in downtown Johnstown and Ligonier, PA. It was the perfect partner for a company that needed oodles of dairy products to stock its Riverside supermarkets. Now, instead of buying those products from outside vendors, Penn Traffic could obtain them from its own dairy division, wiping out the middle men and their markups.

As a bonus, Sani-Dairy brought with it 11 Dairy Dell restaurant/dairy stores that it had been running through a wholly-owned subsidiary. Suddenly, Penn Traffic had a much bigger footprint in the food service world.

1967 Annual Report

1973 Annual Report

Photo from Penn Traffic 1971 Annual Report

1967 Annual Report

Not "Just Another Company"

Even as the dairy division launched, Penn Traffic's other ventures continued to roll forward.

The Penn Traffic department store in State College opened on March 6, 1968. A new supermarket also opened in the Nittany Mall, bringing the grand total to 20 Riverside stores under the Penn Traffic umbrella.

1967 Annual Report

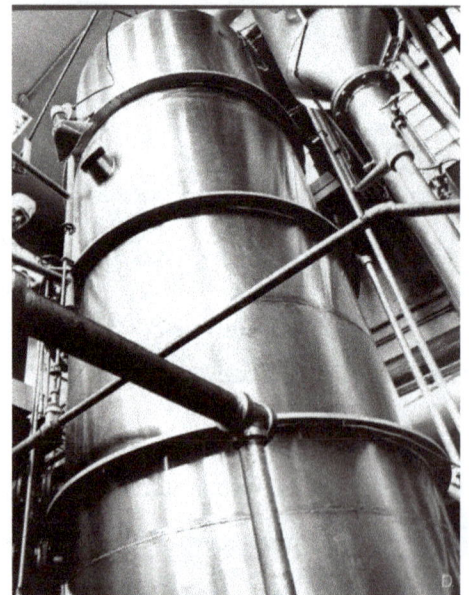
Photo from Penn Traffic 1971 Annual Report

All this churn continued to have a positive impact on the company's bottom line. Total sales in 1968 leaped 22.1%, from $63,353,012 in '67 to $77,322,761.

Dividends were up, as well. For the fifth straight year, Penn Traffic paid an extra dividend over and above the quarterly dividends.

In his letter in the latest annual report, President Edwards called 1968 "a year of substantial progress and achievement." In true Penn Traffic style, he attributed the success to one factor in particular: the people who made up the Penn Traffic family.

Of those 2,712 people, he wrote, "It is to these people, whose energy, talent, and loyalty make it all happen, that this year's report is dedicated. Without these people, we would be 'just another company.'"

Photo from Penn Traffic
1966 Annual Report

Photos from Penn Traffic 1967 Annual Report

137

MONDAY, MARCH 15
IS THE DAY THAT WILL
START A NEW HISTORY

Penn Traffic

GRAND
OPENING

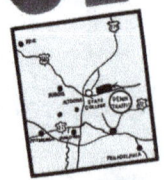

Penn Traffic

PENN TRAFFIC WILL OPEN MONDAY THRU SATURDAY FROM 10:00AM TO 10:00PM

Photo from Penn Traffic 1968 Annual Report

138

Artwork courtesy of Deb Goldie-Rogers

Memory Department

I loved Penn Traffic! When I was little, I always thought I was in New York City at Christmas, looking at the beautifully decorated window. My mother would only shop at Penn Traffic. I remember, as a child, we would go to the restaurant, and I would order stuffing with gravy. It was the best; I can still taste it. As a young girl, my mother (Dorothy Riner Girgos) worked in the gift wrapping department around the holidays. She was very proud that she worked there.

Joanne M Magro

In 1965, Amana blitzed the public with their new kitchen aide, the Radar Range. A major, trusted retailer in each commercial market was selected to introduce the product, and they sent a company representative to demonstrate the microwave...and to assure the public that the cooked food was absolutely SAFE.

The display was located on the fifth floor, immediately outside my Dad's offices, and directly in front of the bank of elevators, so that the public could not avoid the sales pitch. I recall that male customers were dressed in suits and that most women wore small hats. The crowds would listen politely and ask questions, but no one would taste the bacon that the salesMEN (no women) were preparing.

One of the salesmen spied me (I had been visiting my Dad), and asked if I would try a piece. Actually, I had no choice; everyone was watching...so I DID. The salesman then asked the man standing behind me if he would like a piece. He accepted, and I realized that the man was my Dad. At home, however, my Mom was certain that we would surely be ill from the effects of the "radar."

Paula Kellar

I remember going to the Christmas decorated windows downtown with my grandfather and grandmother. They bundled me up in leggings, heavy coat, scarf, hat, and snow boots. I was so amazed by the moving display. I always pressed my nose up against the window to see if I could see more.

Later in life, in high school, I was a member of the Youth (Teen) Advisory Board for two years. We even did a local radio show with WCRO just off the elevators in the female clothing department. Good times.

I was always amazed as a young child at the ladies' restroom on the mezzanine. I still remember the pink tiles and having to put a coin in for the stall door to open. Most women tried to catch the stall door before it flew shut so they wouldn't have to pay.

I think the camera department was on the mezzanine as well. I can remember looking down from the mezzanine onto the first floor where the jewelry and the makeup counters were. I liked checking out the hats and coats that all the women would wear.

JoHanna Haines Hergenrider

I remember having hot fudge sundaes in the restaurant. It was one of those treats we were allowed when we went there to shop.

Betsy A. Pudliner

My aunt would take me to Penn Traffic every Easter and buy me a dress, shoes, hat, purse and gloves. Then, we would go to the restaurant and have a club sandwich and a milkshake. I looked forward to that outing so much and am grateful to have it as a lifetime memory.

Gretchen Redick Rogers

I worked there, and my mom, Eva Johnson, was a waitress in the restaurant. I remember getting my hair done when those big curls were popular, piled as high atop your head as structurally possible. I counted 57 hairpins! AND the insides of the curls were sprayed gold to match my gown.

Linda Palmer

I bought my prom gown there. It was one of the nicest gowns I ever had.
Florence Strushensky

I couldn't wait for school to let out so I could go to Penn Traffic and get a salad with blue cheese dressing. I loved those days so long ago in 1968.
Jean Neiderhiser

My dad bought me a small toby mug--Winston Churchill--by Royal Doulton. It was among the lovely things on Penn Traffic's mezzanine, a favorite browsing spot. I was so pleased with it and still have it. Dad was a Churchill fan.
Jane Oleksak

Photo courtesy of Jane Oleksak

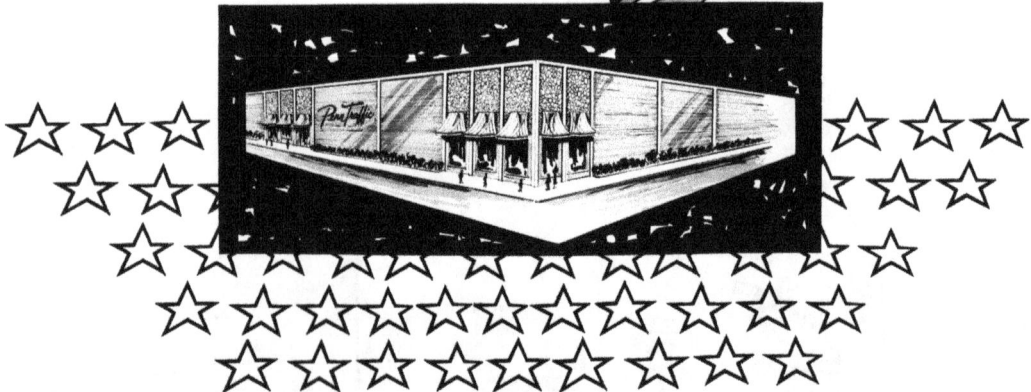

Artwork courtesy of Deb Goldie-Rogers

BARBARA BAXTER
BUYER
YEARS OF SERVICE 26
1956-1982

Once upon a time, Barbara Baxter got to see Pearl Bailey, Carol Channing, and many other stars on Broadway. She saw Paul Newman and his wife, Joanne Woodward, in the bar of the hotel where she was staying. She traveled to New York City so many times, she lost count, and even flew out to Los Angeles and hung around Hollywood.

It was all part of her 26-year career as a clothing buyer for the Penn Traffic Company.

Photo from Penn Traffic 1975 Annual Report

Once Upon a Buyer

Barbara's fairy tale career started with a part-time job as a clerk in the dresses and coats department at the Westwood PT store in 1956. After a while, she moved up to a position as an assistant buyer at the store, working with buyer Laura Beckley.

As an assistant, Barbara helped Laura order women's clothing for Penn Traffic and the PT satellite stores in Westwood, DuBois, and Indiana, PA. Laura and Barbara selected styles from vendor offerings, then determined the best numbers and assortments of sizes to order for each store based on demographics and past and projected sales activity.

As business increased, and Penn Traffic opened new stores in State College and Somerset, the women split their workload in two. "As we added stores, it got to be too much for one person," recalls Barbara. "That was a lot of responsibility, a lot of bookkeeping and traveling to the stores and everything.

"We just had to split it. Laura took women's sportswear and coats, and I got better dresses, moderate dresses, and bridal.

"Better dresses were priced at $100 and over," says Barbara. "Moderate dresses were lower-priced, for people with moderate incomes. Bridals, of course, were individualized. We worked with brides and their families and found what they wanted on trips to New York City."

143

At that point, Barbara became a full-fledged buyer in her own right...and she never turned back. The work was hectic and challenging, but she loved it.

Photo from Penn Traffic 1977 Annual Report

Road Warrior

Barbara never minded the travel, either, though there was plenty of it. As a buyer ordering merchandise for all the department stores in the company, she had to drive around and visit each of them, assessing their needs and making sure the orders she'd placed were properly delivered.

In those days, she drove constantly, shuttling between downtown Johnstown, Westwood, Indiana, DuBois, Somerset, and State College. "The roads weren't always the best, especially in the winter," says Barbara. "But you had to be at those stores on certain days, and that's just what you did."

Barbara's travels also took her farther afield—all the way to New York City. She and the other buyers went there regularly, in fact, to find and order clothing to sell in Penn Traffic's stores.

"We did most of our buying in New York City," remembers Barbara. "Usually, there were four to six people who traveled together, all from different departments, except shoes and millinery. The shoe departments in our stores were all leased and operated by Brown Shoe Company, which took care of its own buying. As for the millinery departments, they worked with a special buying office in New York, separate from the one the rest of us worked with."

Sometimes, Barbara and the buyers would travel to New York by train. Other times, they drove a van or flew to the city. When they arrived, they often checked into the reasonably priced Piccadilly Hotel. "With the limited expense accounts we were given, we had to be careful where we spent our money," says Barbara. "The Piccadilly was reasonable, and the staff there were always very good to us."

Photo from Penn Traffic 1973 Annual Report

The Art of Buying

According to Barbara, a New York-based buying office provided guidance on where to find the best merchandise for each season. Then, she and the other buyers would make appointments with vendors to see the merchandise in person.

"We'd go and see what they were offering and make decisions about what to buy for the stores," says Barbara.

In the process, she and her fellow buyers kept up a grueling pace. "We were busy from eight o'clock in the morning till six o'clock in the evening. And we never stopped moving."

Often, says Barbara, moving meant walking...all over town. "We went a lot of places on foot, since taking a taxi was expensive, and we had to pay out of our own pockets if we went over our expense account allowance. This led to a lot of walking. Maybe I'd be on 26th street and have to be on 58th street for my next appointment. Covering that kind of distance in a short time could be a real workout."

Getting across town was just the beginning. Making buying decisions was challenging in its own right.

Styles were chosen according to season. "Summertime was our big season, so we ordered a wider variety then. Winter was always slower," remembers Barbara.

Next, she had to decide how many of each size in each style to order for each store. "I tried never to buy more than four of a kind for each store," she says. "And the exact sizes we ordered depended on the nature of the style.

"One style might be better suited to smaller figures, so I'd order it in sizes 4, 6, 8, and 10. Another style might be designed for larger figures, so I'd order it in sizes 10, 12, 14, and 16. I also sometimes ordered half sizes, based on what I knew about a store's clientele."

Photo from Penn Traffic 1973 Annual Report

Ordering four of each style per store gave Penn Traffic flexibility in managing its stock. If a particular style sold out, Barbara could always reorder, then adjust her next orders accordingly.

Barbara on Broadway

If Barbara didn't get to see a vendor during her trip to New York, the vendor might send a salesman to Johnstown to show her his wares. But going to New York enabled her to see much more in a shorter time...and take advantage of certain perks that weren't available at home.

"Often, the salesmen in certain vendor showrooms would ask if you wanted to see certain Broadway shows," remembers Barbara. "They would order and pay for tickets, and we'd pick them up at the theater.

"It was very nice that they did that. Theater tickets weren't as expensive as they are now, but they were still pricey.

"I saw lots of shows. *Mame*, for example. I think I saw everything that was on Broadway at the time.

"Going to those shows, I got to see a lot people who I wouldn't have had the chance to see otherwise: Pearl Bailey, Carol Channing, and many other actresses and actors, whoever happened to be in a certain show."

But Broadway wasn't the only attraction that Barbara got to visit during her travels as a buyer.

Photo from Penn Traffic 1977 Annual Report

Hollywood Nights

In addition to her many visits to New York, Barbara got to spend some time in Los Angeles. She and her fellow buyers went in search of new fashions to sell in Johnstown, and did their share of touring on the side.

"When we were done each day, we drove around in our rental car and saw the sights," remembers Barbara. "We got to experience Hollywood and other parts of the city.

"We even drove down to San Diego when Penn Traffic paid for us to stay an extra day. My son had been stationed as a Marine at Miramar in San Diego, and I wanted to see what it was like. On our way back to L.A., we stopped at beaches and explored a little."

Out of Gas

Barbara loved her adventures, but eventually, the buying trips came to an end. She kept working for Penn Traffic after the 1977 flood, buying for the satellite stores, but when Hess's bought those in '82, they didn't invite her to come along with them.

Photo from Penn Traffic 1976 Annual Report

After that, Barbara worked for the Martin's store in downtown Johnstown. She finally retired after nine years, and now lives a quiet life in Upper Yoder.

But she still fondly remembers her time at Penn Traffic.

"I really did enjoy it," says Barbara. "And I liked everyone I worked with.

"I had good clerks in my department. I could go on vacation and know that when I got back, everything had run smoothly without me.

"The bosses were great, too. G. Fessler Edwards was president when I started, and he was very, very nice. So were the vice presidents, Bill and Dick Corben.

"It was a wonderful place to work and shop," says Barbara. "It provided a good living and opportunities to travel for 26 years.

"While it lasted, it was fun."

Photo courtesy of Darrel Holsopple

Chapter Fifteen

The Pook Who Loved Penn Traffic

1969-1976

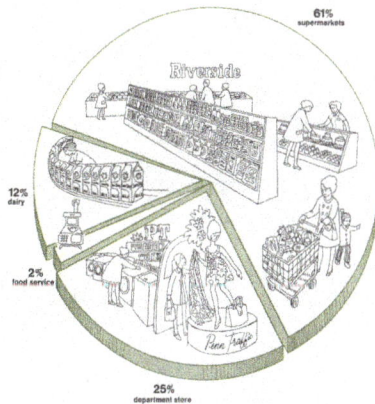

From the Penn Traffic 1969 Annual Report

One thing was clear in the 1970s: the supermarkets were taking over the Penn Traffic Company. In 1969, they generated 61% of sales. That number rose to 64% in 1970...then 66% in 1971...68% in '72...72% in '73...and 75% in 1975.

Meanwhile, department store sales just kept fading. They went from 25% of total sales in 1969 to just 15% in '75.

The company's heart just didn't seem to be in department stores anymore. They hadn't opened a new one--full-line or combination store--since State College in '68. Meanwhile, there were 28 Riversides by 1972...33 by 1975.

Even Sani-Dairy seemed to be on a roll, undergoing a $3.5 million expansion in 1971 which increased production capacity by 300%. By the time it was over, Sani-Dairy had a new 9,000 square foot ice cream facility capable of storing 400,000 gallons of ice cream.

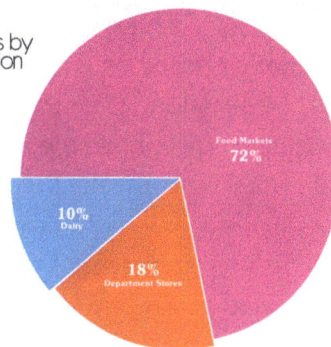

From the Penn Traffic 1973 Annual Report

Milk production was doubled in all container sizes, and the orange juice and yogurt lines were also expanded.

But when it came to the department stores, Penn Traffic just wasn't showing a lot of love. The company did spend some money to refurbish the DuBois PT, but that work was necessitated by flooding from tropical storm Agnes on June 22, 1972.

Otherwise, the department stores seemed underappreciated, especially the downtown Johnstown store. It was still the company's headquarters, but not really the focus of its attention.

When, if ever, would Penn Traffic make a big play on the department store side again? The answer, it turned out, had to do with a white-furred mascot called Richie the Pook.

richland mall

The Pook and Penn Traffic

Richie, a panda-like figure known for wearing a giant yellow bow tie, was the official mascot of the Richland Mall, a new shopping venue in the Johnstown suburb of Richland Township. As the project developed in early-to-mid 1974, Richie popped up with increasing frequency in the media, raising awareness about the new mall.

In the process, he raised awareness about Penn Traffic. After six years without a new department store, the company was opening a full-line, mall-style Penn Traffic store as an anchor of the new Richland Mall.

One end of the mall would be anchored by Sears, the other by Kmart...and right in the middle, across from the oasis of trees and a babbling brook at the heart of the mall, would be Penn Traffic.

Finally, the department store division had something to crow about, a way to boost its profile within the company. The supermarket and dairy divisions had no part of this deal; it was all about the merchandising, marketing, and customer service that the department store people had done so well for over a century.

And Richie the Pook gave it his blessing. When the Richland Mall Penn Traffic opened on October 14, 1974, he was there to mark the occasion. He clowned around with his giant bow tie, patted people on the back with his furry gray paws, and helped welcome the first shoppers through the doors.

After which, the cash registers started making beautiful music, as expected.

Photo from Penn Traffic 1971 Annual Report

"At Least One New Penn Traffic Store"

According to President Edwards' letter in the 1974 Annual Report, business was good at the new mall store. "Activity from opening date through the Christmas season was most satisfactory, and from all indications, the new store has been well received in the area," he wrote. "We are confident that both the new Mall and our Penn Traffic store will be successful."

Photo from Penn Traffic 1977 Annual Report

His expectations were right on the money in 1975. Thanks in part to the performance of the Richland Mall Penn Traffic, the department store division tallied a 14.5% increase in sales for the year.

As noted in the Report to Shareholders in the 1975 Annual Report, this success breathed new life into the department store side of the house. Chairman of the Board Edwards (who'd retired as president) and new company president Paul G. Reitz wrote of a "carefully planned program of further expansion," in which "the Department Store Division will continue its site selection for growth in individual department stores, or in conjunction with Riverside Market operations."

Edwards and Reitz were even more specific than that when it came to the new expansion plan. "At least one new Penn Traffic store will be opened during the year," they wrote. "At this time, several locations are under study."

Perhaps the fact that their predictions didn't pan out shouldn't come as a surprise. After all, they wrote that they were "optimistic for long range economic growth" in the Johnstown area, and we all know how that turned out.

Photo from Penn Traffic 1973 Annual Report

Photo from Penn Traffic 1968 Annual Report

"A Major Eroding Effect"

One year later, in the 1976 Annual Report, President Reitz wasn't sounding so bullish about the department stores...especially the one in downtown Johnstown.

"Unusually warm weather and good economic conditions in early 1976 developed good traffic in our department stores," wrote Reitz. "During the

rest of the year, sales slowed considerably. Four of our seven department stores showed different degrees of gains for the year while three dropped below last year's sales."

According to Reitz, the downtown store was dragging down the division. "Not unexpectedly, our own outlying stores and new competitors have had a major eroding effect on the downtown unit. Being the largest of our department stores, its poor results greatly affect the entire division."

Sounds like the honeymoon was pretty much over for the mother store, doesn't it? But downtown Penn Traffic didn't have anything to worry about, did it?

The company had sold off the Family Host Cafeteria in Altoona and seven Dairy Dell stores in '74, but they were a different story, right? They didn't have the same *history* as downtown Penn Traffic. They weren't the *headquarters* of the entire operation.

Was it possible that Reitz, a Riverside man who'd come with the merger in 1962, might not have the same degree of loyalty to the downtown store as G. Fesler Edwards and those who'd come up through the ranks on Washington Street? Who could say for sure?

Was it possible the Penn Traffic company might be facing a future without the store that gave it its name?

The answer, it turns out, was yes...but not for any reason that

anyone could have predicted.

By the end of 1977, the famous Penn Traffic Department Store in downtown Johnstown would close its doors forever, and no one, but no one, would see it coming.

Photos from Penn Traffic 1975 Annual Report

MEMORY DEPARTMENT

I worked at Penn Traffic over the Christmas holiday in 1970 in the children's and Girl Scout departments.

Bonnie Partsch Donnelly

When I was in high school at Johnstown High (1971), I was envious of the teen advisory board girls, because they got to be part of the Penn Traffic store. My best friend and I would go up to the junior department after school, and there was a jukebox you could play for free. We must have worn out the Rolling Stones' record, "Honky Tonk Woman." At the cosmetic counter, they gave us a sample of Chanel #5 fragrance, and I thought I was so special wearing it to school. When I wear Chanel #5 now, I always think of Penn Traffic.

Mary Lannen

My mom and I always did my school clothes shopping at Penn Traffic. I remember a beautiful pink winter coat that she bought for me, and those had-to-have penny loafers! We spent the day. It was a treat to drive from Windber and get the latest styles. I was in the Class of '73, and all the years of Christmas displays and the perfume counter are sweet memories of home.

Debra Stopko Korhut

I worked there for the Christmas season of 1972 in the "Center Aisle" with Mary Washington. Occasionally, they sent me to the basement to do free gift wrapping. Christmas was always festive, busy, and exciting at Penn Traffic.

My aunt, Helen Replogle, worked there for many years in the furniture department. I remember the computer room took up a whole floor and was very cold, white, and sterile-looking. I'm sure my iPhone has WAY more computing power than all those giant computers did.

Emilie Clawson Hinton

Penn Traffic was my favorite store to shop. My husband was Santa there in the early '70s. I have pictures of me, pregnant, sitting on his lap!

Colleen Kurtz

I was hired for Ladies' Day as a sale clerk in 1974, then moved to the Trim-A-Tree department, which was located on the furniture floor. I was a floater off and on for the following year, then was hired by Mr. "B" in the deli. I loved working for Penn Traffic. I have a lot of good memories from there.

Terri Waddell Hale

Penn Traffic was the most elite store in Johnstown. We had to wear our Sunday best to go shopping there. I remember talking to Santa, trying on and buying shoes, spending time on the mezzanine, and so much more. I liked it so well that when I got older (1971-72), I worked there. First was in the hosiery department with Martha, Susan, and Debbie. Next was the jewelry department with Leona and Margie. I remember the first optic lights (lamps). Fun times and great memories!

Linda Eash

I worked there sweeping and mopping floors and cleaning up the Tasty Kitchen and restaurant after closing time back in '75 and '76. There were two old men on duty, security guards, who took turns sleeping. One would nap while the other made the rounds with a key clock, turning keys in obscure corners all over the store on every floor. They were supposed to pat us down as we left work, but we learned to just "stare them down." I never stole a thing, though. Well, I often found change on the floor while sweeping the restaurant, and I did keep that.

At the time, Penn Traffic had a young African-American woman plainclothes security guard. She used to stand in the greeting card aisle, next to the watches and jewelry. Nobody figured her for a cop!

I truly loved that store and probably explored every nook and cranny of the backrooms at one time or another.

Steve Morgan

Photo by Hesselbein Studio, courtesy of Johnstown Area Heritage Association

My mother's sisters (my aunts) both worked at Penn Traffic in the 1960s and 1970s. Aunt Laura worked in notions and hats, and Aunt Evelyn worked in the second floor sportswear department. I remember my mother buying me all of my school clothes at Penn Traffic in the '70s, and the store had all of the latest fashions.

When I was in high school, I applied to be a Penn Traffic Teen Advisory Board member as a representative from Richland High School. Sadly, I wasn't chosen, and I remember being really disappointed.

The cafeteria at Penn Traffic was also a wonderful place. We would go there after the Christmas parade and get hot fudge sundaes with an animal cracker on top. The Christmas windows at Penn Traffic were magical; just like in the movie *A Christmas Story*. I am so glad that I grew up during those times!

Janice Friedman-Snyder

Photo by Brian Krise

PennTeen

Kathy Baich
577 Dorothy Ave.
Johnstown, Pa. 15906

BULK RATE
U. S. POSTAGE
PAID
Permit No. 145
JOHNSTOWN, PA.
15901

Volume 1

Onward Johnstown Trojans

Ready, two, three, up! The cymbols crash, the trumpets blare and the Johnstown High School Trojan marching and drilling band begins its third season under the superb direction of W. Glyn Edwards. The band once again will entertain its audiences with precision drill half-time shows to keep its school proud.

Since the band does not get the publicity it deserves, we write this article to better explain just how the band functions.

Unknown to many people, these band members sacrificed their last two weeks of vacation to devote them to difficult precision drilling. The rugged rehearsals began at 7:00 and ended at 3:00.

In spite of the extreme hot and cold weather conditions, everyone, having foremost in their minds the good reputation of the band, worked to uphold its high standards.

According to Mr. Edwards, the potential of individual band members of this year's band could make this band one of the best!

New Faculty Welcomed

The students of Ferndale Area were pleased to welcome several new members to their Faculty. Among these are Mr. Woodhead who is a Chemistry Instructor and also serves as a Junior High football coach. Lending assistance to Mr. Woodhead in the Junior High coaching ranks is Mr. Stefanick who spends his school hours instructing students in General Math. The other two faculty additions are found in the Foreign Language Department. Here we find Mr. Mikula who teaches Spanish and who has to his credit a stay in Mexico which lends realism to his teaching. Last but not least we find Mr. Stevenson who specializes in French instruction and whose background is kept secret thus far.

Once again, we, the students wish to welcome the latest additions to our faculty and hope that they find their stay at Ferndale both enjoyable and profitable.

Red Cross Program

During the week of August 4-10, the Red Cross offered a Leadership Program at Grove City College. The 160 delegates were from the Pittsburgh area, Cambria-Somerset county chapters, Virginia, and Canada. The two delegates from Westmont were Terry Owen and Mary Nokes. Terry is a Varsity cheerleader and Secretary of the Student Council. Mary is Secretary of National Honor Society and Treasurer of the Girl's Athletic Association. The girls were chosen on the basis of school leadership and scholastic ability.

The leadership course consisted of classes dealing with handling of groups, assemblies showing how the Red Cross operates on the local, national, and international levels, and recreational functions.

New Principals Start at Township

This year Conemaugh Township started its school year with a new principal and assistant principal. The position of principal was filled by Mr. James L. Herdman. Mr. Herdman received his Bachelor of Science degree from Penn State University, his masters degree from Lehigh University and did additional graduate work at Lehigh University and Lafette College. Previously Mr. Herdman taught mathematics at Easton, Pennsylvania and served as Director of Guidance at Lower Mooreland near Huntingdon Valley.

Mr. George Schmidt, newly appointed assistant principal, graduated from the University of Pittsburgh in 1950. He later went on to do graduate work at the University of Iowa. Mr. Schmidt taught English and Social Studies for 17 years. He served as football and basketball coach at the University of Iowa. Mr. Schmdit also acts as a scout for the Pittsburgh Pirates during the summer.

Four new teachers were also hired. They are as follows: Mrs. Patricia Macchiarolo, mathematics; Miss Evelyn Pellsky, reading; Mr. Thomas Brown, mathematics, and Mr. John D'Antonio, science and mathematics.

Dave Sanders

Richland Student In Portugal

Dave Sanders, a senior at Richland High School, recently came back from a vacation in Portugal. Last May, Dave was selected as an American Field Service exchange student, and on June 20, he left for Porto, a city in the northern part of Portugal, to spend the summer. He returned on September 1, at 2:00 in the morning.

Dave lived with his family on Francelos Beach. He had two "brothers," Rui, seventeen, and Jorje, fourteen; and one sister Isabel, nine. His "father" was a technician in a tire factory and his "mother" was a clerk. Dave could understand some Portuguese, and he toured most of northern Portugal.

He had many fine experiences. The mayor of Porto presented him with a book about Porto. Dave said he liked the food and gained fifteen pounds. He watched Portuguese catch an octopus and said that cooked with rice, it was delicious. Dave remarked that it was a wonderful experience he'll never forget.

C. V. To Get New School

A new senior high school is under construction for the Conemaugh Valley Area School District. Ground was broken last January at the construction site adjacent to the East Taylor Township Elementary School along Route 219. The building will contain 23 classrooms, facilities for home economics, shop, arts and crafts and music along with a library, an 800 seat auditorium and three gymnasiums. It will have facilities for 600 students. Near the school athletic fields for the different sports will be constructed. The project will be completed by June 1, 1969.

2 Ferndale Srs. Attend Program

Two senior students at Ferndale this summer attended colleges through the National Science Foundation's Summer Program for Highly Advanced Secondary Students.

Douglas Gyorke went to Knox College in Galesburg, Illinois. He studied math and chemistry for six weeks. The total number attending was forty, and Doug was one of two from Pennsylvania. He said that he enjoyed himself very much and hoped to be able to go back. In high school Doug is a member of the football team and president of the National Honor Society and the Key Club.

Robert Pickerill

Robert Pickerill attended the University of Kansas at Lawrence, Kansas. His classes consisted of sociology and the elementary numbers theory. This also lasted for six weeks. Classes were two hours in length from Monday to Friday. One hundred and six students were enrolled in the same course as Bob, and four were from Pennsylvania. Bob, like Doug, stated that he would like to attend this school again if at all possible. At Ferndale this year he is president of the Leo Club, treasurer of the JETS Club, and vice president of the National Honor Society.

Starting Soon!

Hey girls, it's time to brighten up to fall! Have a bright new you to go with the bright new fall fashions! Starting soon we will have another five week Beauty Workshop class. Watch the newspaper for the date.

Join us then and meet the new you!

Question Corner

Students from the various schools represented by the Teen Advisory Board: Johnstown, Windber, Ferndale, Westmont, Bishop McCort, Conemaugh Township, Conemaugh Valley, and Richland, were asked to answer the following question:

"Would you date a boy with long hair and ruffles? Why or why not?"

Linda Crain	—Why not? He's still a boy isn't he?
Jill Schonek	—Long hair is OK, but ruffles???
Minda Georg	—I like a date that's 100% boy.
Madalene Komisar	—Yes, because what's important is his personality, maturity, and consideration for me. And as long as hes' clean and neat, too.
Dee Morbit	—No, they remind me of sissies with ruffles.
Tana Tabler	—Yes, if I was sure he was a boy!
Sally Benson	—Yes, because it shows they're certain of their masculinity.
Mary Kay Krumenacker	—No, I'll stick to the oldfashioned kind.
Pam Chapman	—Yes, if he is wearing my favorite "perfume"!
Cynthia Gilbert	—Definitely not. When I walk down the street, I want people to know I'm with a boy and not just with one of the girls.
Karen Stutzman	—Yes, if his nylons don't bag.
Monica Lloyd	—No, I don't care for "dainty" boys.
Marleen Davich	—No, I like masculine guys.
Beverly Yanko	—No, it would be like going out with one of my girl friends.

On the Air . . .

Attention! Nobody should miss the High School Happening featuring the Teen Advisory Board members from the eight Johnstown Area high schools. At 7:30 each Saturday night tune in to WCRO and hear the latest from all the schools.

Hear the girls give the info on all the newest fads, events, and happenings going on; listen to sports figures size up their opponents and give their strategy on future games.

Jump on the bandwagon and join the fun each Saturday night as the Penn Traffic High School Happening radio show comes your way on WCRO.

BMHS Students Attends College

Angela Neilan, a senior at Bishop McCort High School, attended college this summer at Northern Michigan University. Through the National Science Foundation she furthered her studies in physics and mathematics. Angela placed eighteenth in physics and twenty-first in math in a class of forty-four.

Miss Neilan is secretary of the Student Council and an active member of the National Honor Society, German Library, Mu Alpha Theta Clubs and a member of the Yearbook Staff.

PENN TEEN TOPICS

Published monthly by the Twenty-three Member Penn Traffic Teen Advisory Board.

Volume 1 No. 3 September, 1968

Editor—Bonnie Hunter

Reporters—Pattie Peters, Susan Ripple, Arlene Noel and Susan Miller, Windber.

Mary Nokes and Linda Clites, Westmont Hilltop High School.

Lorraine Adams, Barbara Najjar and Kathy Pohlit, Bishop McCort High School.

Leslie Chapple, Susan Salay and Holly Frank, Conemaugh Township.

Elaine Stypula, Sue Walls and Karen Tilton, Richland High School.

Judy Opacic, Kathy Litzinger, Susan Walter, Johnstown High School.

Connie Risko and Marsha Lynch, Conemaugh Valley.

Jill Jenkins, Anna Pappas, Cathy Brant and Ann McLaughlin, Ferndale Area High School.

Fashion Chemistry . . .

Potent fashion catalysts take a new formula, apply it to separates and . . . whooosh . . . it's *the look*! Each part stands on its own with fine authority . . . yet when the combination suits you, you'll "feel" the right mix. Come, stir around our newest arrivals in skirts, shirts, sweaters, vests, pants. Find what fizzes.

Get into the big swing in fashion co-ordinates at Penn Traffic in the Sports Aisle and Junior Colony Hang-Out with such names as Bobbie Brooks, College Town, Villager, Majestic, Garland and many others.

Key Ingredient

Cordoruy is the key ingredient as Majestic sets up a bit of chemistry in this co-ordinate set. It's right in the groove, right in style for this set for school or football. During the day it's a straight skirt with the new wide belt and a long tapered vest with imitation pockets over a contrasting sweater or blouse. Later in the day it's the big swing to tapered slacks and a wide collared blazer with front pockets to warm up to that fall evening at the football field. It's something to cheer about . . . in egg shell, brown or royal blue.

Mix by Kelita

Kelita mixes earthen tones in a three piece plaid outfit for fall fun. It's an A-line skirt with a three button jacket with imitation pockets for school with matching sweater or blouse, for that quick fun change its matching tapered slacks for after school occasions. All together, it's one of the potent fashion catalysts for fall.

Get with the chemistry of fashion . . . come in and brouse through the Junior Colony Hang Out and the Sports Aisle on the Second Floor of Fashion at Penn Traffic.

BECKY SMITH OUTSTANDING ATHLETE

In 1967 Richland High School formed an all girls track team. They practiced long and hard and had a very successful first year. Success followed one member of this team, Becky Smith, all the way to the national Junior Olympics held in Knoxville, Tennessee August 6-8, 1968.

At the Allegheny Mountain Association Amateur Athletic Union Girls Junior Olympics held at Greensburg High School, Becky qualified for the AMA finals in Johnstown June 1, 1968. Becky then competed in the Region 2 Junior Olympic Track and Field Championship Meet at Allegheny College, Meadville. She led the competion in the intermediate high jump and earned an expense paid trip to the University of Tennessee where she competed in the Junior Olympic national championship meet. Becky finished seventh in the intermediate high jump competition with a jump of four feet ten inches.

Becky is a junior at Richland High School and is working under the supervision of Mrs. Renzi.

Annual "Luau" Held at Westmont Hilltop

Students of Westmont Hilltop Senior High School, dressed in "aloha shirts" and "muumuus", together in honor of the great "tikhi" on Saturday night in the gym.

All football players were warmly received at the door by our Varsity Cheerleaders. The girls, dressed in brilliant native garb, presented colorful leis to each football player as he entered the dance. The leis were made of pastel tissue paper flowers over 2,000 in number.

Many Tahitian gals and guys gathered around the great Tikhi or sat beneath the shady palm trees. Some Westy natives grooved to the swingin' beat of the "Blues Bag". Fresh fruit, coconut, punch and cookies refreshed some 200 weary natives through out the evening.

A great big THANKS to our Varsity Cheerleaders for making our "Luau" such a tremendous success.

Small But Tuff

On August 19th Coach John Matsko of the Ferndale Area Yellow Jackets opened the 1968 football season with a two week training session.

This years squad is the smallest since Matsko first accepted the duties as head coach five years ago.

Along with being small, the boys are also very inexperienced as they have only 3 returning lettermen: Larry Speicher, senior and Rick Speicher and Carm Sotille both juniors.

Rick Stem, chosen as captain by his teammates will lead the Jackets through the rest of their 8 game season. The first being taken by the Jackets in a 13-6 victory over Shade.

Conemaugh Township Victory

On September 6, Conemaugh Township kicked off their football season by defeating the opposing Northern Cambria Colts by the score of 13-6. A 20 yard drive was ended when halfback Mel Shroyer broke through for a 4 yard touch down. Quarterback Frank Haines then threw a 40 yard pass to halfback Jim Ellingsworth for the winning touchdown. Russ McCaullif kicked the field goal. Both touchdowns were made in the first quarter. The Colts only touchdown was during the fourth quarter.

Valley Jays

Another football season has opened for the Conemaugh Valley Blue Jays. Along with the new members of the team, the Blue Jays start the season with a new coach, Mike Yewcic. Yewcic has retained 13 lettermen. They are: Richard Calpin, Bob Mesaros, Louis Sandmaier, Ted Roman, Steve Chase, Rick Roebuck, Dave Molnar, Jeff Fyock, Gary Oleksa, Don Patcher, Scott Hagerich, Barron Gimza, and Jeff Hockensmith. An outstanding performance is expected from our back field this year. The outstanding sophomores are Bob Placky and Paul Conrad.

J. H. S. Squad Starts With Bang

The Johnstown Trojans started the '68 football season with a bang by defeating Erie Prep 34-26 at Erie. Returning quarterback, Carl Schneider ran 18 and 1 yd. for two of the Trojan touchdowns. Gary Hrivnak caught a 4 yd. pass from Schneider for the second touchdown of the game. Tony Veney and Alan Andrews ran 5 and 2 yds., respectively for the remaining two touchdowns. Coach Francis "Blackie" Mihalic and his Men of Troy are headed for a big season. The 14 lettermen returning in the Trojan line-up are as follows: John Martin, Gary Gelesh, Nick Sremanak, Dan Meyers, Larry Fabina, Gary Hrivnak, Bronco Keser, Bob Sopchick, Carl Schneider, Ed Rosko, Tony Veney, Bob Ramos, Jon Burgo, and Ed Seman. The Trojans play four home games and 6 away. This Saturday night Johnstown will take on South Hills in a home game at the Point.
of last year.

The Beat Goes On

It is football time and once again the areas high school bands are striking up tunes and figuring out shows to perform for their football games at half-time. Although some people don't realize in order to preform such actions they do, bands begin practicing before school starts. Along with the areas other high school bands, Ferndale Area band members practiced two weeks before school started.

This year the Ferndale Area Band has 70 members. Some of the highlights the band will be doing are the teaberry shuffle, a soft shoe routine, majorettes twirling fire, and a precision drill routine. The Ferndale Area Band's mascot, Carolyn Clark, will be highlighting the band by twirling two fire batons, and participating in the dance steps with the band.

THE 1968 VICTORY RAMBLERS

Windber High's football hopes rest on fifteen returning lettermen on a forty-four man team. Only one lettermen is a veteran with the offensive unit. In comparison with 1967, this year's team will be a little smaller in the line and about the same in the backfield. The line will average 160 pounds compared with the 165-170 last year.

The Ramblers' schedule last year had a 5-4-1 mark, including a one-sided rout over Conemaugh Township when the score read 37-0.

This year's schedule follows:

Sept.	21	Indiana
	28	Punxsutawney
Oct.	4	Somerset
	12	Conemaugh Township
	19	Westmont
	25	Cambria Heights
Nov.	1	Forest Hills
	9	Johnstown

ELEANOR KOHAN
HEAD PIE MAKER
YEARS OF SERVICE 3
1972-1975

Photo by Philip Balko

Every morning, Eleanor Kohan would turn on the ovens in the Penn Traffic bakery and start rolling out the dough. She would switch on the radio, turn on the steamer, and start organizing the ingredients for each recipe from her recipe book.

She did everything according to a proven system. She had at least 10 to 12 pies to make every day, and there was no better way to get them done--and done right.

It was all part of being the head pie maker at Penn Traffic, a job Eleanor did for over two and a half years.

Pies, Pies, Everywhere Pies

Eleanor made all her pies from scratch, following recipes handed down by her predecessors. Those women, Mary Stotler and Mary Karnoski, trained her to do things the old-fashioned way when she came to Penn Traffic from the Harris Boyer bakery in Morrellville in 1972. (She lost her job at Harris Boyer when she got married, because married women weren't allowed to work there.)

"I started out making glazed doughnuts and raisin-filled cookies," says Eleanor. "Then, the ladies in the pie shop invited me to work with them when the girl who'd been helping them quit.

"It was really hectic, but I caught on fast. And I loved it.

"Mary Stotler and Mary Karnoski really showed me the ropes. One thing they taught me was to mix up all the spices for the next day's orders in butcher paper bags. When I had time, after I got all my baking done for the day, I'd put the dry ingredients for each pie in the bags, mix them up beforehand.

155

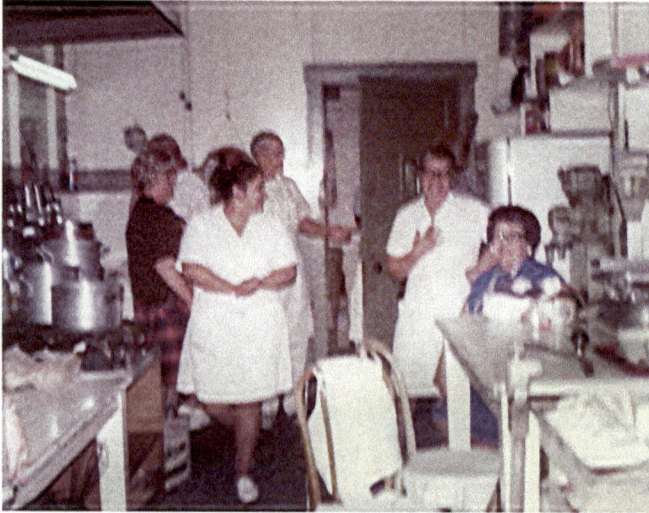

Photo by Eleanor Kohan

"Like if I had 8 pies to make the next day, I'd mix up all the dry ingredients for them the night before. Then, when the orders came, I knew just which packages of spices to use for that number of pies."

Eleanor learned how many cans of fruit filling to use for apple, cherry, peach, or berry pies. She learned how to work with clear gel, a filling thickener used in place of corn starch or flour.

She also learned the ins and outs of stabilizer, an ingredient used to increase the volume of meringue pies and keep them from collapsing.

It was an on-the-job education that turned her into a first-rate pie maker...and prepared her to take over when the two Marys finally retired.

"I worked hard and mastered everything from making dough to taking inventory," says Eleanor. "When Mary Karnoski was getting ready to retire, she said 'I'm gonna put your name in for my job, Eleanor. Out of the girls in the bakery, I think you can do it best.'"

The Value of Pie

From then on, Eleanor spent her workdays as the chief pie maker at Penn Traffic, creating a variety of from-scratch pies for sale in the bakery shop and restaurant. Her pies were so popular, she had to stay organized and work hard to keep up with demand.

"I'd make the pie dough the night before an order and put it in galvanized tins. I used a big steel bowl to mix the 20 pounds of flour, eight pounds of shortening, and eight ounces of salt I needed for a typical batch of dough.

"At first, it took me a long time to mix," says Eleanor. "But I eventually got it down to ten minutes."

Eleanor would roll out the dough for the pie shells on a long table dusted with flour. She would stack and store the shells, then separate them the next day.

She mixed big cans of fruit filling with clear gel and pre-mixed dry ingredients, then spooned them into the shells and covered with dough. Pumpkin and cream pies went without a dough covering; for certain cream pies, a graham cracker crust was substituted for the usual flour-based crust. When everything was put together, she popped the pies in the over to bake.

It was all done according to the instructions in Eleanor's special recipe book, which contained pie recipes developed and handed down for decades by bakers at Penn Traffic.

Photo from Penn Traffic 1966 Annual Report

"I made apple, apple crumb, cherry crumb, pineapple peach, you name it.

"The ingredients, amounts, and directions for each pie were written in a little brown notebook," remembers Eleanor. "But that notebook got so tattered and torn, I had to throw it away. I copied all the recipes into a spiral notebook with a colorful cover, which I still have to this day."

The contents of that notebook, courtesy of Eleanor, are included right here in *Penn Traffic Forever*. Turn to the recipe section of this book and make your own pies (and raisin cookies) just like they used to make in the bakery at Penn Traffic.

The Pie Stops Here

As much as Eleanor loved baking at Penn Traffic, she eventually decided to hang up her white uniform, apron, hair net, and Hush Puppy shoes. She left in 1975 for a better-paying job in the General Services department at Bethlehem Steel.

Her departure was the end of an era. Soon after she left, Penn Traffic started bringing in frozen pies instead of having them made from scratch in the bakery.

"Before I quit, I showed some of the girls there how to make pies," says Eleanor. "But they just didn't like it. It was easier to reheat frozen pies instead of making fresh ones from scratch."

But the frozen-pie era didn't last long. After the flood of July 1977, the downtown Penn Traffic store--and bakery--closed down for good. The home of delicious Penn Traffic baked goods, which people had savored for decades, was gone forever.

But Eleanor still makes them sometimes. "I still love to bake. I don't make as many pies, cookies, or apple dumplings as I used to, but I still make a few from time to time for church bake sales or family or friends.

"And those old Penn Traffic recipes are just as delicious as they ever were," says Eleanor. "Those Penn Traffic bakers really captured the magic all those years ago."

And you can, too, with the legendary Penn Traffic pie recipes starting in the recipe section of this book.

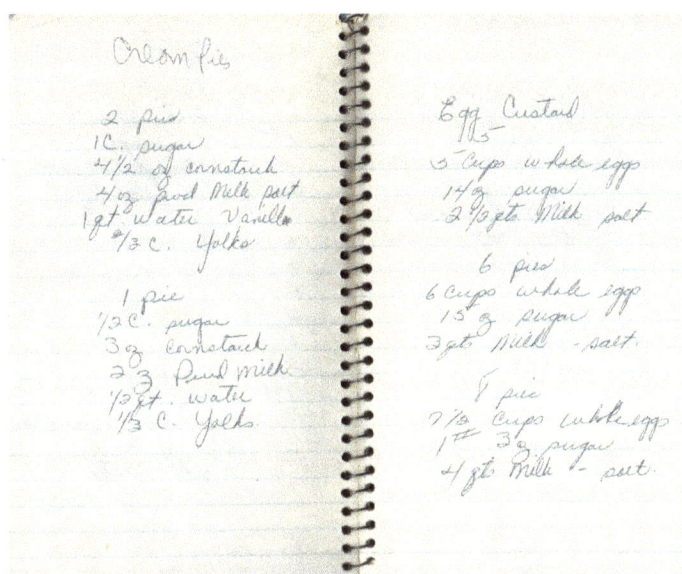

Courtesy of Eleanor Kohan

S. Pecan

10 pies

6 cups sugar
6 " whole eggs
3 1/3 " butter
10 " syrup
10 " pecan

15 pies
9 C. sugar
9 " eggs
5 " butter
15 " syrup
15 " pecan

S. Pecan

1 pie

2/3 C. sugar
2/3 " eggs
1/3 " butter
1 C. syrup
1 C. pecan

2 pies

1 1/3 C. sugar
1 1/3 C whole eggs
2/3 C. butter (melted)
2 C. syrup
2 C. pecan

Black Raspberries

1# dried black raspberries
6 oz currants
2# sugar
1 gal water
4 g clear gel
salt

Raisin
5# Raisin
1 1/2# sugar
3 qt. water
salt.
4 g clear gel

Apples (26# 4 cans)

1 can
1 qt water
1# sugar
4 g clear gel
1 tsp cinnamon
1/8 tsp salt.

1 gal water
1# clear gel
7# sugar
3-4 tsp cinnamon
1 tsp salt

16# fresh apples
2 1/2 # sugar
1 g cinnamon
1/3 oz salt
13 g flour
(10 pies)

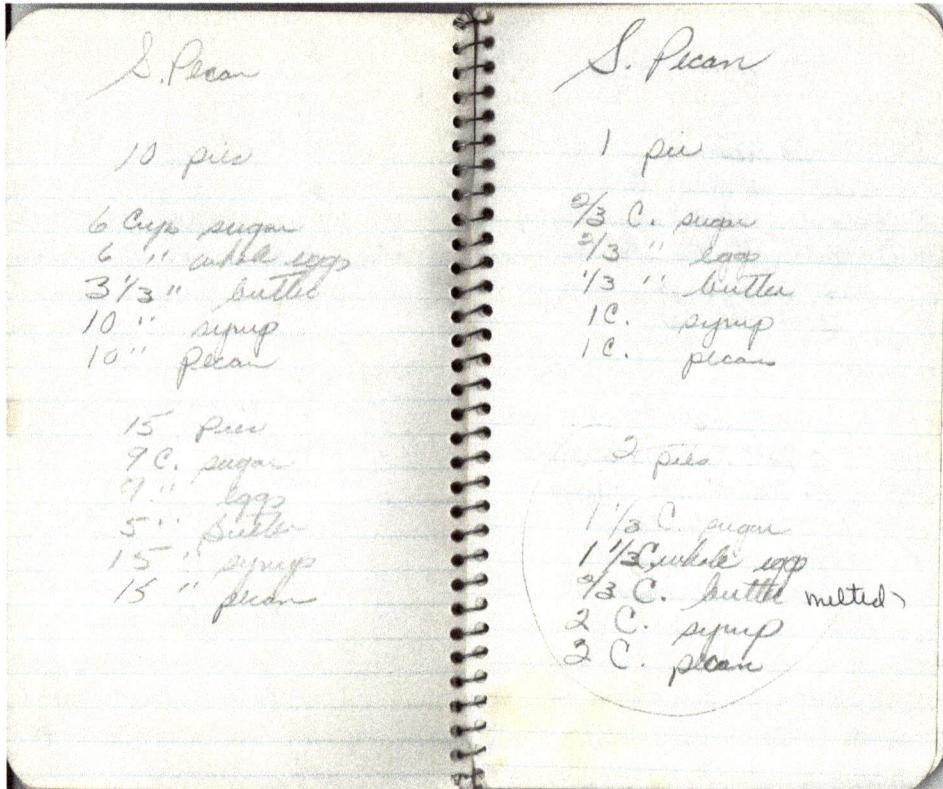

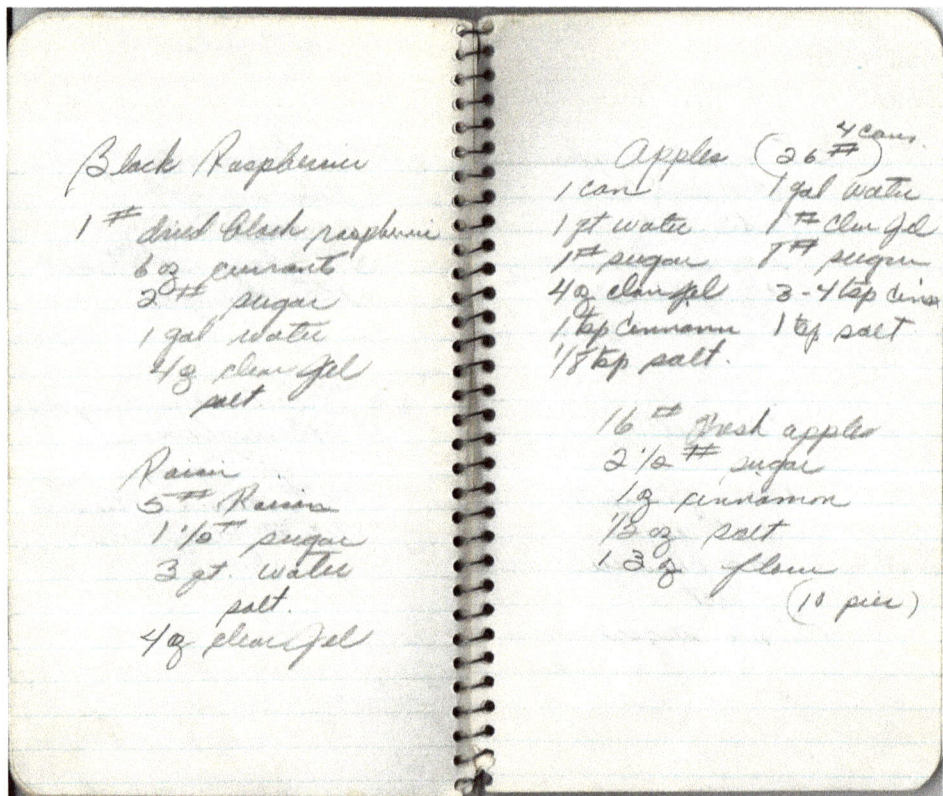

Courtesy of Eleanor Kohan

MEMORY DEPARTMENT

When I was a kid, my Aunt Inez worked on the 5th floor. She would often sneak me in to watch the ladies make candies. It was always a great day when I got to do that! My favorites were chocolate-covered wintergreen patties and raspberries.

Karen Evans

I really liked Penn Traffic. I worked in the lingerie department when I was a teenager.

When I was a little girl, my parents bought shoes for me there. They had a really nice carousel for kids to sit on and be fitted for their shoes. Their windows were really beautiful at Christmastime.

Mary Mcdowell-Cupp

My sister and I loved eating at Penn Traffic. My favorite was city chicken.

Sharon Drenner

My Mom worked in the jewelry department for quite a few years. I loved the store, especially at Christmastime with the decorations, windows, etc.

Barbara Ann Stahl

My grandmother's sister worked in the toddler clothing department for years. We'd take the elevator up to visit her when we were downtown.

Mary Jo Holleran

I went to Saint Patrick's elementary school, and I remember my mother taking me to Penn Traffic for my back-to-school shopping. They carried blouses, uniforms, and even training bras. Penn Traffic's female employees made sure I didn't feel embarrassed getting measured for the right bra. As I grew into a woman, that was our place to shop for those sorts of things. Of course, Penn Traffic was also our stop because they carried everything we needed for joining the Girl Scouts!

They had fine, American-made products, and of course their Santa Clause ALWAYS brought that new baby doll and carriage that was asked for by a certain little girl every year. It's sad that the Penn Traffic store is gone. It was a five-star store.

Michele Kondash-Kolenovic

I worked there for a while in women's accessories and coats. I got my first credit card there with a fifty dollar limit in my teens. It was a wonderful store.

Mary Kay Brant

I have wonderful memories of the magical Christmas windows. The snow would be falling, but we had to go see the animated figures in the holiday windows. It was cold, but the memories are still warm.

Susan Galbraith

Penn Traffic
VIP

GARY KINLEY
SIGHT AND SOUND SALESPERSON
YEARS OF SERVICE 22
1956–1958
1962–1982

Every day at lunchtime, Gary Kinley played pinochle in the lounge on the fourth floor of Penn Traffic, right next to the employee lunchroom. The daily game was a who's who of store notables, often including Harry Steele (head candy maker), Larry Rosen (future Department Store Division president), and George Streiline (head of merchandise receiving and marking). It was such a popular event that if someone couldn't make it, there was *always* someone to sit in for the absentee.

"We did it for years and years," remembers Gary. "There were no stakes, but it was very competitive. The challenge of winning was reward enough to keep us coming back for more."

Photo courtesy of Gary Kinley

Sayonara, Japan

Competitiveness was also one of the reasons Gary worked so hard during his 22 years as a salesman at Penn Traffic. He put his heart into selling all manner of merchandise, and it paid off.

Like the time he won a trip to Japan. "I was one of only 18 salesmen in the U.S. to make it through the Concord Tape Recorder sales plan," says Gary. "Then I sold my quota of Concord recorders and found out I'd won a trip to Japan.

"But my merchandise manager said he was going to take the trip instead of me. I blew my top and went over his head, and that led to all company trips being cancelled.

"I still have the itinerary for that trip to Japan, which would have been the trip of a lifetime. It was going to start off with three days in Hawaii," says Gary.

161

Handbag Romance

Gary started working as a sales clerk at Penn Traffic on his 18th birthday in 1956. He ended up leaving after two years to work at Republic Steel, then came back four years later to pick up where he'd left off.

Eventually, Gary worked his way up to managing the Sight and Sound department, selling cameras, tape recorders, CB radios, televisions, and accessories. That was when he started hitting his stride.

"I sold reel-to-reel tape recorders like hotcakes," says Gary. "I sold the first 8-track tape in Pennsylvania.

"Penn Traffic became the only department store in the country to sell Contax cameras because of me. I proved I had the knowledge to sell those cameras, and the Contax company agreed to let us sell them."

But Gary's favorite accomplishment at Penn Traffic was meeting his future wife, Elaine. "She was working in the handbag department," he remembers. "One day, I was coming through, and she said, 'Gary, come here a minute. An old guy is trying to bother me. Can I borrow your high school ring?'

"So I gave her the ring, and she put it on, and the guy gave up and went away. After that, she and I started to get to know each other better, and the rest is history."

Dr. Ruth to Captain Willie

During his time in the Sight and Sound department of Penn Traffic, Gary met a number of celebrities, including sex therapist Dr. Ruth Westheimer, clown Emmett Kelly, Jr., and Willie Stargell, in only his second year of playing for the Pittsburgh Pirates.

One of Gary's most memorable encounters, however, happened in 1957, during his first two-year stint at Penn Traffic.

Photos courtesy of Gary Kinley

162

"I was on the first floor, hauling some items to the notions department on a long cart. One of the boxes fell off the top of the stack on the cart and landed on the floor there. Guess who was standing there watching? President Samuel H. Heckman.

"President Heckman walked over and asked if I was having trouble, and I said yes. He just said 'That's all right.' Then, he put his cane down and took out the toothpick he had in his mouth. He said 'I'll give you a hand,' and he helped me put the box back up on the cart. When he was done, he smiled and said, 'There you go,' and I said 'Thank you, sir.'"

Sneaking Treats En Route

When the department stores became part of Hess's in 1982, Gary went with them. As a salesman at Hess's in the Richland Mall, he posted higher numbers than ever. He did so well, becoming the company's top salesman, that the

company president even gave him a blank check to do anything he wanted in his department.

But Gary never quite got over Penn Traffic. He still fondly remembers delivering rolls from the bakery to the bake shop on the freight elevator, sneaking a fresh one for himself en route. Likewise, he remembers helping himself to a piece of delicious Penn Way candy when he delivered trays of it to the candy counter.

And, of course, he thinks about those pinochle games in the lounge where friendship and camaraderie were the only true prizes on the table.

Candy counter photo by Hesselbein Studio, courtesy of Johnstown Area Heritage Association

Chapter Sixteen

The Flood That Ended It All

July 1977

Photo from Penn Traffic 1976 Annual Report

It was raining when Dick Corbin left work at the downtown store at 5:00 P.M. on July 20, 1977. He didn't think anything of it.

But then the storm didn't let up. It just got worse, in fact, from 7:00 P.M. to midnight, complete with heavy lightning and thunder. "Around midnight," recalls Dick, "the lightning seemed to be one continuous flash, with the atmosphere seeming almost like daytime."

Meanwhile, the night watchman was noticing the first signs of trouble at the store on Washington Street. He called Store Superintendent Virgil Good at home, claiming there was leakage in the store. Virgil rushed to the scene but didn't notice anything major. As news came in about flooding in other parts of the city, however, he realized the situation was about to get much worse.

He called Dick at 2:30 in the morning. "He told me the river was rising fast," remembers Dick. "He said, 'I think you better get down here, because we're approaching flood stage.'"

Dick took his advice. He leaped into the car with his son Steve, who was home from college, and headed downtown as fast as he could.

165

Another Corbin, Another Flood

"Once I'd made it downtown, my car radio indicated that the city of Johnstown was closed, and no additional traffic would be allowed in," explains Dick. "I continued forward toward the store, and crossing the first river noted that the water was very close to going over the banks.

"As I continued to cross town, I discovered that our main intersection in town had water running-board deep, so I detoured down a couple of streets and made my way to the parking lot across the street from the store. Water at this point in this area was hub cap high."

Determined to reach Penn Traffic, Dick and Steve stepped off the curb. The water was up to their knees, and the current was swift. They held hands as they worked their way across.

Just then, Virgil left the building and met them on his way to move his car to higher ground. Dick followed his lead, moving his car to a lot that was 3 or 4 feet higher than the first.

When they got back to Washington Street, the water was up to their waists. It was harder to get across, but they all made it and got inside the store, where they met the night watchman.

They didn't realize it at the time, but the four of them would be spending the rest of the night in that building. Like Dick's father, Harry, who'd stayed through the night on St. Patrick's Day in 1936, they were about to live through a flood within the walls of the Penn Traffic store.

Photo courtesy of Dick Corbin

The Big Crash

By 3:15 A.M., the water outside was two feet up in front of the doors, though it hadn't entered the store yet. There was still a little time to make some preparations, and the four men set to work.

First, they moved all the elevators to the third floor before the power could go out. Then, they turned off all the gas outlets, starting with the main line. Next, they gathered up all the flashlights, batteries, candles, food, and water they could find

Photo courtesy of William Glosser

and put them in a safe location on an upper floor.

By 3:45 A.M., there was a little water in the basement from a sewer backup, though the rest of the building's interior was dry. But things were getting worse outside, as the water level reached six feet. "Cars were floating down the street, debris was hitting our windows, but they were still holding."

They didn't hold for much longer, though. At 4:00, there was a large crash, and the windows gave way.

Photo courtesy of William Glosser

166

Photo courtesy of William Glosser

As the four men retreated to the mezzanine, things went from bad to worse on the main floor. "The water was now rushing into the store from all directions," says Dick. "It took about 15 minutes for the basement to fill up, and the water continued to rise on the main floor until it got to about four feet.

"Fixtures were floating, glass cases had been overturned and were piling up on each other, merchandise was going in all directions. The whole place went totally dark."

The Rising Stops

Up on the mezzanine, the men considered their next move. Would the water continue to rise? Would they be forced to retreat to higher floors, as Dick's father, Harry, had done in '36?

Fortunately, the answer was no. Soon after the windows burst, the rain stopped, and the water level stabilized.

Around 5:00 A.M., as the first traces of daylight leaked into the building, the men could see that the water was starting to recede.

They cheered, but their relief did not last long. As the water went down, they got their first good look at the damage, and it was "monumental." They had their work cut out for them.

And in some ways, they were in more danger than ever.

Photo courtesy of William Glosser

"They Would Be Shot"

The looters showed up around 6 A.M., wading through the waist-high water toward the Penn Traffic Building.

Dick and the others were watching the doors and saw them coming. "We challenged them as they came to the door with the threat that if they entered the store, they would be shot," remembers Dick. "We had the advantage of being in the dark, so they could not tell whether we had weapons or not.

"We did not. The threat itself was enough to turn these people away, and we did not have one incident of looting in the store. Many other stores in town had high losses by looters, but not Penn Traffic."

Photo courtesy of William Gasior

167

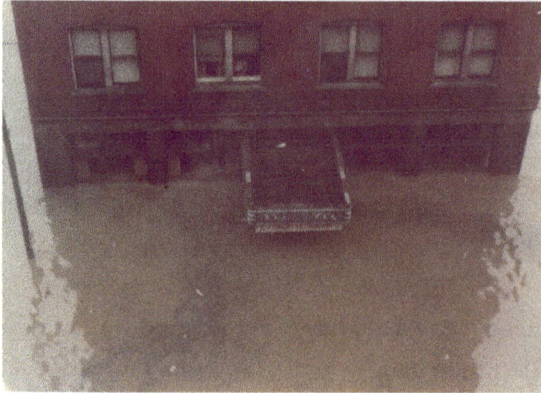

After that first pack of looters moved on, and the water level dropped, Dick and the others barricaded the damaged windows and doors to keep out intruders. With that accomplished, they moved on to make a thorough survey of the damage.

It was ugly, to say the least. At its peak, the water had reached a level of four feet on the main floor, except for the men's department, where the high water mark was at seven feet. The basement, of course, had been completely submerged.

"Everything in the basement was destroyed," says Dick. "On the main floor, all merchandise was damaged, with the exception of the top shelf in the gift department."

Then there were the other downtown properties to consider, all within a mile of the store. Setting out on foot, Dick and his team visited each one.

According to Dick, the nearby garage was undamaged. As for the warehouse, there was three feet of water in the basement, but losses were minimal because much of that space had recently been emptied. "The only merchandise that we lost there was a shipment of General Electric small appliances," says Dick.

The company's office building on the other side of Washington Street between the Hendler Hotel and Flood Museum was another story. That one-story building, which housed corporate offices and the entire accessory division merchandise manager and buyers, was wrecked. "Water in this building was about seven feet high, and we lost all of our office furniture," says Dick. "The filing cabinets were totally immersed, and the records that had been stored in them were in a very muddy condition."

Believing in the Impossible

As Dick and the others--joined by management personnel who trekked into town through the day via the Inclined Plane--finished their damage survey and contemplated the massive cleanup job ahead, they were shaken. It would be a formidable undertaking...maybe the biggest they'd ever faced in their lives.

But they had to get through it, and they knew that they could. After all, their predecessors had completed similar cleanups in 1889 and 1936. Dick's father, Harry Corbin, had been one of those men; if the father could do it, so could the son.

Penn Traffic was depending on them. It was up to them to bring it back to life and get those cash registers ringing the way they had for 123 years.

They believed in their hearts that they could do it. They believed they could clean up Penn Traffic and open its doors to the shoppers of Johnstown again.

Photos courtesy of William Gasior

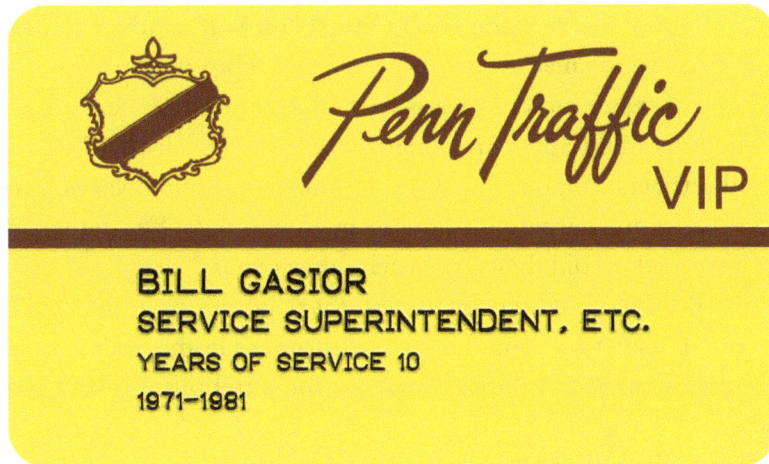

**BILL GASIOR
SERVICE SUPERINTENDENT, ETC.
YEARS OF SERVICE 10
1971-1981**

Photo courtesy of William Gasior

Every two weeks or so, a customer in Woodvale would request a new La-Z-Boy recliner. He would call Penn Traffic and say his chair was broken, and they owed him a new one since it was under a lifetime warranty.

As service superintendent at the time, Bill Gasior had to deal with it. "My guys would go out and try to fix it, and they'd say heck, that thing's destroyed, we have to give him another chair. And we'd give him another chair.

"A couple weeks later, the same thing happened. My guys went out to see the chair, and it was all busted up. The mechanisms were all broken on it.

"I finally asked my guys what was going on with the chairs. They said the guy using it was in the neighborhood of 375 pounds. He was breaking the chair in half just by sitting on it."

Bill went to John Gunter at Penn Traffic and told him about the situation. He asked John if they had to honor the warranty given the circumstances.

"John said, 'Bill, I'll tell you what. At Penn Traffic, the customer's always right, and we aim to please. But I will tell you this. You go ahead and give him one more chair, and that's the last chair he gets.'

"So that's exactly what we did," says Bill.

PT Teamsters

Bill Gasior came to Penn Traffic in 1971 after stints at Glidden Metals in Johnstown and Coleman in Somerset. As service superintendent, he oversaw all appliance and furniture repair, carpet installation, drapery making and installation, mechanical repair and state inspections of company vehicles, delivery truck driving, and men's and women's alterations.

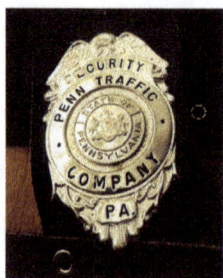

*Photo courtesy of
William Gasior*

Not to mention, he also ran the Penn Way candy manufacturing operation and served as chief of security and chief labor negotiator.

His repair crews operated out of a shop in the Penn Traffic warehouse on upper Main Street and included several specialists. "I had one guy who did refrigeration, one guy who did ranges and microwaves, two guys who did draperies and carpeting, and four guys who did TVs, stereos, etc.," explains Bill. "Very seldom did they cross each other's lines."

Bill's staff did repairs in customer's homes or in the warehouse shops. "If my guys couldn't fix something in a customer's home, they brought it to the shops.

"The appliance repair shop was in the basement of the warehouse. The TV repair shop was on the second floor."

According to Bill, his repair staff shared a common goal, grounded in the company's customer-first philosophy. "We took care of the customers as best we could. We wanted them to be happy and tell others that Penn Traffic takes care of its customers."

That isn't to say Bill and the repairmen always saw eye to eye. After all, he was the designated Chief Labor Negotiator, and they were Teamsters.

Getting Ugly

"We went through a nine-day strike that was not exactly nice," remembers Bill. "This was in the mid-1970s, around '74, '75. There was picketing, sign carrying, weapon carrying. It was nasty."

According to Bill, the Teamsters wanted an increase of 25 cents an hour. The company was willing to give them 15 cents, but not the full 25, so the union called a strike.

The days that followed brought plenty of name-calling, bad feelings, and problems for Bill. For example, when trains pulled up to the warehouse to drop off merchandise, the strikers would interfere. "They'd march around on the railroad tracks and tell the engineer not to put the boxcar in the dock," says Bill. "They did everything they could to get in the way."

In some case, Bill had to seek help from Penn Traffic management. Company executives even ended up transporting merchandise themselves, since the delivery truck drivers were striking Teamsters.

"We had guys like Bill Corbin driving trucks to DuBois," says Bill. "Dick Corbin was driving trucks to Indiana. We still had stores to run, and this was the only way to distribute stuff to them."

As days passed without an agreement, things got ugly. "A couple of union guys flashed guns in their belts," recalls Bill. "One guy brought a baseball bat and leaned it against the wall of the alley that our delivery trucks used. He said 'if any trucks come out of this alley, we're smashing the windshields.'

"I called the police, who were unionized by the way, and told them this guy made threats. I said I'd hate to see any people get hurt if they get hit with that bat.

"So two cops came around, and one said to the striker with the bat, 'Do you have a car here?' The striker said yes. The cop said 'You put that bat in your car, or I'll put it in mine. I don't want to see that out on the street again."

Finally, after nine days of conflict, the two sides came to an agreement. It was a good thing, because Bill was exhausted. "I'd been working 24 hours a day for those nine days to keep things rolling while the Teamsters were out."

But just because the strike was over, that didn't mean the hard feelings and hassles would magically go away.

"Who'll Supply the Wristwatches?"

There were still plenty of bumps in the road between Bill and the Teamsters. Some of Bill's repairmen were determined not to make things easy for him.

"Once, I came up with a new work order to better track their time in the field," says Bill. "I wanted them to record time in and time out at every home service call.

"Some of them were only doing two service calls in an eight-hour day. I told them, 'You guys work 8 A.M. to 4:30. At 4:20, every truck in the fleet is pulled into the garage. So where are you guys at in the meantime, if you're only finishing two calls a day? What are you doing?'

"I said I needed them to fill in this new work order at every call. So then this one guy says to me, 'Who'll supply the pens?' I said 'We'll supply the pens.'

"Then, he asks me, 'Who'll supply the wristwatches so we know what time it is?' I said 'You'll figure it out. Look at the customer's kitchen clock.'

"He said, 'That's their clock, not mine. I want a wristwatch,'" says Bill. "Not only did he not get a wristwatch, but I got him so worked up that he pulled off his tie and threw it across the table.

"Unfortunately for him, it was a clip-on tie. We all had a laugh about that one."

The New Dick Corbin

After years as service superintendent, Bill found himself moving in a new direction, working as an assistant to Dick Corbin, Vice President of Branch Stores.

"I handled operations in the branch stores," explains Bill. "The receiving and shipping guys would all report to me. Building construction and any remodeling, I was in charge of."

Then, in 1980, Dick retired. Larry Rosen, president of the Department Store Division at the time, gave Bill his job. Suddenly, Bill was in charge of all the department stores operated by Penn Traffic.

He loved the work but soon found it kept him away from the office quite a bit. "I would be away three or four days at a time, working out of town at a branch store, and there still lots to do at the central office.

Photo courtesy of William Gasior

"So I ended up hiring an assistant to help with the workload," says Bill. "He oversaw a lot of the stuff in the Johnstown operation because I was on the road taking care of the other stores."

The Dream Job

Bill continued to run the branch stores until 1982, when Crown American Corporation bought Penn Traffic's Department Store Division. As the Penn Traffic stores were absorbed by Crown's department store chain, Hess's, Bill's future was up in the air...but he soon landed on his feet. He was one of the few Penn Traffic employees hired by Hess's after the sale, signing on as director of operations.

Photo courtesy of William Gasior

The new job lasted ten years, until Hess's started having financial troubles of its own. Bill's relationship with the company grew increasingly toxic, until he finally decided to get out.

He ended up in a dream job as executive director of operations at a school district outside Philadelphia. "I oversaw eight buildings, including six schools and a bus garage housing 72 buses. Plus, I was in charge of all maintenance," says Bill.

"Before I retired in 2007, I'd spent $50 million renovating six buildings. I'd built a brand new stadium with an all-weather football field. I'd made a difference and had a great time doing it."

Bill and Dick Reunions

These days, Bill lives in Celebration, Florida, not far from Walt Disney World Resort. But Penn Traffic is still part of his life.

He still reminisces about the good times he had there, like when he got to meet Paul Newman and had a long talk with Strother Martin during the filming of *Slap Shot*. "Strother brought in coffee and doughnuts, and we talked for an hour."

Or when he shopped at the downtown Penn Traffic store as a kid and felt special. "You were treated as a person when you walked in the store," he remembers. "You felt like you were the only person they were paying attention to. It wasn't like 'just a moment' or 'it's over there.' They went with you and picked out what you wanted, how you wanted it. They made sure they did it just right for you."

At least once a year, he still gets together with his friend, Dick Corbin, who also lives in Florida, and they talk about the good old days.

And it seems, for a little while at least, as if the good old days never ended at all.

Chapter Seventeen

Washing Away A Dream

July 1977

And they were wrong.

Marie Neff had to take a roundabout route to work in the days after the flood of '77. "My dad would take me from our house in Hornerstown over to Moxham, and I'd get a lift with someone whose wife worked at the store. Then, we'd go up to the Richland Mall store, where we'd get in a Penn Traffic delivery truck for the ride downtown.

"There were no seats in that truck. You either stood and held on to the side of the truck, or if you found a tire or something, you sat on it. That was a real joy ride, let me tell you," says Marie.

It wasn't fun, but she had a job to do. She was one of many Penn Traffic employees working to get the store cleaned up and reopened...working to get the 123-year-old dream back on track.

Photos courtesy of William Gasior

173

So was Barbara Baxter. "I lived in the Westmont area, and I had to take the Inclined Plane downtown. You couldn't just drive into town on your own.

"At the bottom, there were men waiting, and they told us we had to get tetanus shots at Lee Hospital before we went any further. We did that, trudging through the mud that was everywhere downtown. And then we went to the store," says Barbara.

"When I walked in there for the first time, my heart sank," remembers Virginia O'Herrick, who was also part of the cleanup team. "The whole basement and main floor had been flooded. There was just nothing left."

Photos courtesy of Dick Corbin

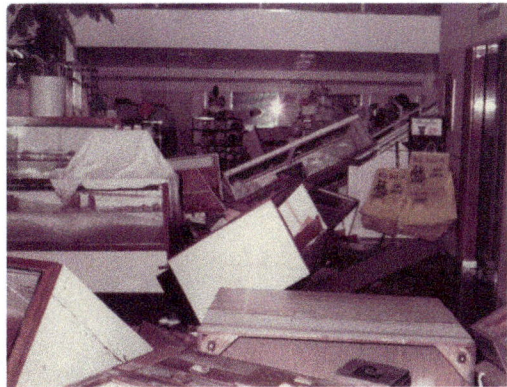

Eleanore Kennell was also shocked when she went to work for the first time since the disaster. "It was terrible to go in and see all that," says. "Just to see all the devastation. You couldn't imagine how awful it was until you went into the store and actually saw it for yourself."

"And the smell was horrible," says Barbara. "I always said it smelled like death in there."

"The smell was just horrendous," says Bill Gasior, service superintendent for the Penn Traffic Company at the time. "When you got in the store with stuff rotting and whatever, it was really bad. There was meat rotting, and the coolers were all flooded. It was bad.

"It was just a mess," says Bill. "Just a mess."

Attack of the Lawn Tractors

Cleaning up that mess turned out to be a formidable task, though a small army of people joined in the effort. Like Marie, Barbara, Virginia, Eleanore, and Bill, many Penn Traffic employees did their part...about 100 in all. They were joined by paid contractors with experience in different aspects of the cleanup, though such people were in great demand around town.

Dick Corbin, who was in charge of the cleanup, hired every qualified contractor he could get his hands on. "Anyone who came in there with a company that had any experience cleaning up, we hired them. If we didn't, somebody else would hire them right away."

Photos courtesy of Dick Corbin

175

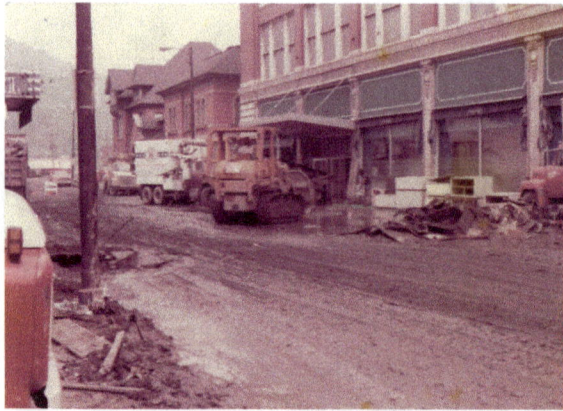

Penn Traffic's small army went to work on the mess, hauling mud-caked debris from the main floor out into the street. There, a bulldozer high lift dumped it into waiting 20-ton trucks, which carried it off to a landfill.

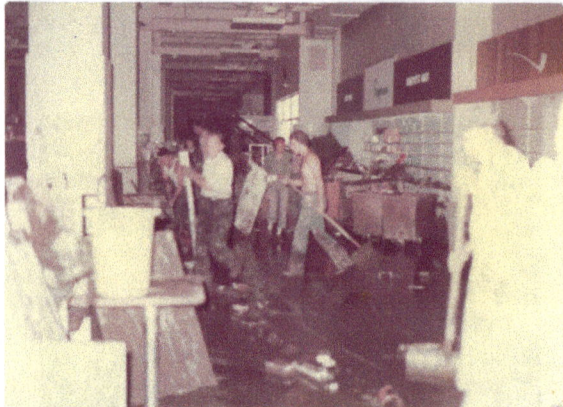

As the debris was cleared away, cleaning crews set to work on the 6-8 inches of mud that covered the floor. They used snow shovels, squeegees, and lawn tractors with snowplows to push it outside. "You just kept on pushing and shoveling the mud and getting it out in the street," said Bill Gasior. "Hopefully, someone was gonna come and pick it up eventually."

Slowly but surely, the crews made headway on the main floor, finishing the worst of the cleanup there in ten days...but the basement was another story.

The Real Problem

"The basement was the real problem," recalls Dick. "It was full of water and knee-deep mud, and we had to get it up out of there somehow or other."

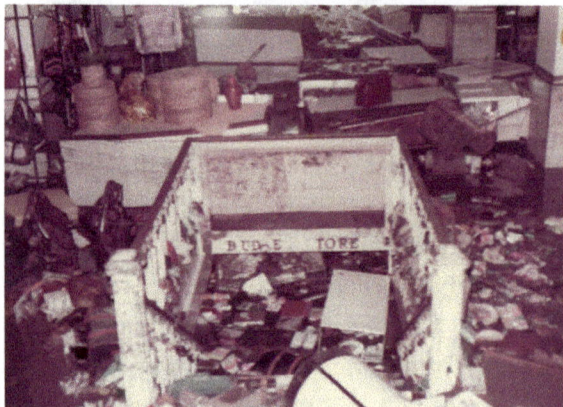

Clearing the basement was vital to the overall cleanup effort, according to Bill Gasior. "All our heating and electrical systems were located down there. We couldn't use the air conditioning until we finished the basement, because the electrical system that powered it was based there."

To get the water out, Dick enlisted volunteer fire companies with pumper trucks. "We had four entrances from the front into our basement, with a fire company and a hose in each entrance," explains Dick. "We also had a fire company in the back of the store, going down through a hole that we'd punched through the wall of the store."

Even with all that help, Bill Gasior remembers the work went slowly. "It was probably a three-day operation," he says. "The hoses would get clogged up with debris. Socks and underwear and everything else would get stuck in them, and we'd have to clear it out."

Photos courtesy of Dick Corbin

Still, pumping the water turned out to be the easy part. Next, the crews had to bring up the debris and mud that was left behind.

"The removal of debris from the basement was strictly a hand-powered operation," says Dick. "Our personnel worked in the basement with boots and gloves in knee deep mud, shoveling, lifting, and destroying fixtures until we finally got down to the floor level."

Once the debris was pulled from the mud, workers put it on a rented mine conveyor that had been installed in one of the basement entrances. The conveyor carried the debris up from the basement, where it was hauled outside for disposal.

That just left the mud to deal with, though that was a challenge in its own right. "All you could do was load it into containers of some sort and get it out of the basement, dump it on the street or haul it away in trucks we had there," says Dick.

A sewer vacuum was also put to use, though it was so powerful that it grabbed workers' arms and legs several times. (No major injuries resulted.)

Two weeks after the basement cleanup had begun, it finally ended. It had taken that long to clear the incredible mess, but at last it was done.

Waterlogged Jewelry

As the cleanup continued, workers did what they could to salvage certain merchandise for resale, with limited success. "We had to be very careful," explains Dick. "Anything that had been damaged, we threw away.

"But jewelry you could clean. If it turned out properly, we could salvage it. And there were some items from the gift department, too."

Everything else that was damaged or dirty went to the landfill or was bought cheap by salvage companies. With each load, the main floor got a little emptier.

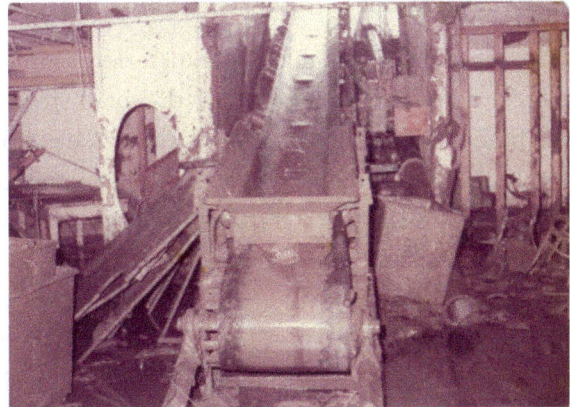

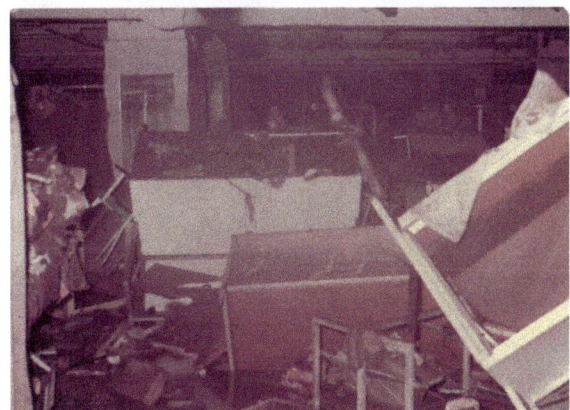

Photos courtesy of Dick Corbin

177

Photo courtesy of Dick Corbin

The upper floors emptied out, too, as undamaged merchandise was shipped to other Penn Traffic and PT department stores. Since the flood, this merchandise had been protected by watchmen with sidearms. When the word came down to ship it, workers covered it to shield it from mud, dust, and odor, then hauled it down and put it in delivery trucks.

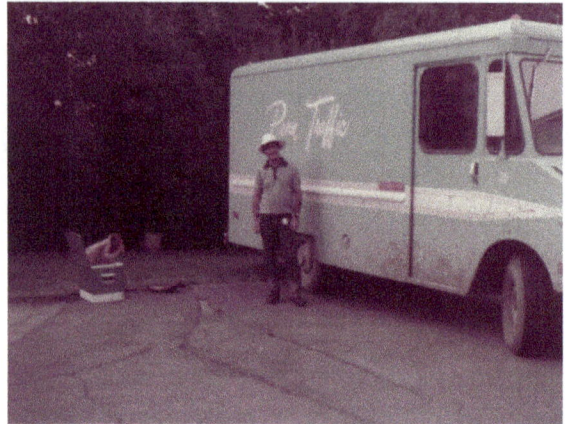

Photo courtesy of Dick Corbin

"As soon as possible, we transferred as much merchandise as we could out of the main store into the branches," says Dick. "Most of it went into the local branches at reduced prices. At the same time, we transferred as many fixtures as we needed from the main store into our branches to accommodate the merchandise."

Muck, Muck, and More Muck

In addition to cleaning the store, crews had to get the off-site downtown properties squared away.

Bill Gasior led the effort to clean up the warehouse on upper Main Street. "The warehouse basement was totally flooded. We had to pump out the water and remove the debris, including ruined ranges and microwaves. Then, we had to get rid of the mud, just like in the store.

Photo courtesy of William Gasior

Photo courtesy of William Gasior

"We did lose some backup stock in the basement, but that was the worst of it. Everything else in the warehouse was okay," says Bill.

His people also cleaned up the garage, which suffered minimal damage, and emptied the small office building's contents, which were a total loss.

Photo courtesy of William Gasior

178

Upstairs Was No Picnic

While all this cleanup was happening, Penn Traffic employees kept the company rolling in the offices on the top floors of the main building. The mother store may have been down for the count, but there was still lots to do.

"We were busy all the time," says Eleanore Kennell. "We had all the other stores, and they were still operating. We had to take care of the financial end of all that for the Department Store Division.

"Sales reports arrived daily, and we had to process them. We had to track all the money that was coming in and going out, as if the flood had never happened," says Eleanore.

In addition, arrangements had to be made to divert new merchandise to other locations. "We had ordered quite a lot of merchandise for our fall season to come into the main store," remembers Dick. "This merchandise had to be diverted to our branches. It was the job of these branch stores to receive and divide and distribute the merchandise

that had been intended for the main store."

The office work underway in the downtown store was important, and the people doing it were glad to be doing their part. It wasn't much fun working in the store building, though, especially in the first days after the disaster.

Marie Neff recall there was no electricity at first. "We had Coleman lanterns on our desks to provide the light to work by."

The lack of working elevators also made life difficult for workers on the upper floors.

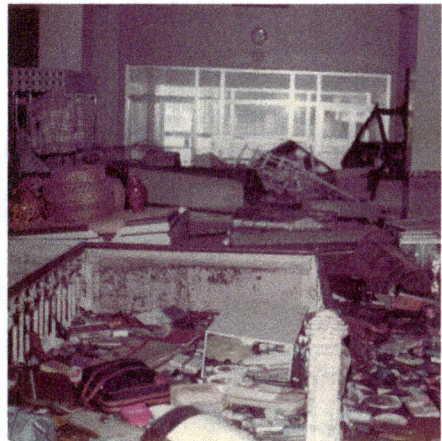

179

"I was on the fifth floor," says Marie. "I had to walk up five flights of stairs to get to the office.

"And I had to walk back down to get anywhere else. The closest working restrooms were on the second floor, so every time I needed to use them, I had to walk down the stairs to the second floor, then back up again. And I had to have at least one partner with me. We weren't allowed to roam the building alone. Maybe they were worried that we might slip and fall or something."

Barbara Baxter remembers that the smell from the mess on the main floor and in the basement was hard to take. "The smell was unbelievable. Even all the way up on the fourth floor, it was powerful.

"The stairwells were all open, and the smell just traveled up through them," says Barbara. "There was no way to close them off so you didn't get that smell through the rest of the store.

"To make matters worse, all the windows in the store had been painted shut at one time. The fumes just

built up in there until a couple truck drivers and carpenters

came and jimmied the windows open so we could breathe," says Barbara.

No More Nasty Surprises?

In spite of the uncomfortable conditions, the Penn Traffic staff worked together to keep the Department Store Division in business. They shared a mission that was every bit as important as the grueling cleanup work that was going on downstairs. They wanted to make sure there were no more nasty surprises on the way that might harm the company.

But a surprise was coming after all, though they couldn't see it. Maybe they should have, since they worked in the heart of the company, close to the decision-making core of executives who planned the organization's future...but the big surprise still caught them off-guard. None of them expected it to happen.

They never imagined that the store on Washington Street, the original Penn Traffic, might not reopen.

Photos courtesy of Dick Corbin

MEMORY DEPARTMENT

The Christmas window displays that were motorized were always a big hit to start off the Christmas season. We would ride the town trolley to the center of town and walk over to Penn Traffic. They always had special dresses for all occasions, and they would gift wrap our Christmas gifts free, finished off with a ribbon and a gold label saying Penn Traffic Company. We would always take time to visit the toy department and see what new toys were there. The women on the sales team always wore dressy clothes, and the male clerks always wore ties. It was always a special place to shop.

Karen Brubaker, President and Owner, O'Shea's Candies

I have lots of Penn Traffic memories, but the very special ones are the pictures with Santa every Christmas. Every year at Christmas, my grandmother and I would take the bus from Westmont specifically to see Santa and have that special picture taken. It was my favorite time with my Mimi.

Linda Brazill

What a great store! I looked forward to when Mom would buy the chocolate Easter candy, bunnies, eggs, etc. I also had the privilege of working in the branch store in DuBois as head of Receiving and Marking. I always waited in anticipation of the unveiling of the great Christmas window displays! Family members worked there as well. It was the area's greatest store! What a loss it was when it closed!

Bill Mickle

How sad when they closed the downtown store after the '77 flood.
Natalie Coleman

We used to eat in the cafeteria once in a while, usually after we'd leave the library (now the flood museum). They had neat hot dogs; the buns were split on top and it looked like a miniature loaf of bread! It's funny what a person can remember from her childhood!
Melanie Hutzell

It goes without saying how magical the window displays were, but my best memory was when my grandmother, Annie Patton, worked the Salvation Army kettle in front of the store for many years because others didn't like to go way off down there. She didn't mind because it was just a block from home. Back in the 50s, I'd go with my grandpa to take her a bucket of hot coals from our coal stove that she'd put by her feet to help keep her toes from freezing as she stood out in the cold. She always said the customers and employees at that location were the nicest and most generous. I remember one year a woman gave her a pretty blue and yellow hand-crocheted shawl for Christmas that she just treasured.
Debbie Vick

Growing up in the 1970s, I spent a lot of time with my grandparents--in fact, every chance I could get. I spent many weekends with them during the school year and many weeks during the summer. They had a large, grand house on Union Street in downtown Johnstown during a time when neighbors not only knew each other but were friends. Hot summer nights were spent sitting on the front porch talking to the neighbors or walking uptown. During those days, you could even leave the front door unlocked without worries.

My Grandfather worked at Sparrows Point, Maryland during the week, so I only saw him during weekends. His employer was a subcontractor who built and repaired smokestacks for Bethlehem Steel. Most of the time, it was only my grandmother and I and her parents who lived upstairs in their own apartment. It was not unusual in those days to have more than one generation living in the same house. My great-grandfather was a retired baker. After retiring from Penn Traffic many years before (I have the gold pocketwatch they gave him upon retiring), he opened the Ideal Bakery in Cambria City.

My grandmother, however, had the best job in the world a youngster could imagine. She worked at the Candy Kitchen on the fifth floor of the Penn Traffic building making Penn Way chocolates.

In the 1970s, Penn Way was one of the premier candies in town. It wasn't the cheap, waxy-tasting dollar store chocolate that people are used to today. My grandmother had a dark green candy bowl with a lid. I think every family had the same style in those days, as I have seen a few here and there at garage sales and antique stores. The best thing about this bowl is that it was always full of chocolate-covered cherries or peanut butter brittle. My parents were very strict about my extracurricular eating habits, but when I was at my grandmother's, it was game-on.

It took an expert hand to remove the lid of this bowl without it making any noise, but the reward was worth the risk. Better yet were the times when I got to visit my grandmother when she was at work. Penn Traffic, or "PT" as it was affectionately known, was the crown jewel of Johnstown and its retail trade. It was a huge store with window displays out front, a mezzanine that could be seen from the first floor, and a constant hustle and bustle.

I have many memories of Penn Traffic, from the joy of Christmas shopping in the crisp night air, looking at the displays in the huge front windows, to spending time just riding the elevators for the fun of it. Once in a while, when my grandmother couldn't find someone to watch me, her fellow employees were not just "family," but my fill-in babysitters. I remember going from department to department as each person would secretly keep an eye on me for her. I know they didn't appreciate it when I tore the tags off clothing.

Years after the 1977 Johnstown Flood, I spent lots of evenings in the basement of the PT building working on a train display that I helped volunteer with that was later displayed at the former Richland Mall during the Christmas season. It was a desolate and spooky place at a time when the building had not yet fully recovered from the flood and become occupied. I still remember the elevators running up and down during the night by themselves.

But the best memory of all will still be that dark green candy bowl, always full of Penn Way candies that grandma would always keep stocked. My grandmother and "PT" are both long gone, but the candy bowl still proudly sits on top of the bar in my home. I know it's not worth anything, and it sits empty. To me, it's priceless, and without Penn Way candies, I just can't bring myself to fill it with anything else. And fortunately, I still have all my teeth!

Brian J. Ensley

Photo by Brian J. Ensley

183

Photos from Penn Traffic 1972 Annual Report

SHIRLEY BLOUGH
PENN TRAFFIC RESTAURANT WAITRESS
YEARS OF SERVICE 10
1967–1977

Waiting tables was a way of life for Shirley Blough at Penn Traffic. For most of ten years, she served customers in the store's restaurant, filling orders and getting to know people from all over Johnstown and beyond.

She joined Penn Traffic after waitressing for three months at the Golden Key, an eatery once located in the building now occupied by the Szechuan Restaurant on Main Street. Penn Traffic hired her the day after she applied, which just happened to be the busiest day of the year in the restaurant.

Photo by Philip Balko

"It was the day after Thanksgiving," remembers Shirley. "They served turkey, stuffing, mashed potatoes, and cole slaw, and there was a huge line all day."

On that first day, Shirley was asked to work as a relief girl, filling in for other waitresses when they took a break. It was a good thing she came to love the job, because she ended up doing the same thing during most of her ten-year career at Penn Traffic.

But things weren't always easy during her first shift. "It was so busy, I got mixed up as to what went where. I remember the manager telling me to sit down, and another girl having to straighten out my side of the dining room," says Shirley.

As rocky as Day One was, Shirley still made a good impression. From then on, she worked full-time in the dining room, putting in 40 hours a week.

And the Penn Traffic restaurant became like a home away from home for her.

A Full Menu

Shirley remembers the restaurant as a bright, airy place. "The walls were brightly colored," she says. "And the back wall was covered by a full-length mirror.

"The tables were all white, and so was the lunch counter. Everything looked bright and welcoming."

185

Shirley spent most of her time in the main dining room, which had rows of booths and tables. Sometimes, she also worked at the lunch counter, which was located in the middle of the restaurant space. A section of smaller tables occupied an area near the counter; these tables seated two people at a time and were often used by customers ordering coffee, snacks, or small meals.

Behind the scenes, food was prepared in a fully staffed kitchen. Beverages and desserts were made in a soda fountain situated between the kitchen and dining room; all orders were picked up from the kitchen in the fountain area. As for baked goods, they were delivered straight from the Penn Traffic bakery.

Whatever customers ordered, they seemed to love it. The restaurant was busy every day for breakfast, lunch, and dinner.

"We served everything. A full menu," remembers Shirley. "Roast beef dinners, fish dinners, turkey dinners, spaghetti, hamburgers and French fries, chicken a la king. Sandwiches and soups were popular, and there were daily specials, too. Some happened every week on the same day.

"And you could top it all off with an ice cream sundae or ice cream soda or milkshake from the soda fountain."

All-Star Crew

With so many menu choices and a steady flow of customers, a large staff of cooks and waitresses was needed on a daily basis.

According to Shirley, the dining room was divided into two parts--a large side with five waitresses on duty, and a smaller side with four. As a relief girl, Shirley worked mostly on the smaller side, though she occasionally filled in at the lunch counter, which required its own dedicated waitress.

Three waitresses worked at the soda fountain during each shift, preparing drinks and desserts and passing out finished orders to the dining room crew.

As for the kitchen, Shirley says there were several cooks manning the stove and several more on the steamer.

And most everyone working in the restaurant was a full-time Penn Traffic employee. "They weren't afraid to pay people in those days, and there was more than enough work to go around.

"On Mondays and Thursdays, we worked from nine in the morning till nine at night. On other days, we worked till five P.M. And we were busy the whole shift. There wasn't much down time."

Photos from Penn Traffic 1966 Annual Report

Often, empty tables were rare. The place was filled with the hum of conversation and the clatter of silverware and dishes. The waitresses in their white blouses and black skirts (and, in later years, red uniforms with white aprons) hurried from table to table, tending to each customer's needs.

And Shirley loved every minute of it. She loved it so much that even a new job elsewhere in the store couldn't keep her away for very long.

Getting Personal

After spending several years in the restaurant, Shirley was invited to work as a personal shopper in the store. She decided to give it a try.

"There were three of us," she says. "A woman named Bunny Harris was the head of our group.

Photo courtesy of Shirley Blough

"People would see something on sale in an ad or hear about it or whatever, and they'd call the store. Then the personal shoppers would buy and ship the requested item."

Sometimes, the requests involved gifts. Once, for example, Shirley got a call from a group of priests in Loretto who wanted to order Christmas gifts for some retired nuns. "I had to decide what to buy the nuns, then wrap and mail it. I ended up sending them special writing paper and pens."

Ultimately, though, Shirley decided personal shopping wasn't for her. "I'd lie awake at night worrying about what to get somebody.

"I had enough on my mind worrying about my three children, who were all teenagers at the time. And, honestly, I preferred working in the restaurant."

So Shirley went back to work in the dining room, where she was welcomed with open arms. She stayed there until the store closed after the 1977 flood, and never regretted going back.

Wonderful Treatment

According to Shirley, Penn Traffic was "one of the nicest places you could ever work."

She fondly remembers the personal attention that she and her co-workers received. "We were treated wonderfully there. The restaurant managers took good care of us. They even knew our children by name.

"On our birthdays, we got a paid day off."

The kindness of Penn Traffic was perhaps most evident when Shirley had an accident at the store. She ended up in the hospital for 11 days after falling down some steps on her way to serve coffee and doughnuts for an early morning after-Christmas coat sale.

"I got cards from everybody at the store, from staff to bosses," recalls Shirley. "Everyone sent me get-well wishes, and every card had money in it. Those are the kind of people who worked at Penn Traffic."

Photos from Penn Traffic 1972 Annual Report

Memory Department

My grandmother was a big, big shopper. She would drag me from one end of downtown Johnstown to another, back and forth, trying things on. My reward was going out to lunch. Sometimes, we went to Wooolworth's. But if it was a big day, we got to go to Penn Traffic. And oh my God, it was just a special place. So special.

I loved their stuffing and gravy, it was the best. That was my favorite. And they had really good hot fudge parfaits.

Debra Heidingsfelder Knobel

Penn Traffic was THE store in Johnstown. I shopped there a lot, because of the quality. Glosser Bros. always had good sales, and you could find things for children for school. But if you wanted a gift or good clothes or good merchandise, you went to Penn Traffic. You always knew it was going to be good merchandise.

They carried everything from furniture to appliances down to nickel and dime things. When you went in there, you could do all your shopping under one roof.

It was definitely a big loss when the store closed. From then on, we had no good store for shopping in downtown Johnstown. There was a Penn Traffic in the Richland Mall, but it just wasn't the same. Everybody missed the original Penn Traffic.

Jane Dunbar

I worked at Penn Traffic for 12 years, mostly in the accounts payable office on the fifth floor. I loved working there, I loved my work. Everybody knew one another. It was like one big family.

The managers were all very nice. It was the same with the employees in all the departments. They always had smiles on their faces. They were always very friendly. I still miss working there with my Penn Traffic family.

Olga Blanar

I'll never forget getting lost in Penn Traffic when I was little. For some reason--maybe

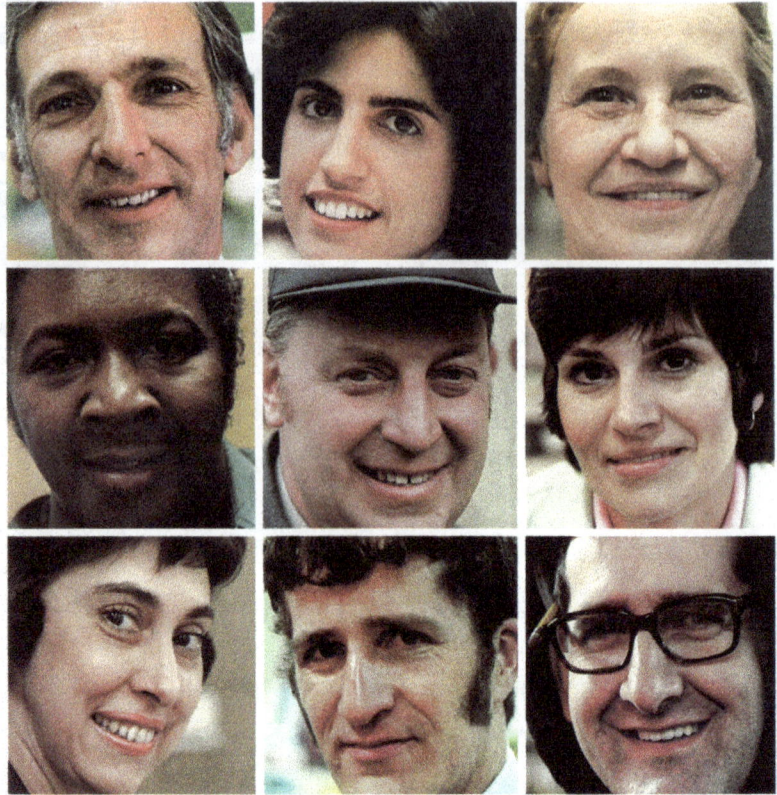

Photos from Penn Traffic 1974 Annual Report

my parents were talking to somebody, I don't know--I was walking around the toy department by myself. Then, I realized I was lost. I knew where I was, but there weren't adults around that I knew. I must have started to cry or something, and this tall man came over, wearing a suit. He put his hand down and said, "Come with me, Paula." I said, "I'm not allowed to talk to strangers," and then he picked me up. I was truly terribly scared. He turned out to be a friend of my dad's, a co-worker named George Streiline. He took me to my parents, and I remember Mom saying "I told you not to walk away from me."

Paula Kellar

The Easter bunny came at Easter. He would walk through the store, and the kids liked that. They would come to the fourth floor where they had the infants and children's department. The Bunny always visited that department, and it was a big deal. You could always tell when he was around.

Eleanore Kennell

On Thursdays, they made banana cream pie in the restaurant. It was my favorite, the best pie I ever ate. They made it every Thursday, and I couldn't wait. I would go and ask if it was ready. They'd say it was still warm, it wasn't ready to serve. But as soon as they served it, I hurried down for pie. I loved it so much, I'd have a couple of pieces!

Pat Fenchak

Chapter Eighteen

Closing Time

July-August 1977

Barbara Baxter didn't realize it was the end of an era until after she cancelled her trip.

It was not long after the flood, and she and some other buyers were getting ready to make a buying trip to New York City. "We were scheduled to leave on Sunday," remembers Barbara. "On Friday, the managers called a meeting and said that we were to cancel our reservations. There would be an important meeting on Monday that we had to attend.

"So that's what we did. We canceled our reservations and went to this meeting," says Barbara. "That was when they told us we had 10 days till the downtown Johnstown Penn Traffic store would close.

"For those 10 days, we weren't allowed to do anything. We weren't allowed to stock the sales room. We couldn't sign invoices. So we would go in there at 8:00 in the morning and sit there all day and do nothing."

"Like a Death"

Marie Neff was as blindsided as Barbara when she finally found out. "We felt like we would clean up and go on with business as usual," says Marie. "Mr. Gunter, the controller, even went on TV and said we were going to reopen.

"But then he went on TV again the next day and said no, we weren't. So we knew then it was the death knell.

"And that was exactly what it was like to us," says Marie. "It was like a death."

Shirley Blough also heard about the closing for the first time on TV. "They didn't call and tell me not to come back in to work at the restaurant. It was understood," says Shirley.

191

"They Went With the Dairy"

Why exactly did Penn Traffic's management decide not to reopen the downtown store?

According to Eleanore Kennell, the decision was based on the expectation that the downtown Penn Traffic wouldn't be profitable in days to come. "Financially, it was slowly deteriorating," she says. "At that time, the steel mills were starting to leave. Johnstown was losing jobs and money, and earnings at the store had declined as a result.

"The downtown Penn Traffic was part of a downward trend, and management thought that trend would continue."

At the time of the flood, Dick Corbin was on the Penn Traffic Board of Directors, which made the decision to close. "I was involved in making that decision," he says. "I can tell you, we didn't make it in a hurry.

"We were considering Johnstown as a whole. The Johnstown area was pretty damaged. There was a question as to how well the downtown would be able to reestablish itself.

"Even before the flood, business had not been increasing in downtown Johnstown. It seemed to be a real problem trying to develop the downtown store while facing competition from the shopping centers and other factors involved.

"In the long run, we didn't feel it was going to be worth it or profitable or anything to reopen downtown. It was more of an opinion than anything else, trying to consider many diff factors. But the downtown was a mess."

According to Bill Gasior, an insurance problem finally forced the issue. "The downtown store was on the same policy as Sani-Dairy. The insurance was all under one umbrella," explains Bill.

"So there was only enough payout on the policy to save one of them. The company had to decide whether to save the store or the dairy.

"In the end, they went with the dairy," says Bill.

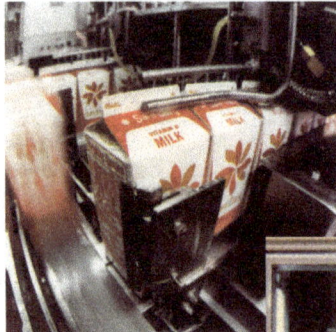

Photo from Penn Traffic
1977 Annual Report

Photo from Penn Traffic
1977 Annual Report

Photo from Penn Traffic
1977 Annual Report

Photo from Penn Traffic 1973 Annual Report

Photo from Penn Traffic 1973 Annual Report

Already Gone

After the Penn Traffic Company announced its decision, employees and shoppers adjusted to the thought of life without the mother store. For the first time in 123 years, one of the pillars of the downtown Johnstown business district would cease to function as a full-line department store.

As the reality of it sank in, people realized just how big a loss they were going to suffer. There would be no more restaurant, candy kitchen, or bakery; no more Christmas display windows or Men's Day sales or fashion shows or sitting on the mezzanine watching people shop on the main floor below.

Things would never be the same.

The building would remain in use as the company's headquarters, but all the merchandise would be gone. The familiar sights and sounds and smells of the original Penn Traffic Department Store would disappear forever.

In fact, they were gone already.

Loose Ends

The closing meant that certain employees, like Shirley Blough, would lose their jobs. Some were able to find work at the branch stores, but others were out of luck.

For example, the delivery truck drivers were no longer needed, because the company would stop making deliveries now that the downtown store was closed. "We went by seniority," says Bill Gasior. "The younger guys, we had to lay off. We cut some furniture guys, too, because most furniture sales had been done through the main store.

"But we moved our warehouse to the Trigona building in the Geistown Cloverleaf, and I was able to add a couple guys there. That saved a few jobs," says Bill.

A number of Department Store Division people who were working in the administrative offices held on to their jobs, too. They had their hands full keeping the branch stores running and dealing with the aftermath of the main store's closing.

Photo by Philip Balko

"We had to get things cleaned up," recalls Marie Neff. "We had a lot of loose ends to tie up in the accounts. Not the present accounts in the accounts receivable from the public, but we had a lot of accounts from different manufacturers. It took us a while to clear that up."

Barbara Baxter's duties weren't much different than they'd been before. "I continued buying for the branch stores," she says. "The downtown store was finished, but I went on buying for the other stores just like before the flood."

Life in the Penn Traffic Building went on like that for the next few years. A new status quo settled in at the Department Store Division, as people got used to the changes and made the best of them.

But the new status quo, like the old one, wouldn't last. And neither would the Department Store Division.

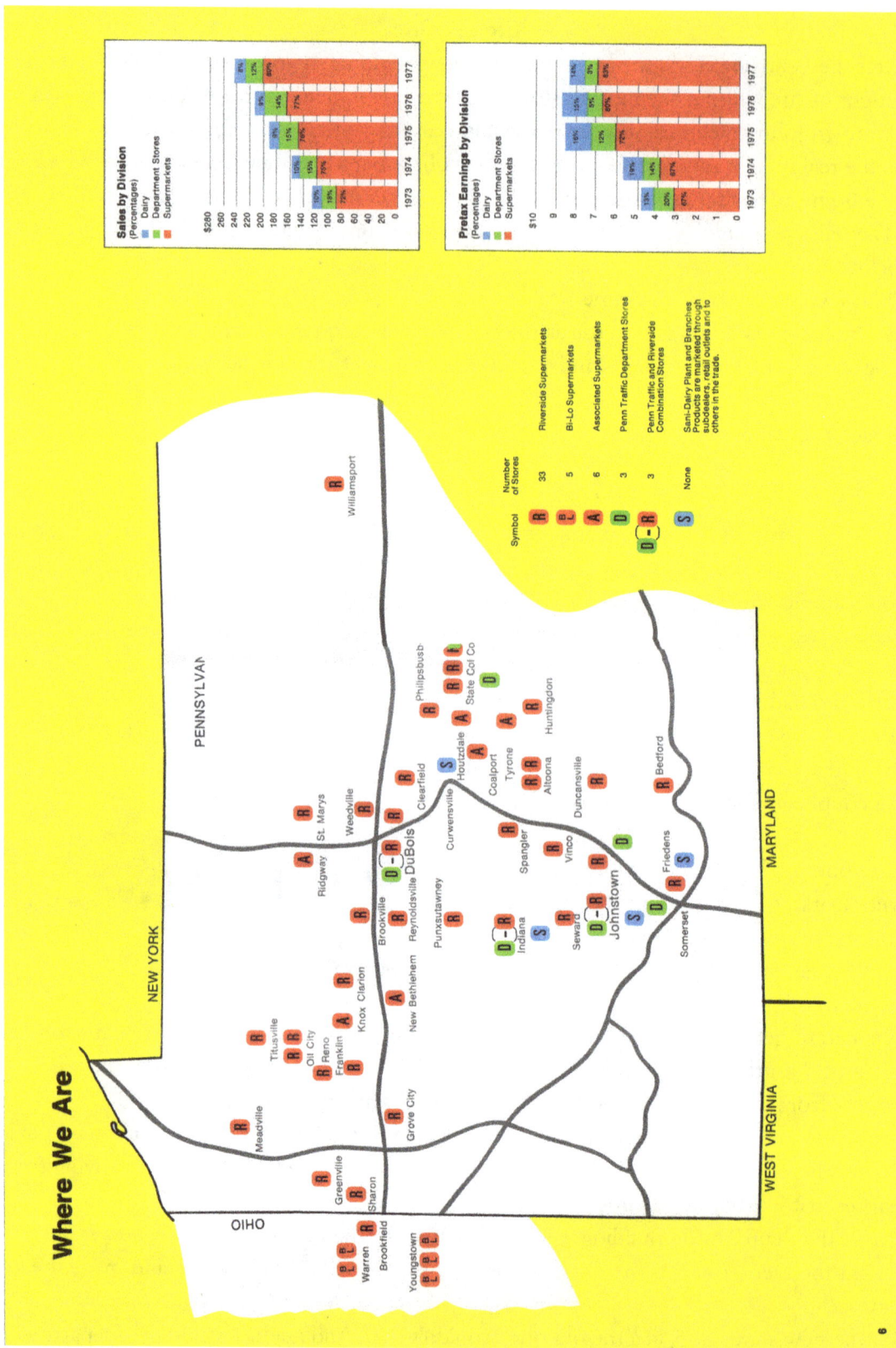

Graphic from Penn Traffic 1978 Annual Report

PAT BAUMBAUGH
CANDY COUNTER TO CORPORATE OFFICE
YEARS OF SERVICE 17
1969–1986

Sometimes, Pat Baumbaugh felt like a jinx. It seemed like every department or office she worked in at Penn Traffic ended up closing.

Or maybe it was just a job hazard that came with working for the Penn Traffic Company in its waning years. Either way, it made for an interesting 17-year career as she jumped from job to job to keep from sinking.

The Goodies They Made

Pat applied at Penn Traffic in 1969 after her husband was laid off from the Woodvale steel firm Griffith and Custer. Penn Traffic quickly hired her and put her to work at the first floor candy counter.

It wasn't long before she moved to the bakery shop, where she worked as a sales clerk and cashier. Her responsibilities soon increased, though, when she left the front lines of the sales counter for a behind-the-scenes job as secretary for the bakery and candy kitchen.

"I took care of all the paperwork and invoices for the bakery and candy kitchen," says Pat. "Along the way, I got to spend time in both places and got to know a lot about the people who worked there and the goodies they made."

Big Dippers

According to Pat, Harry Steele was the head candy maker in the kitchen, the one who knew all the secret recipes for Penn Way candy. The rest of the crew consisted of four or five dippers, including Dilly DeMarco, Myra Liegel, and Boots Goenner.

The team worked together in the chilly kitchen, crafting legendary hand-dipped chocolates. When Pat wasn't busy with her secretarial duties, she watched the time-tested process in action.

Photo © The Tribune-Democrat, courtesy of Park Cover

"In the back room where Harry worked, they had great big trays," remembers Pat. "When they made their chocolate-covered candies, they made the centers in a form. They put the forms in corn starch, and then they stuffed them with the filling for the candy centers. That gave the candies their shapes.

"Next, they dipped the formed centers in melted chocolate," says Pat. "Then they put them on the big trays to cool and harden."

Making other candy products was more involved. "At Easter time, they would make special chocolate eggs," says Pat. "They were filled with coconut, maple, or fruit, and decorated on top. They always made them in halves, then put the halves together and sealed them. Then they weighed the finished eggs to make sure they weighed the right amount."

The result? Pure heaven, according to Pat, who got her share of samples during her rounds.

"They kept discards in tins in a side room," she remembers. "I would go in there sometimes and help myself to a piece. It was always fresh and delicious."

Taking the Cake

Pat also snagged occasional samples in the bakery when her duties took her in that direction. It was hard not to, when she got a whiff of the incredible aromas wafting out of the place.

"It smelled wonderful up there," says Pat. "Especially on Fridays when they baked bread twice.

You could smell it throughout the store. People would rush down to the bakery shop right before closing to get the fresh bread when it was delivered from upstairs."

According to Pat, the bakery staff made cookies, cakes, cream puffs, eclairs, pies, rolls, and more. And they did it the old-fashioned way. "Everything was always hand-made. They never used machines."

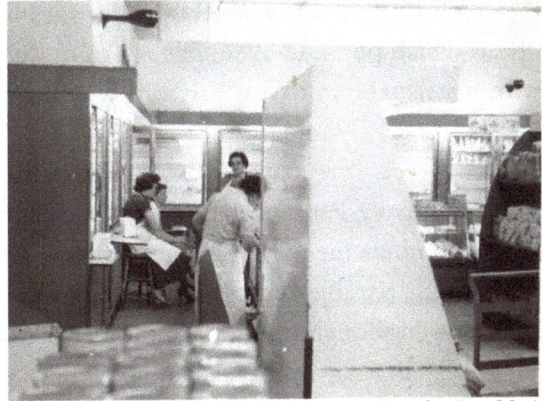

Photo by Arne Magi

One Jinx After Another

After a few years, however, this delicious phase of Pat's career came to an end. The Penn Traffic Company decided the bakery wasn't profitable enough and closed it. Then, they transferred Pat to the personnel office, where she worked for Personnel Director Ed Goddard.

That job didn't last long, because the downtown store closed for good after the 1977 flood, and the personnel office downsized. (Pat's jinx strikes again?) This time, Pat ended up in the accounts payable office, working with the PT branch stores in Westmont, Richland, Indiana, DuBois, and State College.

Photo courtesy of Pat Baumbaugh

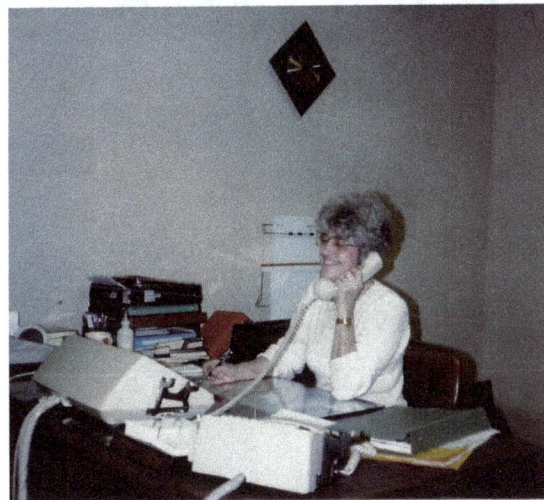

Photo courtesy of Pat Baumbaugh

Photo courtesy of Pat Baumbaugh

But Hess's bought the branch department stores in 1982, casting Pat adrift one last time. Luckily, she found a home handling invoices and issuing checks in Penn Traffic's corporate office, which still had plenty of work from the thriving supermarket division.

At least until a leveraged buyout by a New York City investment group got everything stirred up...at which point, in 1986, Pat got out. Retiring from Penn Traffic after 17 years, she went to live with her daughter in West Virginia, where she found work as a church secretary.

Pinochle with the Dippers

Eventually, Pat moved back home, renting an apartment in Richland Towers. She smiles when she remembers the good old days at Penn Traffic, from the bakery to the personnel department to accounts payable and the corporate office. Her memories of the candy kitchen are especially sweet...even though she never did learn to play pinochle with the dippers.

"I liked going up to the candy kitchen on my lunch hour," says Pat. "The dippers were a fun lot, they were fun to be around. They would sit and play pinochle for pennies on their lunch break, and I would watch.

"But the more I watched, the more confused I got. I just couldn't learn the game.

"To this day, I don't know how to play pinochle. They play it in my building every Tuesday and Thursday, but I can never join in. Maybe if the dippers gave me another lesson, I could finally get in on the game," says Pat.

Memory Department

The first job I had after serving in the army was working as nighttime cleaning crew. I remember my boss, Jean Kiepert. She was the nicest boss I've ever worked for. I worked there until Hess's bought them out, and I went to college. It was a great place to work back then from 1979 to '81. I was working there the night that John Lennon died. I heard it on the TV in the electronics department.

Wade Richard Plouse

I remember shopping for clothes by myself and signing to charge them with no ID other than that the clerk knew me from shopping there with my mother. Then I would meet my brother or sister on the mezzanine and go to the cafeteria for ice cream. The last stop would be the nut counter for a dollar's worth of redskin peanuts for my dad and fifty cents' worth of Spanish peanuts for me.

Claire Montoya

I have the usual memories of Santa, decorated windows, the toy section on the fourth floor, etc., but I also have a story about the Penn Traffic Building after it closed in 1977. Sometime around 1980-81, a model railroad club was formed (maybe twelve people) and began construction of a large portable Lionel train layout in the basement of the Penn Traffic Building.

I was still in high school (North Star) at the time, when my best friend invited me to tag along with him and his dad who were members of the club. This was no ordinary train layout. It measured 82 feet by 16 feet and ran ten trains simultaneously! From that day on, I knew I wanted to be a part of this.

We typically met once a week for several hours in the evening, though a few of the members put in a lot of "overtime" to keep the schedule on track (pun intended).

Our first move was one floor up to the main floor of Penn Traffic. If memory serves me, this was done in time for the Halloween parade and was open to the public that night. The floor was wide open except where they partitioned off for the Gondolier Restaurant and had blocked off the main staircase. At this time, the rest of the building had not been remodeled. On a break, my best friend and I went exploring. The elevators were still in service, and we stopped at a few floors. All was empty and quiet. All that was left were memories of my youth, shopping there on Saturday mornings, and a roaming night watchman.

We then took the show on the road using two trailer trucks. It was displayed in the Richland Mall (down from Kmart) for Christmas. It was also displayed at the Johnstown transit building and in Ligonier for Fort Ligonier Days. At some point, my schedule prevented me from participating in the club, but what a great time we had while it lasted.

Paul Pokos

Photo © The Tribune-Democrat

FRANK ROBISON
BUYER
YEARS OF SERVICE 19 3/4
1962–1982

Did you know that one of the men who greets you at Wal-Mart in Richland was once a buyer for Penn Traffic?

Frank Robison has been working as a greeter at Wal-Mart for 11 years. His Penn Traffic career, which began in 1962, lasted 19¾ years.

Frank started as a department manager in the Indiana PT store, then moved on to buy linens and domestics for that unit. After a while, Penn Traffic recruited him as a buyer for the men's department companywide, a job that led him to move to Johnstown and work in first floor offices in the main store on Washington Street.

It was a job he held for the rest of his time with the company. "I bought men's furnishings," remembers Frank. "Dress shirts, neckwear, hosiery, underwear, socks, umbrellas, and wallets. Anything other than suits, which were up on the second floor.

"I also bought luggage. In those days they had Samsonite, American Tourister, Pierre Cardin, and other brands."

For a while, he also bought all boys' merchandise for the company. "That's when I found out about having to buy white shirts and navy pants for the parochial school children," says Frank.

As Penn Traffic added more stores, the volume of merchandise Frank bought got higher and higher. "I was probably up to two or three million dollars a year at least," he says.

201

Photos from Penn Traffic 1975 Annual Report

Some of what he bought was "on control"-- merchandise ordered regularly and considered part of standard inventory because demand for it was consistent. "White shirts, Gold Toe socks, and Jockey underwear were all on control for us," explains Frank.

Other merchandise, he had to find and buy from vendors during in-store visits or out-of-town buying trips.

New York State of Mind

Like Barbara Baxter, Frank often traveled to New York City in search of merchandise for Penn Traffic's stores.

"New York City was the retail hub in those days," recalls Frank. "Manufacturing might have happened elsewhere, but vendors' offices were in New York. I usually went there once a month."

During his buying trips, he kept up a hectic schedule. "When I got there, I had my itinerary all lined up for the week. I knew everyone I was going to see from Monday morning right through Friday afternoon.

"I gave myself 45 minutes to an hour at each vendor, and that was it. Then I had to move on to the next one.

"I usually grabbed sandwiches along the street for lunch. Sometimes, in the vendor showrooms, they'd say we might work over during lunch, and they'd ask if I wanted to have a sandwich with them in the showroom. I'd say that's okay as long as there's no obligation. I figured hey, I'm not gonna be bought out by anything like that. It can come back on you."

Free lunches weren't the only things he was offered. "Vendors tried to give me lots of stuff, but I had to be careful. I didn't want to be bought by anybody. I felt that if they were giving me something, what were they wanting in return?

"Once in a while, I'd get tickets to a Mets or Yankees game, or maybe one of the salesmen would invite me home for dinner with his family, and I'd go. But I was real careful on that stuff, because they could always go to management and say, 'This Frank, I got tickets or whatever for him, and I think he needs to give us a little more business in return.'"

50 Cents on the Dollar

After the day's meetings, Frank usually ate dinner and returned to his hotel room. "I didn't get out much at night. I had a lot of work to do, writing orders up and getting them signed and getting them to the vendor."

He always went the extra mile to get good deals for Penn Traffic. "I wanted to buy the best merchandise I could get at the lowest price, so Penn Traffic could make a profit.

"For most of what I bought, we made 50 cents on the dollar, which was very good," says Frank.

Photos from Penn Traffic 1973 Annual Report

In return, Frank had a steady job he enjoyed and earned a good living from Penn Traffic. "I really liked working there. They treated me well. I wasn't making millions of dollars, but it was a nice living for raising a family.

"They paid for health insurance and provided vacation time. And I got along well with everyone. I never had a problem with them. I think I could've had a job there for as long as I wanted, if the stores hadn't been sold."

The sale of the Department Store Division to Crown American Corporation in 1982 effectively eliminated Frank's job as a buyer for Penn Traffic. He interviewed for a job with Hess's-- Crown's department store chain, which was absorbing the Penn Traffic stores--but that didn't pan out. He ended up working as a manager at the Joseph Hornes store in the Monroeville Mall.

"Hornes carried elite merchandise," says Frank. "It was a higher grade store than Penn Traffic."

After seven years, Hornes was bought out. Frank's road led him to Wal-Mart, where he's still working today at the age of 81.

Show Me the Candy

Frank works Monday through Thursday, greeting shoppers and handling various chores at the Wal-Mart Supercenter in Richland Town Center, where the Richland Mall used to be. He says the world of retail has changed a lot, but his experience at Penn Traffic still serves him well at Wal-Mart.

And the old days continue to pop up in funny ways during his daily life. "Customers still recognize me from Penn Traffic," says Frank. "They see me at Wal-Mart and ask if I have any Penn Way candy. I just tell them sorry, I don't. We're fresh out."

Photos from Penn Traffic 1972 Annual Report

Chapter Nineteen

Hess's Takes Over

1982

What would a Penn Traffic Company without department stores be like? The answer became clear in 1982.

At the end of the 1981 fiscal year--January 1982--the company sold off its entire Department Store Division to Crown American Corporation for $7.3 million in properties.

John Kriak, secretary and treasurer of Penn Traffic at the time, handled the deal. "Essentially, I swapped Penn Traffic stores for Crown real estate.

1983 Annual Report

"Crown gave us seven parcels, including a shopping center on Scalp Avenue in Richland that housed a Riverside market. Until then, that shopping center was owned by Crown.

"In return, I transferred to Crown all the assets of the department stores, except the Penn Traffic Building in downtown Johnstown. The assets I transferred included all the remaining inventory for the department stores, as well," explains John.

Bill Gasior found out about the deal from a friend of his who ran a security company. "He called and said, 'You guys were sold. Hess's bought you. We were just hired to put guards at all your department stores.'"

Photo courtesy of William Gasior

205

If there was any doubt about the change that had just happened, it was put to rest when Department Store Division President Larry Rosen stopped showing up in the Penn Traffic offices. It wasn't long after that when the news finally broke.

The Penn Traffic and PT branch stores (and PT Sports in Westmont) were now in the hands of Hess's Department Stores, a subsidiary of Crown. Just like that, Penn Traffic was out of the department store business...which had been its *only* business for so many years. The Penn Traffic and PT stores, which had been a part of the retail landscape for so long, were about to become extinct.

All this in spite of the vote of confidence a mere two years earlier, when the company had opened the first new Penn Traffic store since 1974.

The Love Is Gone

In 1979, the company had launched a Penn Traffic department store in Somerset, PA. Unfortunately, the store didn't do as well as expected and died an early death.

According to Barbara Baxter, the closing was premature. "The company didn't really give it a chance. They said the customers in Somerset weren't supporting it, but that wasn't fair. It takes time to get people in a store and get them used to it."

When it came to a proven producer--the Penn Traffic store in State College--the company's executives had been more supportive. They had extensively remodeled that store, applying a "new look" developed to modernize the store's appearance and increase sales. According to the company's 1978 Annual Report, similar renovations were on the drawing board for the Westwood and DuBois units.

Even with these improvements, sales in the Department Store Division continued to disappoint. The company took one last gamble in that direction, opening a clothing-only store in the Butler Mall, but it quickly failed. According to Bill Gaisor, who was in charge of the branch stores by then, it opened and closed in less than a year's time.

There just didn't seem to be any good news in the department store realm anymore. It is any surprise that the company dropped it like a hot potato in the deal with Crown American?

Expansion Strategy?

1983 Annual Report

The way it sounded in the message from then-President Guido Malacarne in the 1981 Annual Report, the decision to dump the department stores was the result of cold, hard numbers. "At the end of fiscal 1981, the Department Store Division was using approximately 17% of the Corporation's gross assets to produce 7% of our consolidated sales and less than 1% of our net income," wrote Malacarne.

"The main reason for the division's poor performance in 1981 and prior years was the lack of sales volume necessary to cover the division's central office buying and management expenses."

According to Malacarne, the company had considered an "expansion strategy" as an alternative to selling the division, a strategy that would have led Penn Traffic to spend $10-$15 million on new or existing stores. This strategy was rejected, he wrote, "because of our lack of confidence that the department store business would generate an appropriate long-term rate of return."

The 90-Day Plan

Soon after the deal with Crown American was done, the fates of the Penn Traffic and PT stores became clear. The Penn Traffic mall-based stores in Richland and State College were kept open and converted to Hess's stores. The PT combination stores in Westmont, Indiana, and DuBois, plus PT Sports in Westmont, were all closed.

And plenty of jobs were lost in the process. Though Hess's interviewed Penn Traffic employees, they didn't hire many of them for the new Hess's stores.

Barbara Baxter was one of those interviewed. "Hess's interviewed me, but I knew before I went in to the interview that I was never going to have a job with them. They wanted cheap help, and I wasn't it. Most of my coworkers I talked to weren't willing to take a cut in pay just to have a job, either. That was the end of it," says Barbara.

Marie Neff was one of those who ended up jobless after the sale, though the writing had been on the wall for some time before that. "I'd been cleaning up old accounts from the downtown store since the flood, but that work was finally winding down. By 1982, I'd been cut to two days a week because there really wasn't anything left to do. Then Hess's bought the stores, and I was out of a job."

Pat Baumbaugh lost her job, too. "I'd been working in Accounts Payable for the department stores. When Hess's took over, they didn't want me."

According to Bill Gasior, Hess's had a plan to get rid of the majority of Penn Traffic department store employees within 90 days. Bill was one of the lucky ones, hired by Hess's to serve as director of operations.

"I handled operations for 15 Hess's stores and security for 22," says Bill. "I really had my hands full then, managing renovations and store closings and transferring Penn Traffic inventory to Hess's stores."

A Company Without Department Stores

Meanwhile, in the Penn Traffic Building on Washington Street, things got a little quieter. The desks once occupied by Department Store Division personnel were empty. Little by little, the work related to the sale of the division to Hess's wrapped up, and mentions of the department stores became fewer and farther between.

Soon, the department stores were just a memory. Business went on in the corporate offices on Washington Street, in the building that had been just such a store, but the business was all about supermarkets and Sani-Dairy now. The company's 128 years in the department store business were over.

Years earlier, chief accountant Elit Felix had said that the Riverside merger of 1962 was probably the worst thing that Penn Traffic had ever done. He'd said Riverside was bigger and more powerful and would eventually close down the department stores.

Elit had been right. As hard as it was to believe, Penn Traffic had become a company without a department store. Eighteen years later, it would stop being a company altogether.

Photos from Penn Traffic 1972 Annual Report

Penn Traffic VIP

JOHN KRIAK
EXECUTIVE VICE PRESIDENT
SECRETARY TREASURER
YEARS OF SERVICE 17
1976–1993

Photo by Philip Balko

John Kriak is the last Penn Traffic executive who still works in the Penn Traffic Building on Washington Street...though the company itself is long gone these days.

John, who once served as Executive Vice President Secretary Treasurer of Penn Traffic, runs his business consulting firm, GroupGenesis LLC, out of offices on the second floor. Though he left the building in 1993, he came back in 1999, and he's been there ever since.

He's the "last executive standing," a man with memories of some of the company's darkest days, and connections to times past when things were brighter.

Something To Do With Transportation

Back in 1976, John was a certified public accountant working as an audit manager for Price-Waterhouse in Pittsburgh. A Johnstown native, he came back to town to visit family and friends, attend local meetings of the National Association of Accountants, and serve in the 28th Military Police unit of the National Guard on Walters Avenue. During one such visit to town, he ran into Penn Traffic's treasurer, Carl Kopp, who tried to recruit him to come aboard as assistant treasurer.

At the time, Price-Waterhouse was considering relocating John to New York City. Faced with the two possibilities, John chose the opportunity in Johnstown. "My dad had retired at that point, and my wife Bonnie's mom was still in Johnstown. Being there for family was important to us," remembers John.

His co-workers in Pittsburgh didn't know much about his new employer, though. "When I told the guys at Price-Waterhouse that I was going to Penn Traffic, they said, "Oh, good. Penn Traffic must be something to do with transportation.' They assumed that, because I'd done a lot of work with the US Steel transportation group.

"I said no, it's a department store and supermarket company. I said it's a publicly traded company in Johnstown, my home, and I've decided to relocate there," says John.

Drowning the Golden Age

Coming back to Johnstown when he did, John witnessed the final days of the downtown store's golden age. "It was exciting to be there," he recalls. "The department store was in full bloom at that time. There was no reason to believe it wouldn't stay in business."

But everything changed the following year, when the flood of '77 slammed into the place, and the company decided to close it for good.

The flood also led John to set up shop inside the Penn Traffic Building, since his offices in the company's one-story office building across the street were destroyed.

It was the start of a new era for John and the company. "The flood had a powerful impact on Penn Traffic. Not only did it lead to the closure of the downtown store, but it changed the direction of the whole company."

One such change was the conversion of the closed store into non-retail rental space. "After the closing, I put together a plan to put the vacant space in the Penn Traffic Building to other uses," says John. "We were able to bring in the I.R.S. and the federal courthouse, and Laurel Holdings took a floor, as well. They used the space for building wire harnesses."

From Crown to GroupGenesis

In the years that followed, John continued working in the corporate offices, managing Penn Traffic's real estate holdings, and being available to the Sani-Dairy division. Then, in 1979, he played a role in the company's next major transaction--the acquisition of 21 Quality Markets by the Supermarket Division.

1989 Annual Report

Three years later, John set up and completed the sale of the Department Store Division to Crown American Corporation. He was on the front lines of the landmark deal to trade the Penn Traffic and PT stores for six Crown American properties, permanently removing Penn Traffic from the department store business.

In 1993, as the company relocated its headquarters to Syracuse, New York--a move that John helped make possible--he decided to quit rather than leave Johnstown. He went to work for Crown American, where his first assignment linked back to the sale of the Department Store Division in 1982.

"The first thing Frank (Pasquerilla) had me do was go to Allentown to help with the liquidation of the Hess's department stores," says John. "This was the same Hess's chain that had absorbed all the Penn Traffic and PT stores.

"We swapped the Hess's department stores with May Co., which owned Kaufman's, Hecht's, and other chains. We did it to get May Co. into Crown American's real estate in the malls."

John stayed at Crown until 1999, when he left to start his business consulting company, GroupGenesis LLC. His search for office space led him full circle, to the second floor of the Penn Traffic Building.

"Of all the places I could have gone, I came back to the Penn Traffic Building," says John. "It was a place I knew and loved. Darrel Holsopple, whom I'd hired, was still the building manager. I felt right at home, and I still do."

A 300-Year Building

Just as, at one time, it was hard to imagine the Penn Traffic Building without Samuel Heckman, it's hard now to imagine it without John Kriak. There's even a community room in the basement that bears his name.

Ask him if he's planning to move elsewhere, and you'll get an emphatic no. "I'm here because I know the building, and it provides comfortable space, plus basement parking. The parking's an immense benefit to me.

"It's the only heated garage in Johnstown. The pipes are all down there, and they keep it warm in the winter and cool in the summer."

There is still lots of empty space in the upper floors of the building, which is owned by South Korean businessman Chung Ho Park. Attracting new tenants has been an uphill battle since the June 2012 departure of the National Drug Intelligence Center, which occupied the entire third, fourth, and fifth floors of the building (plus storage space on the mezzanine and elsewhere).

But John still has hope that the building will play a significant role in Johnstown's future. "I appreciate the building. I look at it as something that was built at the turn of the century which is still viable and a significant asset to the community."

It's not as if the building's coming down any time soon. "This is a 300-year building," says John. "When they built it, they built it to last.

"The structure is solid. Nothing I know of could ever blow it down. It might blow through it, but it will never blow it down.

"Plus, it has redundant boilers and diesel backup electric power. It's a fortress.

"This building will be here another 200 years, at least. It will continue to stand as a testament to the accomplishments of the Penn Traffic company, its support of the community, and the special place it held in the hearts of so many shoppers down through the years," says John.

Photo courtesy of Darrel Holsopple

Photo by Philip Balko

Memory Department

I have so many memories of Penn Traffic. First, I remember going to lunch there every week with my grandmother between my ages of 5-10. I would always have a club sandwich (they were the best.) I also got red Jell-O cubes with whipped cream on top for dessert. I loved those days with my Grandma.

Secondly, when I was 13, my parents got me a Penn Traffic charge card for my birthday. I think it had a $30 limit per month. Oh my god, I thought I was such a grown up.

Lastly, I remember the furniture department. They had rooms set up like a real house and my mother and I would always love to go through those rooms. I had a great childhood and these are part of those memories.

Randy Ruder

I had a boss at Penn Traffic named Mike Wolf who still, to this day, was one of the best bosses I've ever had. The man who managed the kitchen was named Hans Ervig. He either dyed his hair very, very black, or it might have been a toupee.

Steve Morgan

When I became pregnant with my first baby, Penn Traffic hired me over Christmas to work in the gift wrapping center. It was really a great experience.

Mary McKenzie-Buck

Remember the elevator operators sitting on a little "jump seat" or standing. (I wonder if there was a written job description?) I at one time thought I might apply.
Natalie Coleman

My then boyfriend/fiancé and I went to the area on the first floor where tobacco products were sold to buy his dad cherry blend as a Christmas gift to roll his cigarettes.
Sharon Tomera

I remember they had a nice area where you could sit and feed your baby. I appreciated that when I had my first child.
Kathy Kmetz

My uncle, Frank Ostheim, worked on the top floor. I used to go up there, to the "office floor," to say hello.

I also remember that the shoe department had one of those X-ray machines to check your feet.

When I was a teenager, I became friends with Mildred Noon. She was a buyer in the gift department, if memory serves me correctly. When I think about it, it seems I spent a lot of time in Penn Traffic!
Kathy Weaver

I worked for a short time on the fifth floor right next to the candy kitchen. They were the best people. Harry was the boss. He used to give me almond bark when they made it. OHHH! It was the best. The peanut butter cups were out of this world. I loved going to the budget store. I found great sales for my mother. Margaret Benson and Ruth Sexton were the two ladies I worked with. That department store was the greatest store along with Glosser Bros.
Carmen Stutzman

Penn Traffic VIP

ELEANORE KENNELL
CONTROLLERS OFFICE &
CORPORATE OFFICE
YEARS OF SERVICE 23
1969-1992

When Eleanore Kennell worked in the controller's office of the Penn Traffic Company, she put together the annual reports. Every year, she (and a cast of helpers) put the booklets together by hand, then mailed them to 3,000-4,000 stockholders. She still remembers handling stacks and stacks of loose pages delivered by the printing company, putting them in order and assembling them for shipping.

Decades later, at the age of 90, Eleanore is still putting together booklets. Working as a volunteer at the Cambria County Fairgrounds, she assembles premium booklets for the fair in much the same way, from stacks of loose pages on tables arranged around the room.

She says the work helps keep her feeling young and reminds her of her 23-year career at Penn Traffic.

Keeping Pace with Progress

Eleanore moved to Johnstown from Akron, Ohio in 1967 when her second husband, an attorney, went to work for Frank Pasquerilla. Her husband died two years later, in 1969, and Eleanore found a job at Penn Traffic.

She worked in the controller's office in those days, supporting John Gunter, the company's controller. "I started out as a clerk, more or less, doing nitty-gritty stuff," explains Eleanore. "But as time went on, I learned how to do higher level tasks and progressed to the position of administrative assistant to the controller."

John Gunter photo from
Penn Traffic 1976 Annual Report

Her boss, Mr. Gunter, had been in the service in World War II, but he wasn't stuck in the past. He always made it a point to keep up with the times when it came to his work. "He thought you had to keep pace with progress, you couldn't stand still," says Eleanore. "He always encouraged me to learn new things and apply them to what I did in the office."

Penn Traffic Pep Rallies

As Eleanore embraced progress, she also embraced life in the big store. "It was a busy, exciting place, and I loved working there."

She enjoyed the professional atmosphere, which extended from employee's attitudes to the clothes they wore to work. "The company's philosophy was 'the customer always comes first.' We employees really took that to heart.

"The way we dressed was part of that professional, courteous image. When I was first hired, women wore dark dresses, and men wore dark suits. Later, that changed to colored dresses for women and sportscoats and pants for men. But women still couldn't wear slacks."

To get the staff in the right frame of mind, Penn Traffic occasionally had morning pep rallies for them. "They had them once a month or so," remembers Eleanore. "Someone would work up a theme, and the advertising department would pull together an in-house promotional campaign. Then we'd have the event, and it would be a lot of fun."

Hats-and-Gloves Saturdays

Though Eleanore spent most of her time in the controller's office (near the infants and children's department on the fourth floor), she did get to roam other parts of the building during the course of her day and enjoyed the store's many attractions.

She liked stopping by the candy kitchen, for example, and checking in on the women who were dipping chocolates. "They'd slip you a free sample," says Eleanore. "And it was always out of this world."

She loved the bakery and usually ate lunch in the restaurant, sometimes sitting at the counter if she was in a hurry. "The service at the counter was faster," she says.

Eleanore also got a kick out of observing the people who came and went at the store. "Older women would come in and have the 99 cent special lunch and go up and sit on the mezzanine all afternoon. There were chairs up there and a glass railing, so they could sit and watch the people doing their shopping on the ground floor.

"Saturday was the big day when all the ladies and their children would come in dressed up. The ladies wore their best clothes, complete with hats and gloves, just to come to Penn Traffic and shop."

When it came to shopping, Eleanore made the most of her employee discount, picking up clothes after the end of her shift.

Photo from Penn Traffic 1966 Annual Report

216

Photo from Penn Traffic 1966 Annual Report

"The women's department was very up-to-date, very modern. The buyers were up with the times. I got lots of good clothes there.

"The more expensive items were in a special area. Other items were out on tables on the floor, and you could rummage through them to find what you liked," says Eleanore.

Where's Eleanore?

The Penn Traffic Building was Eleanore's home base, but she also got to travel from time to time. While working for the Controller, she oversaw the company-wide inventory count, which happened twice a year.

"Inventory was a big deal," she remembers. "We closed all the stores for the day, and the employees had to make lists of everything they had in stock.

"I had to go to each store to oversee its inventory, which I enjoyed. I liked getting to meet all the people I normally only talked to on the phone."

Once the information was all tabulated in the stores, it was compiled in the controller's office. "That's how we determined if the company was profitable," says Eleanore. "Sometimes, you could tell right away. Other times, it took a while to see where the data was leading."

1968 Annual Report

Skirting the Storm

Years later, after the company merged with P&C Foods in Syracuse, New York, Eleanore moved to a new job in the Johnstown corporate office, one with many more opportunities for travel.

"I got used to getting on a plane and going somewhere at a moment's notice," says Eleanore. "If they needed somebody to go and do something, they would ask me. They would call and say, Eleanore, we need you to go to New York. So I would go to one of the grocery or department stores and get the money for the plane ticket. Then, I would drive to Pittsburgh and get on a plane and go to New York.

"I wasn't afraid to do that. It was part of the job and I enjoyed it. I knew my way around flying enough that I could do it. Not all of the people at Penn Traffic were able to do that kind of thing, though," says Eleanore.

Sometimes, Eleanore traveled to deliver paperwork related to the company's 401k plan. Other times, she had to deliver proxy statements for members of the board of directors to the Syracuse office. "They had a chauffeur pick me up at the airport and take me to the office. I had the proxies in a case that was handcuffed to my arm. I had to uncuff the case and hand it over to the person I'd been instructed to give it to. Then, they took me back to the airport, and I got on a plane to go home."

Unfortunately, flying conditions weren't always the best. "Once, I was flying with John Kriak in a private plane to Fort Littleton outside Philadelphia. It was a horrible day to fly, but we had commitments to meet.

"Boy, coming down out of the clouds that day was an experience and a half. We ended up dropping to what seemed like three feet off the ground. Then, going home, we had to skirt a huge thunderstorm. We ended up going all the way down around South Carolina to get home," says Eleanore.

Secret Charity

In addition to her travel-oriented work, Eleanore served as a kind of secret fairy godmother around Johnstown, doing good deeds on behalf of Penn Traffic.

"The company did a lot of charitable work anonymously," recalls Eleanore. "They would give help where it was needed, and they didn't always want recognition for it.

"For example, if there were people whose house had burned down, and they'd lost all their clothes, Penn Traffic might make sure they at least had a change of clothes.

"These good deeds might not be big enough to warrant a tax writeoff. The company did them just because. Penn Traffic was very community-oriented.

"The bosses would ask me to respond to a certain request, and they would give me the resources to do what was needed.

"They did a lot for the YWCA, for example. I ended up volunteering there and served on the Y's board of directors. When the Y needed something, I would pass along the request, and Penn Traffic would empower me to grant it."

Never Retired

Eleanore retired from Penn Traffic after 23 years, in 1992. She went on to manage costuming for the theater department at the University of Pittsburgh at Johnstown, then retired from that in 2002. But she never stopped working. Even in her 90s, she still regularly assists her daughter, Pat,

the office manager at the Cambria County Fairgrounds. Pat also worked at Penn Traffic in the early 70s, selling electronics, TVs, and records.

She watches her mother as she assembles booklets for the fair and smiles proudly. "This is all stuff Mom used to do for Penn Traffic. There's so much she knows from working there that helps us at the fairgrounds. I love to pick her brain."

"And I love to keep busy." Eleanore smiles back at her. "I love to help in any way that I can. That's never changed."

Memory Department

My mother's family initially lived in Prospect, just up the viaduct behind Penn Traffic. She worked as a waitress in Penn Traffic's restaurant. My father grew up in Brownstown. One day, he and his buddies were walking around town looking for fun (or trouble) and stopped in at the restaurant in Penn Traffic. That's how Dad and Mom met.

Mom used to get all dressed up to go downtown for shopping on a Saturday and took my sister and me along. Besides going to a few different stores for specific purchases (Reiser's Butcher Shop for meat...I think this was on Franklin Street somewhere), we'd always end up at Penn Traffic and often stopped for lunch at the restaurant.

Penn Traffic was also the first store Mom would take me to for my Easter suit (the only suit that I would own and be able to wear for a year when a suit was called for). I can remember when I was in about the sixth grade and in the men's and boys' department, that a certain salesman with a moustache was waiting on my mom and me. (He knew my father, too, and was the only man I knew that called Dad "Ted"...but then Dad had a number of nicknames that I didn't understand, like "Sam" and "Pitch.") My mom agreed with my choice of a suit, and the salesman and I were headed to the changing room to try on the pants as my mother called out across the floor, loud enough for anyone to hear within 20-30 feet, "Make sure you check how those pants fit in the back. He's got a rear end on him like a girl's," which is EXACTLY what a young man of the age of a sixth-grader wants a bunch of strangers to hear!

When I was earning enough money from my job as a paper boy, I wanted to show my independence and love for my family members by buying Christmas gifts for Mom, Dad, my sister, and maybe one or two of my favorite uncles or aunts. So, I would walk from our home in Dale to downtown to buy Christmas gifts at Penn Traffic.

I can remember one year when I was attempting to buy a fuzzy white sweater for my mother, and the woman asked me what size I wanted, and I didn't know. Between the two of us and looking around at other women in the store, we came to a conclusion about size based on my pointing out a woman who appeared to be about the same size as my mother. One just didn't get individualized attention like that at just any store one walked into.

Sure, we bought some things at Glosser Brothers (I bought my first set of ice skates there on my own with money earned on my paper route), but when our family thought of shopping, Penn Traffic is where we went first.

Ed Petrick

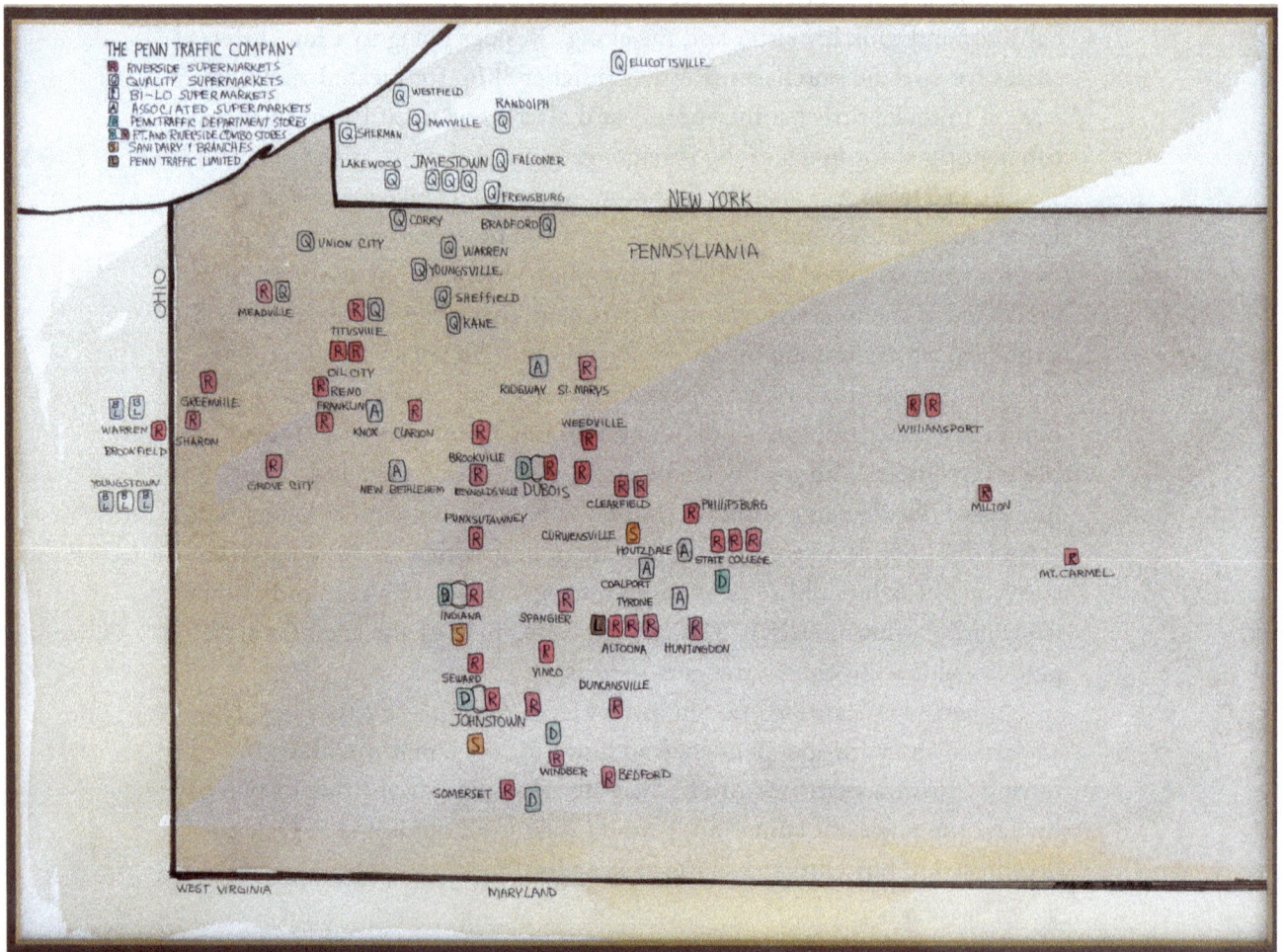

Photos by Philip Balko

Chapter Twenty
The Long, Slow Slide
1983-2010

The saddest part of the story is already over. In the ways that matter, the Penn Traffic we knew and loved ceased to exist after the closing of the downtown store in 1977 and the sale of the branch department stores in 1982.

For all intents and purposes, the twists and turns that followed were part of the life of a different company, one that was called Penn Traffic, one that evolved from Penn Traffic, but one that wasn't really the Penn Traffic we cared about.

When this Penn-Traffic-in-name-only company finally died in 2010, was there an uproar from the public? Did people churn out angry, tearful letters to the editor of the *Tribune-Democrat*, mourning the loss of a local institution as they had when the downtown store closed in '77?

Not a chance. Because the *real* Penn Traffic was already long gone by then.

Ups and Downs

After the sale of the Department Store Division to Crown American/Hess's in 1982, the Penn Traffic Company's focus turned more than ever to supermarkets. The company owned and operated 47 Riverside and BI-LO stores, supplied 15 other independently owned and operated Riversides, and also supplied one additional contract market. Then there were the 21 Quality Markets, acquired by Penn Traffic in 1979, and the affiliated 200,000 square foot distribution center in Jamestown, New York.

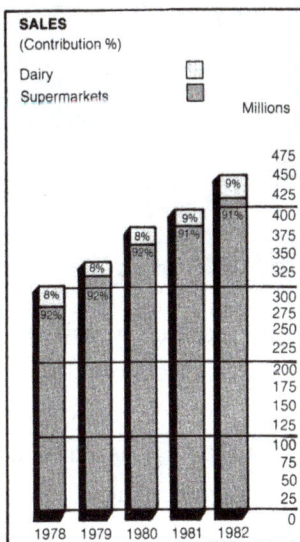

Chart from Penn Traffic 1966 Annual Report

221

In the fiscal year ending January 29, 1983, supermarkets accounted for 91% of Penn Traffic's total sales, which reached an all-time high of $462,425,000. Compare that to sales of $285,951,000 five years before, in the fiscal year ending January 28, 1978. That represented an increase of 61.83% in just five years.

Clearly, the supermarket business was doing fine...but the gravy train didn't last. Penn Traffic opened 17 stores in 1983, only to close 19 in 1984.

As profitability declined, the company shifted its focus to wholesaling and discount superstores. It was operating four superstores by May 1985, with three more in the works.

But supermarket acquisitions ramped up again in 1986, when Penn Traffic bought 15 stores from Glosser Bros. in Johnstown. These stores would be operated as a subsidiary by Penn Traffic's DuBois warehouse.

Then, in 1987, an event of seismic proportions struck the company. A New York City investment group--Miller Tabak & Hirsch & Co.--executed a leveraged buyout of the company. Penn Traffic had just fallen down the rabbit hole into the cutthroat world of high finance.

The Six Billion Dollar Man

Photo from Penn Traffic 1989 Annual Report

Buying Penn Traffic was the first in a series of moves by Gary Hirsch, the head of Miller Tabak & Hirsch & Co., that would enable him to build a $6 billion grocery store empire.

Soon after buying a controlling interest in Penn Traffic and becoming chairman of the board of directors, Hirsch took the company private for $131 million through Miller Tabak & Hirsch & Co. The following year, he raised $25 million by taking Penn Traffic public again...and then he really got busy.

Hirsch acquired three more supermarket companies and made them all part of Penn Traffic. He bought P&C Food Markets, based in Syracuse, in 1988 for $219 million; Big Bear supermarkets, based in Ohio, in 1989 for $341 million; and Grand Union markets, also in '89, for $1.2 billion. The resulting empire, which stretched

from Georgia to Vermont and constituted the seventh-largest food retailer in the U.S., was valued at $6 billion.

"Gary used Penn Traffic as a base and eventually acquired 600 stores," explains John Kriak. "He assembled the management team that would run this enormous company.

Supermarket photos from Penn Traffic 2002 Annual Report

222

"But he stripped many of the functions from the component entities, the individual companies within Penn Traffic. And sales went down in the process."

Photo from Penn Traffic 1992 Annual Report

A Mountain of Debt

By the early 1990s, cracks started to appear in Hirsch's empire. Thanks to the junk bond financing he'd used to make his acquisitions, he'd put the companies he'd purchased in debt to the tune of $800 million, sticking them with brutally high interest payments. Grand Union, for example, was slammed with a $150 million annual interest burden; meeting that obligation prevented the company from upgrading store interiors or pricing its goods competitively.

"It was an overextended leverage debt," says Kriak. "Also, there were problems because of the way they cut costs out of the organization. It totally decimated the top line."

Still, Hirsch kept adding to his empire, using the same tricks to acquire more stores. In 1993, he bought Peter J. Schmitt Co., which included 27 supermarkets. He picked up 12 more later that year when he bought Insalaco Markets Inc. in Pittston, PA.

Then, in 1994, he acquired 45 Acme Markets in Pennsylvania and New York from American Stores Co. for $95.7 million. It was the last major acquisition by Penn Traffic, and the last year in which the company turned a profit.

By early 1995, Penn Traffic had 285 retail and wholesale food stores in its portfolio. It also had a mountain of crippling debt that just kept getting bigger.

By July 1994, the company's long-term debt exceeded $1.1 billion. Profits dropped by $79 million in 1995...$41.4 million in 1996...and $61 million in 1997. Penn Traffic hadn't paid dividends on its stock since going public in 1987, and didn't expect to any time soon.

Bankrupt

As the debt load continued to weigh Penn Traffic down, its component companies were forced to raise prices at the expense of sales. Operating income plunged.

In 1997, Hirsch brought in a new chief executive--Phillip Hawkins of California-based Vons Supermarkets. Hawkins slashed 325 employees (including longtime division heads) and switched to cheaper meats...but it was too little, too late.

Competitors like Wegmans Food Markets and Kroger pulled ahead, and Penn Traffic never recovered. Losing ground fast, the company sold off Sani-Dairy to Dean Foods in December 1997 for $37.5 million. It was a drop in the bucket, given the dimensions of Penn Traffic's developing crisis.

Photo from Penn Traffic 1997 Annual Report

Unable to turn the company around, Hawkins ended up resigning in 1998. Then, in 1999, for the first time in its history, Penn Traffic filed for Chapter 11 bankruptcy protection.

Samuel Heckman would have been rolling over in his grave, if this version of Penn Traffic had had anything in common with his beloved company other than a name. The headquarters wasn't even in Johnstown anymore; Hirsch had moved it to Syracuse, to the P&C offices, effective June 30, 1993.

Bankrupt Part 2

Under the terms of the bankruptcy plan, Penn Traffic shed $1.13 billion in debt by closing more than four dozen stores and selling its creditors majority ownership in the company.

Penn Traffic emerged from bankruptcy in mid-1999. "We've stabilized this company and we're moving forward," said Joseph V. Fisher, company president and chief executive officer. "This is the bright new beginning."

Maybe Gary Hirsch knew better. Just after the close of the 1999 fiscal year (January 29, 2000), he announced his retirement from Penn Traffic. As the mess he'd started headed for catastrophic new phases, the former chairman of the board and executive committee made himself scarce, leaving others to try to clean up after him.

Three years later, in May 2003, Penn Traffic filed for bankruptcy protection again, with debts totaling $337 million. President Fisher, who'd been so optimistic back in '99, resigned in August of that same year.

This time, it took the company two years to emerge from Chapter 11...but things only got worse after that. Losses kept piling up, with no relief in sight.

Bankrupt Part 3?

Finally, it all came crashing down. On November 18, 2009, Penn Traffic filed for bankruptcy protection once more...its third filing in 10 years.

This time was different from the first two, though. According to the Syracuse *Post-Standard,* Penn Traffic "informed the court it wanted to be out of business completely by mid-February." The *Post-Standard* also reported that, "Filings showed Penn Traffic was bleeding multi-million dollar losses at a frightening pace."

As it became clear that Penn Traffic was for sale, potential buyers came forward. The best offer was $85 million dollars in cash from Tops Markets, plus forgiveness of $70 million in claims against Penn Traffic.

In January 2010, Tops, based in Buffalo, New York, ended up getting approval from the bankruptcy court, the creditors' committees, and all parties involved. The deal was done.

The Bitter End

The Penn Traffic Company would soon be no more. Its assets would be transferred to Tops, as would most of its store-level employees. Its corporate offices would close, and its executives would have to find other work.

Its website would remain, providing information about the bankruptcy, but little trace of the company would survive elsewhere. It had finally run its course, 156 years after its humble beginnings along the Pennsylvania Canal...though, of course, the true heart of the company had been gone for years.

Those of us who loved Penn Way Candy, the Christmas windows, the fresh-baked pies, the restaurant, and the mezzanine had already had our hearts broken long ago. Though it was true, we had never forgotten and would never let go of the magic for as long as we would live.

And the force of our love for Penn Traffic would someday bring it all back to life in this book in your hands.

Even our packaging takes on a new look

Penn Traffic

Penn Traffic

Penn Traffic

Penn Traffic

Penn Traffic

Penn Traffic

WE'RE OPEN
UNTIL **9** TONIGHT

Artwork courtesy of Deb Goldie-Rogers

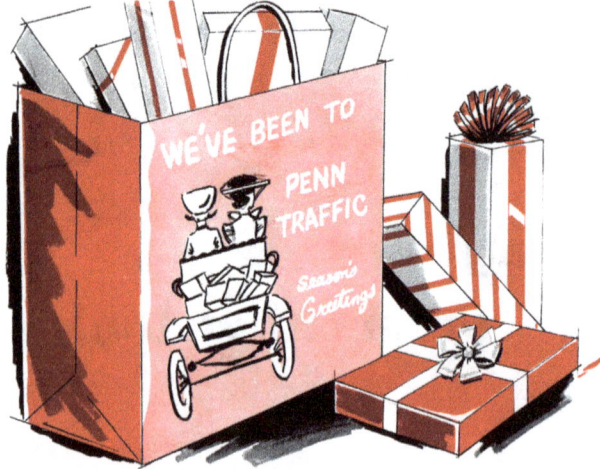

Artwork courtesy of Deb Goldie-Rogers

MEMORY DEPARTMENT

I loved it at Penn Traffic. It was the Macy's of Johnstown.
Kristin Marie Hershiser Clemens

I remember going to see the Christmas window display at Penn Traffic and then getting our picture taken with Santa.
Brian Edwards

My mom worked there for years in the kitchen and bakery. They had some amazing cakes.
Chuck Gutilla

Going to lunch there was special. I loved their little café. And there were so many good deals in the store.

I especially enjoyed going there for shoes on sample day. That was when the men's shoes that had been on display--which were always size 8--were marked down to clearance prices. I loved it because size 8 was my size.
Paul A. Ream

The Easter Bunny would always bring Penn Way chocolate bunnies and coconut eggs to fill our baskets. A special family Easter treat was the solid chocolate egg with nuts!
Ann Trexler

I worked in Johnstown after graduating from Cambria-Rowe and shopped at Penn Traffic every payday after work.
Karen Frantz Kozicki

My grandfather Henry Fritz worked here also and that's where my grandparents met. OMG! I just realized I am Penn Traffic's fault!
Linda Goble

After moving to Morgantown, West Virginia, I visited a bakery there called Ray's Pastries. It turns out that Ray was one of the main bakers at the Penn Traffic bakery.
Arlene Carolus Bennett

I loved the mashed potatoes, gravy, and stuffing in the Penn Traffic restaurant. Then, I always got a cold fudge sundae for dessert.
Judy Hess Gill

Chapter Twenty-One

Return to the Store

2015

It's been over three decades since the Penn Traffic department store in downtown Johnstown closed its doors forever. Wouldn't it be great to see what the building looks like inside after all these years?

If you had the chance to revisit the place, you couldn't find a more perfect tour guide than Darrel Holsopple. Darrel has been in charge of the building for 31 years, serving as Director of Real Estate Operations for the Penn Traffic Company and the current owner, Newfield Properties.

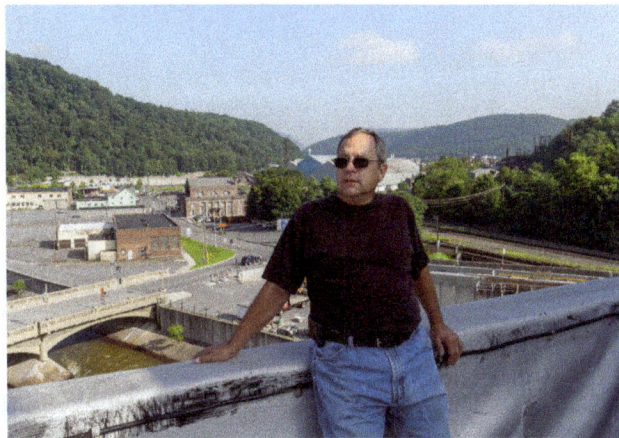

Photo by Philip Balko

Over the years, Darrel has remodeled, refurbished, and renovated just about every square inch of the place. He's seen tenants come and go, and he's been through a lot of ups and downs.

Nobody knows the Penn Traffic Building better than Darrel. That's why we picked him to take you on a tour in the pages that follow, exploring the old building from end to end and top to bottom, seeing what's new within those historic walls...and hunting buried treasures from the store's fabled past.

On your own, you could never see everything that Darrel's about to show you. You wouldn't have access to all the floors, and you wouldn't have keys to all the doors. Even if you did, the place has changed so much that you wouldn't necessarily know what used to be where...and you wouldn't have any idea where

229

to find the hidden treasures left over from the old days. It wouldn't be a very satisfying experience, in other words.

Lucky for you, Darrel found the time in his busy schedule to take you around. So get ready to go where few Penn Traffic fanatics have gone since the closing of the store. Get ready to see things you've wondered about since the old days. And keep your eyes peeled for surprises, because you just never know what you might glimpse in the shadows in a big old building like this with such a rich history.

Enjoy the tour...

Up on the Roof

Your first stop is the building's roof. It's a huge space with panoramic views of the city of Johnstown...big and open enough that it served as a picnic ground from time to time.

"We used to have summer picnics up here sometimes," remembers Darrel. "On a nice day, we'd bring up a table and chairs and grill, and the office staff would eat lunch up here. We'd have 12 or 15 people, and it was really nice.

"That was back in the days after the store closed, when this building was the corporate headquarters of the Penn Traffic Company."

Look in one direction along the Little Conemaugh River behind the building, and you see the Gautier Mills that were once part of Bethlehem Steel.

Photo by Philip Balko

Look the other way along the river, and you see the adjacent brick building that once served as the Bethlehem Steel dispensary and employment office. In the distance beyond that lies Point Stadium.

Cross the roof to the Washington Street side, and you see the buildings in the heart of downtown Johnstown, from the former Lee Hospital and City Hall to the Crown American Building and Ameriserv.

Walk along the length of the roof to the far end, and you're facing the Public Safety Building next door. In the distance, past the

Post Office and bus station, the spires of St. John Gualbert Cathedral point the way to the Franklin mills that once roared day and night in the name of Bethlehem Steel.

Air Conditioning Central

Now that you've walked the perimeter of the roof and taken in the amazing view, turn toward the middle. A large, elevated enclosure of corrugated gray metal dominates that area--the shed that houses the building's central air conditioning system.

Photos by Philip Balko

231

When you walk up the metal stairs and enter, the first equipment you see looks relatively new, brightly painted and polished to a shine. But then Darrel leads you through a big gray door and into another room where the equipment is clearly much older.

"It's original, from when they first installed the system in 1953." He points at a giant green cylinder that looks like it just fell off an old moon module. "It's the fan that pushes the cooled air down into the building."

The fan assembly rests on a set of industrial-strength springs that reduce the vibration passed down into the building by the giant machine. "It used to be, down on the fifth floor, if you had a coffee cup sitting on the table, it would jitter all over the place from the vibration," remembers Darrel.

Other traces of Penn Traffic's past are also on display in the shed, including antique doors and tags on the wall that predate the shiny equipment in the main room by decades.

Photos by Philip Balko

All's Well That's Stairwells

Follow Darrel out of the shed and look around. There are several raised brick structures situated between the air conditioning building and the perimeter of the roof --the enclosed penthouses at the top of the elevator shafts.

According to Darrel, the building has six passenger elevators and three freight elevators, plus three stairwells. He leads you into one of them, and you get another glimpse at Penn Traffic's distant past.

As the door closes, you see the almost-original railing of one of the stairwells that winds through the building. Touch the worn wooden railing; it's been here since the structure was rebuilt after the fire of 1905. The elaborate metal scrollwork on which it rests was designed and installed over a century and a decade ago.

Lean over the railing, and you can see all the way down to the first floor, ninety-plus feet below. But don't lean *too* far; building codes were different in 1905, and the railing is only about waist-high.

Three Floors and 100,000 Square Feet

Follow Darrel down a flight to the fifth floor and take a look at around at what used to be the top level of the Penn Traffic store. Once upon a time, this space was occupied by the Penn Way candy kitchen, the accounting office, the sign shop, Penn Traffic's corporate headquarters, and more. There's no visible trace of any of that, but remnants of the National Drug Intelligence Center (NDIC) are plain to see.

Walk down a hallway and through a door, and the lobby of the top level of the NDIC opens up before you. From the looks of the lobby area, you could almost believe the NDIC is still here and going strong. The walls are paneled in rich, dark oak, and everything looks clean and well-preserved. You almost expect employees to troop through the turnstiles on their way to another day of work at the agency.

Turn right after the turnstiles, and you enter a giant space that was once an NDIC "cubicle farm" swarming with workers. Empty and silent now, it looks vast...and somehow new, as if the workers and their cubicles were only recently removed.

Photos by Philip Balko

233

"At its height, NDIC leased 100,000 square feet in this building out of a total of 184,650," explains Darrel. "They occupied the entire third, fourth, and fifth floors and had over 200 employees."

Doubling back, Darrel leads you through a doorway into what used to be the main computer room for the NDIC. Like the cubicle farm space, it's empty now, but you can still see the remnants of the self-contained cooling system.

"Everything had to be sealed off from the outside world," says Darrel. "You couldn't have open ductwork leading directly outside, especially in the server room. Security was always a major concern."

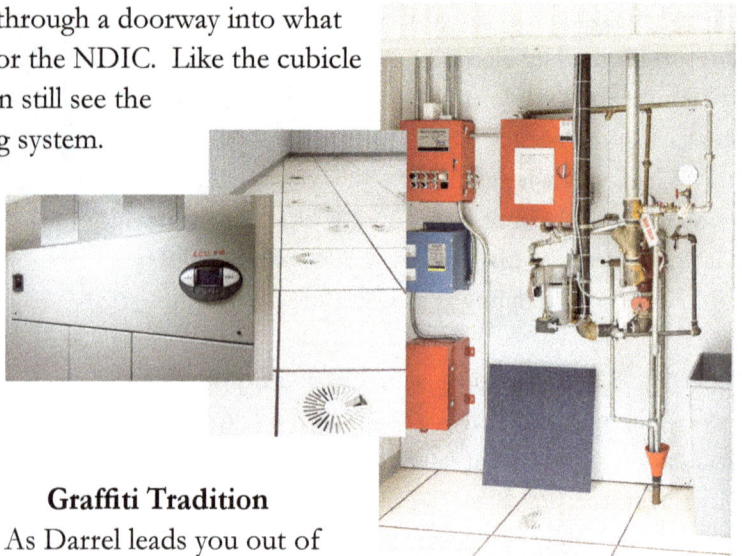

Graffiti Tradition

As Darrel leads you out of the main NDIC area on the fifth floor, he offers to show you around the two other floors that were once dominated by that federal agency.

Why not make the trip downstairs more interesting, he suggests, and have a look at something from the very old days in the bargain?

With that, he escorts you into an ancient freight elevator, one that dates back to when the store was rebuilt after the 1905 fire. Instead of today's push buttons, the elevator has old-fashioned Otis controls that require the operator to manually guide the car from one floor to the next. Darrel demonstrates, cranking the handle to make the elevator car drop... then stopping it suddenly between floors.

"Look at that." He points at the brick wall of the elevator shaft, which is covered in ancient graffiti. "Employees put their names up there ages ago. It used to be a store tradition."

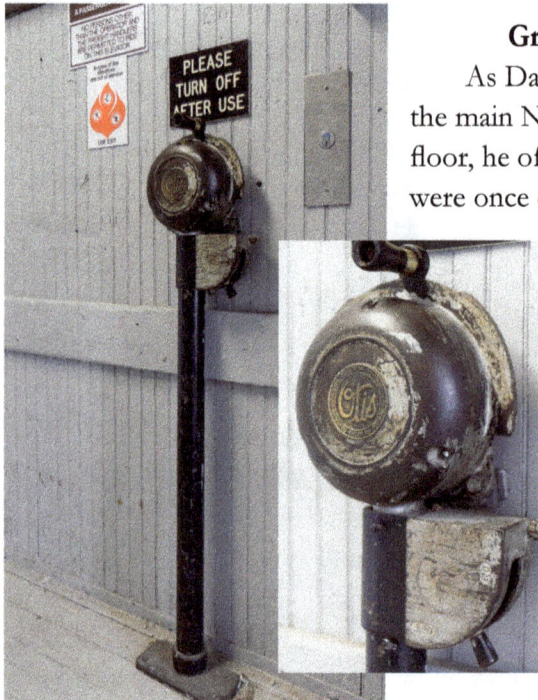

Darrel cranks the handle again, and the car lurches downward. It stops at a door this time, which he proceeds to pull open.

You're on the fourth floor, now, about to enter what was once the domain of NDIC's leadership.

Photos by Philip Balko

234

The Corner Office

The first thing you see when you approach the office suite is a revolving door that once had a metal detector inside. The alarm still goes off if you give it a push, though you don't need to; these days, you can just walk around it.

When you do, you see a massive plaque with the agency's name, still mounted on the wall. It's so heavy, according to Darrel, the wall had to be specially reinforced to support it.

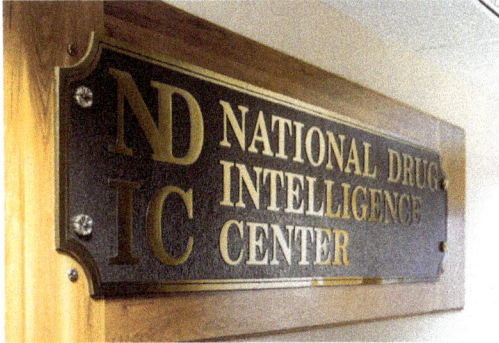

Turn left at the giant plaque, and you find yourself facing big glass doors with the NDIC logo on them. Pushing through, you enter a lobby with a big, white desk where the receptionist used to sit. Again, everything looks polished and fresh, as if the agency only pulled up stakes a few days ago.

Passing the big desk, Darrel leads you into a huge corner office with burgundy carpeting and a stunning view of downtown Johnstown. "This was the office of the director of the NDIC," he explains. "Before that, it belonged to the president of Penn Traffic."

Photos by Philip Balko

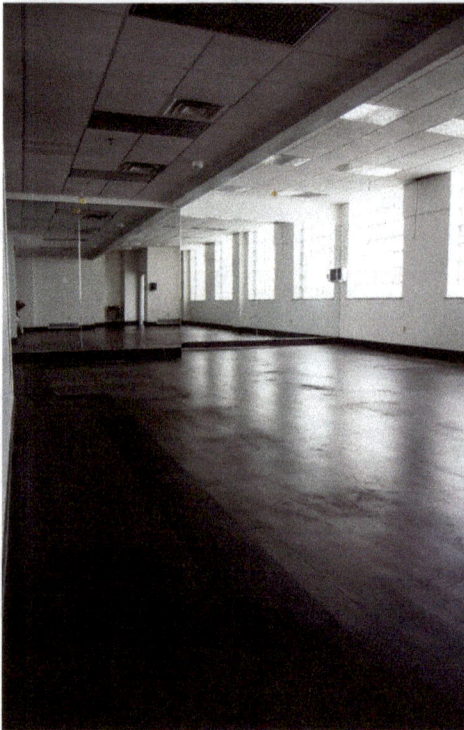

Adjacent offices are also big and carpeted, though none are quite the size of the director's office or have the same color carpet. "These belonged to assistant directors and other officials," says Darrel. "Before that, Penn Traffic vice presidents and executives worked here."

As Darrel escorts you out of the executive offices, he talks about how NDIC's offices had the highest security and first-class workplace conveniences, including a fully-equipped workout facility.

He takes you there for a look, hiking down a hallway. On the right, you see a big, bright room that was once full of exercise equipment used daily by NDIC employees.

"The treadmills were wired for 220 service," says Darrel. "Can you imagine that? And they had full men's and women's locker rooms. It was really something."

As Darrel leads you through the maze of hallways, he tells you more about the agency's expansion in the building over the years.

"They started by occupying the fifth floor," he recalls. "Then, they expanded onto the fourth floor. Eventually, they took all of four and part of three. Finally, they took all of the third floor, too, plus storage space on what used to be the mezzanine."

Third Floor's the Charm

When you've finished on the fourth floor, Darrel takes you down in the passenger elevator (no freight hauler this time) to the third. Here, you wander through featureless hallways, past locked doors where NDIC employees once worked in secure solitude. Whatever's behind those doors, Darrel doesn't offer to show it to you.

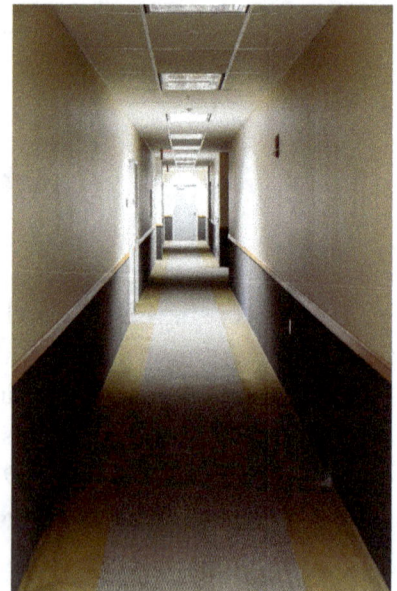

Suffice it to say, the entire third floor was once NDIC turf. Together with the fourth and fifth floors above, that makes for an impressive footprint, a testament to the talent and resources that were dedicated to the agency's headquarters. But it wasn't the only federal agency with a sizable presence in the building.

Photos by Philip Balko

236

Black Lung Was Here

Follow Darrel down to the second floor, traverse a few hallways, and you come to a giant, open space. Like the fifth floor cubicle farm of the NDIC, this was once occupied by cubicles, desks, and office equipment. Since then, it's been emptied and stripped to the bare walls, floors, and ceiling.

"This used to be the Department of Labor's local Black Lung office," explains Darrel. "They moved across town to the Tech Park, and we gutted and cleaned up what they left behind. We can build out this space to suit a new tenant."

Before the Black Lung office could move, the floors in the new Tech Park space had to be reinforced to support the great weight of the office's many paper files. That was never an issue in the Penn Traffic Building, though.

"The floors were already strong enough here," says Darrel. "Since this was originally a department store, the load per square foot is much higher than in a typical office building. Everything's highly reinforced."

Darrel points out the high ceilings, cross-beams, and support pillars. "Those all look the same as they did when the store was here, except for the ductwork and sprinklers. This is a great place to see the bones of the store, without any kind of covering."

To the Mezzanine

Leaving the former Black Lung office, Darrel leads you to an elevator. You ride down to the ground floor and walk through a door into what turns out to be the base of one of the ancient stairwells. Looking up, you can see all the way to the distant top on the fifth floor, ninety-odd feet above.

A short tunnel leads to a door that opens outside, at a freight dock where merchandise was once unloaded into the store.

Next, Darrel takes you up a set of stairs to the mezzanine...what's left of it, anyway.

Photos by Philip Balko

It doesn't look at all like the broad balcony of the old days, with the glass railing where shoppers could gaze down at the main floor below. There's a full wall where that railing once ran, and the space leading up to it is stacked with items in storage, not artfully arranged with seats for ladies eating lunch.

"We tore all the glass out and studded the walls up to reduce the risk of fire," says Darrel. "If you took the wall out now, you'd see above the ceiling of the courtroom on the main floor."

In the rooms once occupied by Penn Traffic's photo studio, optometrist, post office, and other tenants, nothing but empty space, dusty shelves, and bare walls now exist. The NDIC used these rooms for storage, but they've been vacant since the agency departed.

If you look hard enough, though, you see traces of the old store here and there. One room, for example, is lined with crumbling cork walls. In the days of the store, it was used as a freezer for the restaurant.

Photos by Philip Balko

A Palace of a Bathroom

Then there's the ladies' bathroom, where the past of Penn Traffic comes to life even more vividly. There aren't many places in the building where you can almost imagine that you're back in the old days at the store, but this is one of them.

The toilets and the stalls are long gone, but the marble walls and floor remain. So do the sinks and mirrors, and the fancy wallpaper that lines the entryway.

The curved glass shield that stood in the doorway, keeping passersby from looking in, is gone. You can still see the shell of what was once a palatial bathroom, though, an old-fashioned ladies' lounge designed with comfort and class in mind.

"This was an elite bathroom for female customers back in the day," says Darrel. "All the partitions were marble. An attendant would greet you when came in.

"After the store closed, we split it between men and women. But eventually, we just tore out all the toilets and urinals and made it one big storage space for NDIC."

More Treasures of the Store

When you're done taking in the grand bathroom, Darrel leads you down to the main floor, where he unlocks an out-of-the-way stairway. This is perhaps the greatest treasure you've seen yet.

It doesn't look like it's been open in a long time. The paint on the walls is peeling, and the stairs themselves look thoroughly worn. The metal handrails are caked with dust, and the lights don't come on when Darrel flips the switch.

But you can tell this corner of the building hasn't been remodeled. For some reason, even as seemingly everything else in the place has been gutted and rebuilt, this one stairway stands apart, as if frozen in a time warp.

Look at the treads on the stairs. If you were ever in the store during its heyday, you'll recognize the design instantly.

The metal rails are the same, too. You probably gripped them yourself in the old days on your way from the main floor to the mezzanine.

Photos by Philip Balko

Then there's the light fixture hanging at the top of the first flight. Does it look familiar? It should. The same exact style of fixture hung all through the store in the 1950s, 60s, and 70s.

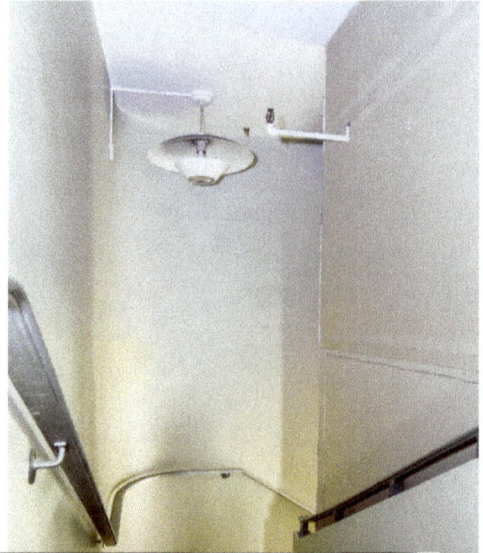

Take a deep breath as you gaze at this little forgotten corner of the past. Everything about it reminds you of the store, doesn't it? It almost makes you wonder: if you walked up those steps into the darkness, might you somehow emerge in the height of the glory days of Penn Traffic, with the store humming and twinkling all around you?

Photo by Hesselbein Studio, courtesy of Johnstown Area Heritage Association

The Basement Complex

Next, Darrel leads you downstairs to the basement. You find yourself in a big, airy room with oak wainscoting and a doorway leading into an adjacent room.

The sign by the door reads, "John M. Kriak Community Room."

"Back in the old days, this was Penn Traffic's grocery store," says Darrel. "By the time I got here, it was storage. Then, John Kriak said he wanted a community room in this space, so we built one and named it after him."

Leaving the community room, you step through a doorway into a parking garage that used to be the Budget Store. According to Darrel, the garage includes 50 spaces for rent to the building's tenants and is fully heated. "All the steam lines run through here, so it's cool in the summer and warm in the winter," says Darrel. "It's 70-some degrees year-round."

To create this garage, which happened before Darrel was hired by the company, Penn Traffic personnel had to take down walls and remove a central staircase leading down from the main floor of the building. You can still see the big, ridged plate covering the hole in the ceiling from which the staircase once descended.

You can also see the grid pattern left behind when the original tile flooring was pulled up.

Near the middle of the garage, there's an enclosure with a big door, a kind of garage within the garage. It's a high-security structure called a sally port, used to transport prisoners into the building for court appearances. There's an elevator inside, so the prisoners can go straight from a vehicle up to the courtroom without entering an open space with room enough to make a run for it.

Steamed Up

Crossing the basement, you enter the adjacent boiler room. It's been in continuous use since the building's construction, though the equipment has been updated through the years.

"This was coal-fired at one time," says Darrel. "There's still a hole back there where they lifted out the ashes with a hoist.

"When I first got here, there were two long steam boilers, three feet in diameter, that ran the length of the room. Ten years ago, I swapped those out for two much smaller boilers. Just one of those new units is enough to heat the whole building, doing the same work that it used to take two of the old boilers to do."

Photo by Robert Jeschonek

Leaving the boiler room, you head for the door to the stairs. Beside it, propped against the wall, is a genuine antique--a huge evergreen arch that once hung in the store at Christmas time.

"We had more of those but got rid of them through the years," explains Darrel. "That's the last one."

The First Floor Shall Be Last

Finished with the basement, you follow Darrel upstairs to the first floor. Passing through the hallway, you notice you're walking on marble.

"That marble flooring has been here forever," says Darrel. "It dates back to when the store was rebuilt after the big fire."

Two of the highest profile current tenants are located here--the Johnstown Division of the U.S. District Court for the Western District of Pennsylvania and the local office of the Internal Revenue Service. Both are locked down tight, so you won't be going in, but that's all right. Darrel assures you they're nothing like the main floor of Penn Traffic that once sprawled through this entire area of the building.

Still, there's definitely an elegant look to the main lobby between the courtroom and I.R.S. It does harken back to classy Penn Traffic atmosphere that greeted generations of shoppers.

Photo by Philip Balko

Photos by Philip Balko

An etched mirror on the wall depicts various local landmarks. Tasteful decorations are displayed on accent tables and mounted on walls. The highly polished inlaid flooring has a retro look, with a pattern of black diamonds over rose marble. The building directory is presented on gold tags under glass on a waist-high pedestal.

And in an alcove by the elevator, a stone plaque is etched with the old Penn Traffic seal of quality, a nod to the building's past.

Fittingly, it is here that your tour ends, in the elegant and brightly lit lobby with the seal of quality on display. You shake hands with Darrel and wave goodbye, stepping out onto the sunny sidewalk. It's been a long trip from the roof to the basement and the lobby; time now for a cup of tea or coffee somewhere, to let it all settle in.

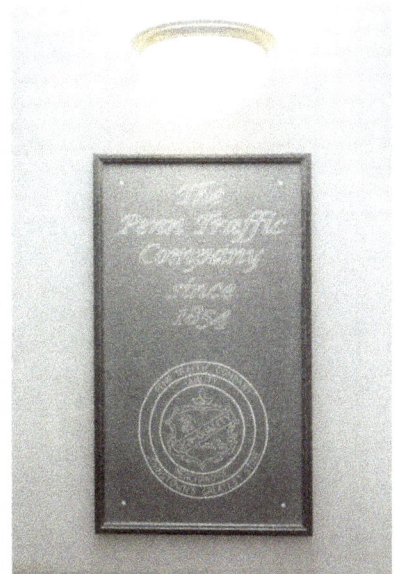

But first, you can't resist, can you? You have to walk to the corner closest to the Public Safety Building and reach up to touch the sign there, the one that forever identifies this building as the place you loved.

The one with the Penn Traffic logo on it, emblazoned there in flowing gold script as if the store within those walls never closed and never will for as long as that building yet stands.

Photos by Philip Balko

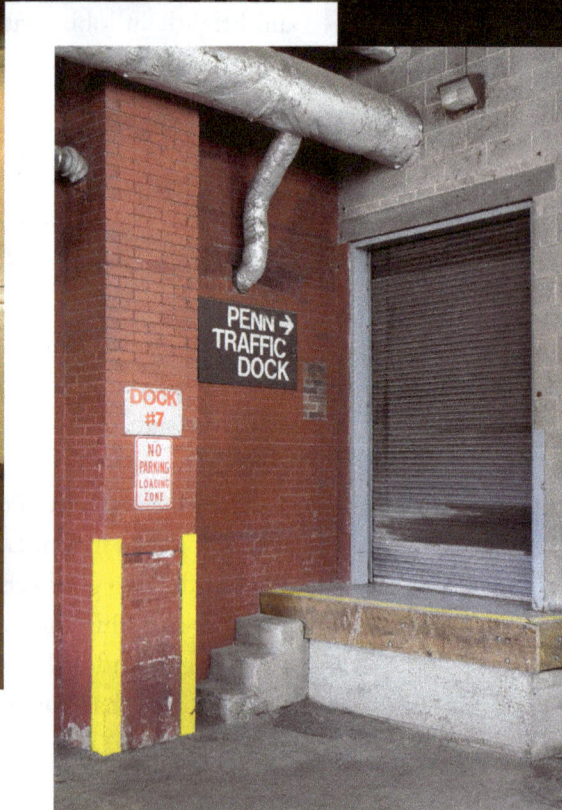

Photos by Philip Balko

Chapter Twenty-Two

Lullabye on Washington Street

Photo by Philip Balko

So now you know the whole story of Penn Traffic, from beginning to end. You've taken a rare behind-the-scenes tour of the Penn Traffic Building as it stands today. And you've met (or reunited with) some of the guiding lights and keepers of the flame, whose memories have brought the store and its times back to life for us all.

What else is there to say or do in the name of Penn Traffic? Our beloved downtown store has been gone since 1977...the company's other department stores since 1982...and the company itself since 2010. Many generations have grown up without ever setting foot in a Penn Traffic store or even hearing about one. It hardly seems possible that Penn Traffic has any relevance in today's world beyond the nostalgic reminiscences of a bunch of "old-timers."

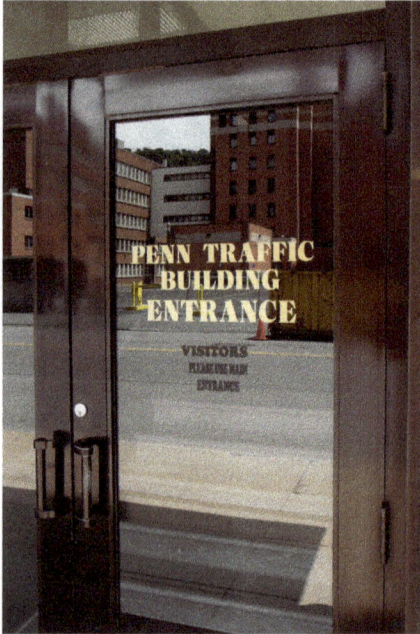

But here's the thing. The stories and symbols of Penn Traffic have *power*. They're a kind of magic, preserving ideas that our society has temporarily abandoned, transmitting them forward to a time when they're needed the most.

They remind us of a better way to do business, in which true customer service is always front and center. They remind us that simpler lives and ways of doing things can be more enriching than complicated lifestyles revolving around technology and multitasking.

They remind us that of all the duties and distractions of life and work, our shared memories and connections to each other are what matter the most.

They remind us also that even the greatest of human enterprises are imperfect and someday fall to dust. That all things in this world must end...but dreams and ideas can last forever, and be reborn and rediscovered as if they are entirely new.

So maybe the best thing we can say or do in the name of Penn Traffic is to keep its story alive, sharing the magic so we increase the chance that the ideas behind it will be reborn in future generations.

And maybe someday, we'll walk into a store just like it again, or more likely, a store like nothing we've yet seen, where the Penn Traffic way is at the heart of every interaction between employees and customers.

And who knows? Maybe it will be in the same place where Penn Traffic once grew and thrived.

The 25th Guest

Remember the employee reunion from the start of this book? Two dozen former employees of Penn Traffic showed up to celebrate their careers at the store and company. Twenty-four men and women came together to hug and laugh and tell stories.

But did you notice there was one more guest at the reunion?

Photos by Philip Balko

One indispensable guest around whom all the others gathered? One who, without a single word, made the event special beyond all words?

That guest, the Penn Traffic Building, still towers downtown, as vast and solid as it ever was in its glory days of being a store and company headquarters. As long as it stands, it sparks nostalgia in those of us who remember the old days...and curiosity in those of us who don't. And where curiosity begins, investigation follows.

Perhaps that investigation will lead to inspiration. Perhaps it will spur someone to tap its power...and what better place to do that than the building where it evolved?

Perhaps you're even that someone. Perhaps you're smart and determined enough to use the magic of yesterday to jumpstart the glories of tomorrow.

Until then, Penn Traffic will continue to sleep, and dream, and wait. The whisper of passing traffic along Washington Street and the rushing of the Little Conemaugh River behind it will be its lullabye.

But as you read this, it stirs. The more of you who read this, the more it stirs. Until one day, you...yes, *you*...walk up and touch the handle of the front door...*you*, the one with the plan and the will to make it happen, the plan to use the best of the past to make the most of the future...

And in that instant, Penn Traffic will wake and stare out at the world from its five floors of windows, wondering where the two of you should start first.

Photos by Philip Balko

Photo courtesy of Johnstown Area Heritage Association

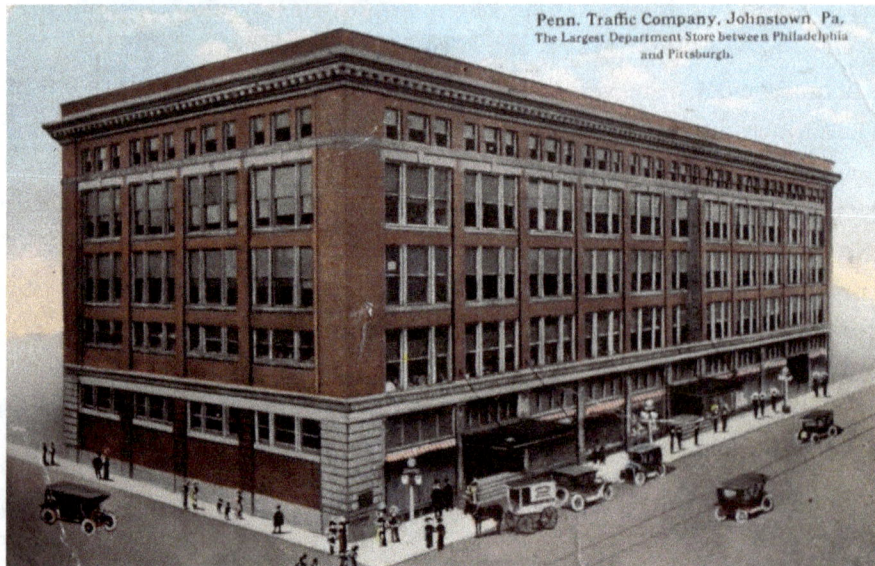

Chapter Twenty-Three

Penn Traffic Recipes

Penn Traffic might be gone, but its legacy of delicious cooking and baking lives on in the pages that follow. Thanks to Eleanor Kohan (head pie maker, 1972-1975), recipes for authentic Penn Traffic pies have survived to this day, just as they were handed down to her after being perfected by generations of bakers at the store's bakery. Those recipes, and those for various cookies and nut bread, are printed here for you to use in your own baking adventures. As a special treat, Eleanor has provided the official recipe for Penn Traffic cole slaw, just as it was prepared in the store's legendary restaurant.

And there's one final bonus in this set of recipes, as well--a recipe for Penn Way hand-dipped peanut butter cups, as handed down from Penn Way's longtime head candy maker, Harry Steele. This lost treasure comes to us from Elaine Kinley, a friend of Harry's who learned it long ago and kept it safe all this time for us to enjoy.

So please, make the most of this very special collection of recipes. Use it to bring back the taste of Penn Traffic in your own kitchen, and pass it forward so future generations can savor it, too. Remember, this represents the accumulated wisdom of decades of daily baking, mixing, and candy-making in the Penn Traffic kitchens and bakery. It's a gift from those dedicated men and women that you'll only find here, in the pages of this book.

Penn Traffic Pies and Dumplings

During her years as head pie maker at Penn Traffic, Eleanor made stacks of pies every day. She practiced the art of pie-making so well, she could just about do it in her sleep.

Photo by Philip Balko

She remembers it clearly to this day, and stays in practice by continuing to bake up pies in her own kitchen in the West End of Johnstown. Everything she does follows standards and traditions established by a long line of Penn Traffic bakers. Like a craftsman, she still lives by the ways her mentors taught her and the experience she gained while following in their footsteps.

Now, here, she passes it along to you. The recipes that follow are copied straight from the personal notebook she used in the bakery at Penn Traffic. She gives them to you in the hope that you'll keep alive the memories--and smells and tastes and textures--of the grand old downtown department store.

Just remember: baking times may vary according to oven.

Penn Traffic Pie Crust

As you prepare the pie recipes in this recipe book, you can save a few steps by using premade pie crusts...or you can try the official Penn Traffic pie crust recipe passed along by Eleanor right here. Remember, this recipe makes more dough than you'll need for the crust of one pie; if you're only planning to make one pie, set aside the rest of the dough and keep it in the refrigerator until you're ready to take a crack at some more pies.

Ingredients:
5 lbs. flour
1 tbsp. salt
2½ lbs. shortening
1 cup corn syrup
1 cup hot water
1 cup cold water

Directions:

The day before baking, mix corn syrup and hot water, then cold water. Stir well with a whisk and put in the refrigerator for 24 hours to chill.

The next day, mix flour and salt. Add shortening. Slowly pour in the corn syrup/water mixture from the day before. Mix thoroughly with your hands until dough forms.

Store dough in a cool place.

When ready to make a pie, roll out enough dough to fill a pie plate. Place the dough in the pie plate and press it into the indentations of the plate. The shell is now ready for filling.

Apple Pie
Ingredients:
1 large can of apples
1 quart water
1 lb. sugar
4 oz. Clear Jel
1 tsp. cinnamon
1/8 tsp. salt

Photo courtesy of Park Cover

Directions: Mix dry ingredients. Drain juice from apples. Mix water and Clear Jel. Bring juice from apples to a boil, stirring in the water/Clear Jel mix. Add spices and apples to this mixture, set aside to cool.

Add filling to unbaked pie shell. Roll out dough for top pie crust and put on pie. Using pastry wheel, make a letter "A" in center of top crust. Then, crimp the edges of the pie and brush with beaten egg whites.

Bake at 425° for 30 minutes.

Variations: To make other fruit and berry pies, substitute 1 lb. canned, frozen, or fresh fruit or berries, plus 1 quart juice from the same fruit or berries instead of water. If juice not available, use water.

Lattice Top Crust: After pouring filling into unbaked pie shell, roll out lengths of unbaked pie dough. Place one layer of dough lengths across the top of the pie. Then, place another layer on top of them in a criss-cross pattern. Bake as directed.

Crumb Pies: After pouring filling into unbaked pie shell, cover with crumbs, prepared as follows:

Crumb Ingredients:
¼ cup brown sugar
1 cup flour
½ cup butter
1 tsp. cinnamon

Crumb Directions: Mix crumb ingredients like pie dough, kneading into little balls, or "crumbs." Spread over pie filling and bake at 350° for 35-40 minutes.

Apple Dumplings
Ingredients:
1 apple for each dumpling (preferably Jonathan, Grannysmith, or another variety with some tartness in the flavor)
Penn Traffic pie crust dough (see recipe above)
½ cup sugar
1 tsp. cinnamon
¼ tsp. butter
1 egg white

Directions: Peel and core 1 apple for each dumpling. Roll out Penn Traffic pie crust dough and cut into squares. Make each square big enough to cover an apple when folded.

Place apple, small end down, in center of a square. Mix sugar and cinnamon. Pour 1 tsp. sugar/cinnamon mixture into center of apple (where core was removed). Put ¼ tsp. butter on top of that mixture in center of apple.

Brush all edges of dough square with water. Pull up all four corners of square so they meet in the middle. Poke joined edges in middle with fork, then brush with egg white. Bake at 350° for 30 minutes.

Pumpkin Pie
Ingredients:
1 small can pumpkin
¾ cup egg yolks
¾ cup egg whites
1 cup white sugar
½ cup brown sugar
1 tbsp. flour
1 tsp. cinnamon
½ tsp. nutmeg
½ tsp. ginger
1 can condensed milk

Photo by Philip Balko

Directions: Mix eggs and pumpkin. Mix cinnamon, nutmeg, ginger, and flour. Combine wet and dry ingredients and pour filling into unbaked pie shell. Bake at 450° for 15 minutes, then lower the temperature to 350° and bake for another 50 minutes.

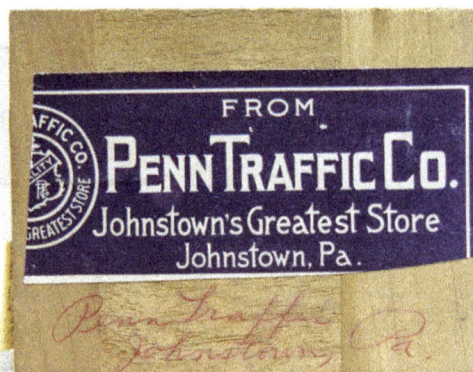

Southern Pecan Pie
Ingredients:
2/3 cup sugar
2/3 cup whole eggs
1/3 cup butter, melted
1 cup corn syrup
1 cup pecans
Directions: Mix all ingredients and pour filling into unbaked pie shell. Bake at 350° for 30-35 minutes.

Easy Mincemeat Pie
Ingredients:
1 jar mincemeat
1 cup apple pie filling
Directions: Chop apples in apple pie filling. Mix all ingredients and pour filling into unbaked pie shell. Bake at 350° for 30-35 minutes.

Shoo Fly Pie
Filling Ingredients:
1 cup boiling water
½ cup molasses
1 tsp. baking soda
½ tsp cream of tartar
Crumb Ingredients:
¼ cup brown sugar
1 cup flour
½ cup butter
1 tsp. cinnamon
Crumb Directions: Mix crumb ingredients like pie dough, kneading into little balls, or "crumbs."

Photo by Philip Balko

Filling Directions: Mix all filling ingredients and pour into unbaked pie shell. Spread crumbs on top of pie. Bake at 375° for 45-50 minutes.

Cream Pies
Filling Ingredients:
½ cup sugar
3 oz. cornstarch
2 oz. powdered milk
1 pinch salt
1/3 cup egg yolks
½ quart water

Filling Directions: Mix ingredients. Cook on stovetop at high heat, stirring constantly, until mixture thickens. (Be careful not to overcook and burn mixture.) Remove from heat and set aside to cool.

When filling mixture has cooled, pour into baked pie shell and refrigerate.

Variations:

Banana Cream Pie: Slice 1 banana into baked pie shell. Pour cream pie filling over that and refrigerate.

Pineapple Cream Pie: Pour cream pie filling into baked pie shell. Spread canned, strained pineapple on top of that and refrigerate.

Cherry Cream Pie: Pour cream pie filling into baked pie shell. Spread canned cherry pie filling on top of that and refrigerate.

Lemon Pie
Ingredients:
5 ¼ oz. sugar
2 ½ oz. Clear Jel
1 pinch salt
1 ¼ oz. lemon powder
1 ½ oz. egg yolks
1 pint water

Directions: Mix ingredients and add filling to baked pie shell. Refrigerate.

Quarter Century Club photo courtesy of the Johnstown Area Heritage Association

Penn Traffic Bakery Raisin Cookies

Pies weren't the only goodies Eleanor made in the bakery. She also made raisin-filled cookies and raisin bars to die for...and kept the recipe.

That recipe, which follows, is exactly what she used at Penn Traffic, right down to the huge batches. To make smaller quantities for your own cookie fans, just reduce all the amounts by the same percentage, and *voila!*

Once you've mixed everything together and rolled out the dough, fill it with raisins (or whatever you like, for that matter). You can even use cookie cutters to make holiday cut-outs and sprinkle them with sugar, etc. Then bake in the oven for 20 minutes at 350°...and let the deliciousness begin!

Ingredients (dough):

12 lbs. sugar

1½ lbs. powdered milk

9 lbs. shortening

4 oz. vanilla

2 caps Butter-All

3 oz. salt

2 quarts eggs

2 quarts water

20 lb. cake flour

10 oz. baking powder

Directions: Mix ingredients by hand until they thicken into dough. Store dough in a cool place until ready to make cookies.

Ingredients (raisin cookies):

2 lbs. raisins

2 cups sugar

4 oz. cornstarch

Water

Directions: Mix cornstarch and water until it thickens. (Add water slowly. Stop before mixture becomes too watery.) Mix raisins and sugar in a pot and cover with water, then bring to a boil. Lower heat and slowly add cornstarch/water mixture, stirring constantly with a wooden spoon. Cook for 1½ hours. When filling is thick enough, remove from heat and set aside. To determine correct thickness, dip wooden spoon into filling and lift it out above the pot. If the filling does not drip from the spoon, the thickness is correct. Remove pot with filling from heat and set aside, allowing it to cool.

Roll out dough.

Photos courtesy of Eleanor Kohan

Cut rounds with a cookie cutter. Use a spatula to place each one on a foil-covered cookie sheet. Spoon cooled filling onto rounds of dough, then cover with additional rounds. No need to brush with water or egg whites; edges of dough will melt together and seal during baking.

Bake at 350° for 20 minutes, then set aside to cool.

Penn Traffic Coconut Cookies

During her years in the bakery at Penn Traffic, Eleanor also made a lot of coconut cookies following the recipe handed down to her. Here are the ingredients for a large batch; adjust as needed.

Ingredients:

2½ lbs. powdered sugar
1 lb. oleo
1½ lbs. shortening
2½ lbs. macaroon coconut
¾ oz. salt
1 oz. powdered milk
1 oz. vanilla
1¼ lb. eggs
6 oz. water
5 lbs. flour
3¾ oz. baking powder

Directions: Mix dry ingredients in one bowl. Mix wet ingredients in another bowl. Then, combine contents of both bowls and mix into dough. Use a heaping teaspoon of dough for each cookie, dropped onto a greased cookie sheet. Bake at 350° for 10 minutes.

Photos courtesy of Eleanor Kohan

Penn Traffic Bakery Nut Bread

Eleanor was also known for the delicious nut bread she made in the Penn Traffic bakery. Here's the recipe, handed down to her by the bakers who trained her. Remember to adjust the ingredient amounts to suit your needs.

Ingredients:

5 oz. powdered milk	1 lb. 14 oz. sugar
6 cups water	¾ oz. salt
3¾ lbs. flour	3½ oz. baking powder
5 oz. shortening	12 oz. walnuts
½ pint eggs	¼ cup corn syrup

Directions: Mix powdered milk and water, then combine with other ingredients. Pour batter into small greased bread pan and bake at 350° for 30 minutes. Remove bread from oven. After bread has cooled, brush on warm corn syrup, heated briefly (a few seconds) in microwave oven. Sprinkle with crushed walnuts if desired.

Penn Traffic Spice Cake

In addition to the pies, cookies, and nut bread she made, Eleanor baked up a mean spice cake (also known as poor man's cake). As with all the other goodies she prepared, this cake follows the exact recipe handed down to her by the longtime bakers at Penn Traffic, who'd perfected it through decades of experience.

Ingredients:

1½ cups brown sugar	1½ tsp. baking soda
6 oz. shortening	1/8 tsp. salt
1 egg	1/8 tsp. nutmeg
1 cup raisins	1/8 tsp. allspice
1½ cups water	1/8 tsp. cloves
3 cups flour	1 tsp. cinnamon
Ice with maple icing	

Directions: Mix dry ingredients. Boil raisins and water until raisins soften (approximately 10 minutes). Drain raisins, reserving liquid. Mix dry ingredients (flour, brown sugar, baking soda, nutmeg, allspice, cloves, cinnamon) and set aside. Mix raisin juice and dry ingredients in mixer. Add raisins to this mixture last. Pour batter into a greased 9" x 13" cake pan. Bake at 350° for 30 minutes.

Penn Traffic Restaurant Cole Slaw

During her time as head pie maker in the Penn Traffic bakery, Eleanor Kohan traded certain recipes with the cooks in the Penn Traffic restaurant. Here's a prize recipe for the restaurant's famous cole slaw, just as it was made in the store--in large batches for the many daily customers who craved it. To whip up a batch for a non-institutional group, adjust each ingredient to a smaller amount. Otherwise, put everything together as you see here, and savor the goodness of old-time Penn Traffic restaurant slaw!

Ingredients:

50 lbs. cabbage, chopped fine
2 bags carrots (for color), grated
3 small onions, chopped fine
4½ cups tarragon vinegar
6 cups salad oil
6 quarts salad dressing
7¼ lbs. sugar

Directions: Mix vinegar, salad oil, salad dressing, and sugar in a bowl until sugar dissolves. Mix cabbage, carrots, and onions in a separate bowl. Combine wet and dry ingredients and refrigerate.

Penn Way Peanut Butter Cups

And now, we come to a legendary Penn Traffic treasure, lost and now found again for all the candy-lovers among us.

Years ago, after the closing of the downtown department store, the Penn Traffic Company decided to stop making and selling Penn Way candy. According to Bill Gasior, who oversaw the candy-making operation, Penn Way just wasn't profitable anymore. The company had tried selling the candy in its branch department stores, but the demand wasn't there the way it had been at the downtown store.

Around this time, Bill decided to have a look at Penn Way's secret recipes, which were locked away in the filing cabinet of his office. He only had one copy of them...though he was lucky to have even that. For many years, the recipes had existed only in the mind of the head Penn Way candy maker, Harry Steele, who'd refused to write them down. Worried about losing the recipes forever when Harry retired, Bill had hired a helper for Harry and instructed him to learn and copy down the recipes. The helper, Marlon Boratko, had encountered resistance from Harry but finally succeeded, presenting Bill with the compiled recipes. At which point, Bill had locked them up for safekeeping.

But when Bill decided to check on the recipes--the only copy in existence of the secret Penn Way candy recipes--they were gone. "If you asked me where all those recipes are today, I couldn't tell you," says Bill. "They were taken out of my locked file cabinet in my office. And I didn't have another copy. I'd made the mistake of trusting the wrong people."

Lucky for us, one Penn Way recipe did survive, in the mind of Penn Traffic alumni Gary Kinley's wife, Elaine Kinley. Long ago, according to Elaine, Harry Steele himself had shown her how to make Penn Way's famous peanut butter cups. She used that recipe many times through the years and never forgot it.

Now, she has written it down for use in this book, so at least a little of the Penn Way magic can continue to delight future generations.

Penn Way Hand-Dipped Peanut Butter Cup Recipe

(Note: Hand-dipping isn't necessary if your hands are too warm.)

2 lbs. chocolate wafers and 18 oz. peanut butter, smooth.

Use that amount. If making more, use that same amount again. Two lbs. should roughly make approximately 36 cups.

Depending how big you make the peanut balls.

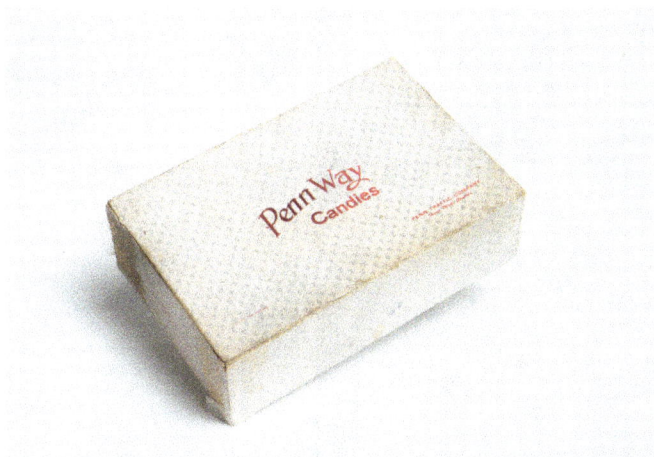

Photo by Philip Balko

You need peanut butter papers and peanut butter mold. Get these at a candy supplier. Usually, 12 cups to a mold.

Take 18 oz. peanut butter, mix in large bowl. (*Not* plastic.) Whip by hand with 6 tbsp. light Karo syrup. Mix till it thickens. If it's too sticky, it needs more Karo, a little bit at a time. Whip till you can roll the peanut butter into small balls (about the size of a hazelnut).

Place the peanut butter balls on wax paper. Roll them all at one time and set aside.

Next, melt your 2 lbs. of chocolate wafers in a double-boiler. *Do not* let water hit the chocolate. Line paper in each mold. Take off water.

Drop 1 tsp. of melted chocolate in cup. Don't let chocolate get too hot. If it's too hot, it will be thick, and it won't drop well.

Next, place a peanut butter ball in each cup, on top of the chocolate.

On top of the peanut butter ball, drop 1 tsp. of chocolate to fill the cup. Smooth out chocolate. Tap the mold on the table to take out any bubble that might have formed. Take your spoon and put a little twirl or curl on top.

Continue to fill all the molds.

Place in freezer (level) for about 3 minutes, no longer.

Take the hardened peanut butter cups out of the molds and put them on a cookie sheet in a cool place until you are ready to store them.

Note: If the chocolate gets too cold to work with, reheat in the double-boiler.

Later, for storage, put in containers. Put waxed paper between the layers. Continue to make more peanut butter cups if desired. Use the same ingredients and amounts for each batch.

Store in a cool place.

Good luck!

WHERE BUT AT PENN TRAFFIC CAN YOU FIND 110 PATTERNS IN DISTINCTIVE CHINA

Only a truly great store like Penn Traffic can offer you such a tremendous selection of world-renowned dinnerware patterns, including the famous names of Lenox, Haviland, Wedgwood and Syracuse. The complete selection of china patterns makes it possible for you to find the perfect pattern to reflect your individual personality. Come browse around and choose from this truly great selection on our modern new Mezzanine.

Sonata by Syracuse, 5-pc. place setting, 17.95

Wedding Ring by Syracuse, 5-pc. setting, 16.95

Camelot by Royal Doulton, 5-pc. place setting, 12.95

Glen Auldyn by Royal Doulton, 5-pc. setting, 19.95

Platinum Elegance by Schumann, 5-pc. setting, $16

True Love by Flintridge, 5-pc. setting, 26.50

Crissy Rose by Flintridge, 5-pc. setting, $18

Brookdale by Lenox, 5-pc. setting, 26.95

Wakefield, by Lenox, 5-pc. setting, 27.95

Milburne by Lenox, 5-pc. place setting, 27.95

Glenwood by Noritake, 5-pc. place setting, 5.50

Rosay by Noritake, 5-pc. place setting, $6

Asia by Wedgwood, 5-pc. place setting, 37.95

Plaisance by Haviland, 5-pc. setting, 26.95

A. Rhodora by Lenox, 5-pc. setting, 27.95

B. Ladore by Haviland, 5-pc. setting, 26.95

Penn Traffic

Visit our selection of lovely gift items, including imports at 20% savings. Main Floor

See our collection of crystal and stemware to complement your beautiful china. Mezzanine

SHOP PENN TRAFFIC TODAY 9:30 to 9. BY MAIL OR PHONE 535-3581

260

Acknowledgements

You probably don't know how close you came to not having this book.

When I started researching it, Penn Traffic's history was scattered to the four winds. (The *four hundred* winds is more like it.) Just *finding* the photos and facts and stories took a major effort.

No centralized archive of Penn Traffic materials existed. The company was long gone, as were many of its prominent figures. So much time had passed that many of the visual and written records that had once been preserved had been lost or destroyed.

But because so many people had a strong interest in seeing this book published, it became a reality, as if by magic. Photos, artwork, and documents came out of the woodwork. Eyewitness reports unfolded in e-mails, Facebook posts, and recorded interviews. One person with special memories led to two... two led to five...five led to ten.

Against all odds, in spite of the loss of so much evidence and so many members of the Penn Traffic family, a story started to take shape. An *epic* story spanning over a century and touching thousands of lives and fates. A story captured for future generations thanks to the foresight, generosity, and kindness of so many heroes of the Penn Traffic Company. *Penn Traffic Forever* would not exist without them.

Everyone mentioned in this book deserves recognition, from the individuals who were personally interviewed to those faithful Penn Traffic Facebook followers who provided recollections for the Memory Department chapters. Special thanks goes out to those who went above and beyond in providing information, guidance, photos, artwork, relics, and even recipes, including: Darrel Holsopple; John Kriak; Eleanor Kohan; Gary and Elaine Kinley; Jean Jucha; Katherine Moser; and Paula Kellar. *Extra*-special thanks goes to Dick Corbin, who single-handedly provided the biggest and most valuable treasure trove of Penn Traffic materials, without which this book would not be nearly so entertaining and enlightening. (Your grandfather, Penn Traffic architect and driving force Samuel H. Heckman, would be proud, Dick.)

Thanks also to Jennifer Pruchnic, Esther Vorhauer, and the entire reference staff at the Cambria County Library for their excellent support of my research for this book. While we're on the subject of librarians, Scott Pyle of the Carnegie Downtown and Business research library in Pittsburgh also deserves credit for his contributions.

Additional documents and photos were provided through the efforts of Kaytlin Sumner and Marcia Kelly of the Johnstown Area Heritage Association. Thanks to them and all their associates for their help with this project.

Then there's fantastic Phil Balko, photographer and photo editor par excellence. When it comes to indispensable collaborators, Phil takes the cake and then some. For Phil, as with me, this book has been a labor of love. He has given generously of his time for very little reward, save the satisfaction of preserving the story of Penn Traffic for current and future generations. If you ever cross paths with him, be sure to shake his hand, buy him a frosty beverage, and thank him for his hard work on this book. (Also, recommend him to your friends and relatives for future photographic services.)

As always, the biggest thank you goes to my wife, Wendy Jeschonek, for her boundless support, love, and understanding. Her contributions and sacrifices during the creation of this book are too many to count. I couldn't have done it without you, babe.

I also owe a special thanks to the man who gave my research for this book the first push: the one and only Bill Glosser. Bill (more commonly associated with another Johnstown department store you might have heard of) was the one who introduced me to John Kriak, my first connection to the Penn Traffic story. *Todah rabah,* Bill.

Finally, thanks to all the members of Penn Traffic Nation out there for keeping the story alive for all these years. I wish we could get together for stuffing and gravy and sundaes in the restaurant...or fresh candy from the Penn Way kitchen...or a cup of tea on the mezzanine...or just one more unveiling of the big Christmas window display on the corner of the Penn Traffic Building on a snowy December night.

But I guess this book, which is for you after all, and *about* you, is the next best thing.

October 9, 2015, Johnstown, Pennsylvania

About the Creators

Robert

Author and editor Robert Jeschonek grew up in Johnstown and spent many happy hours in the Penn Traffic Department Stores in downtown Johnstown, Westmont, and the Richland Mall. Since then, he has gone on to write lots of books and stories, including *Long Live Glosser's, Christmas at Glosser's, Easter at Glosser's, Fear of Rain,* and *Death By Polka* (which are all set in and around Johnstown). He's written a lot of other cool stuff, too, including *Star Trek* and *Doctor Who* fiction and *Batman* comics. His young adult fantasy novel, *My Favorite Band Does Not Exist*, won a Forward National Literature Award and was named a top ten first novel for youth by *Booklist* magazine. His work has been published around the world in over a hundred books, e-books, and audio books. You can find out more about them at his website, www.thefictioneer.com, or by looking up his name on Facebook, Twitter, or Google. As you'll see, he's kind of crazy...in a *good* way.

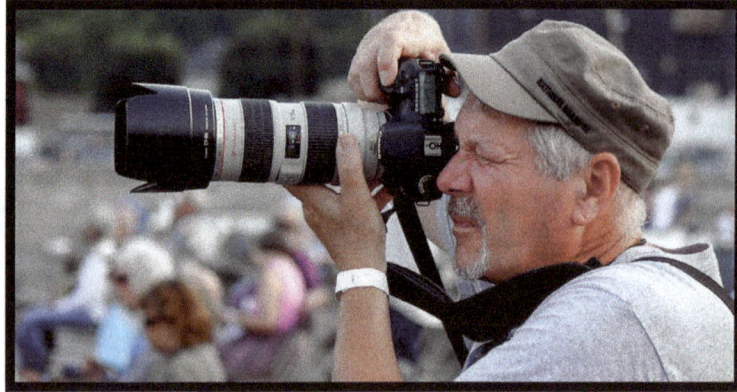

Philip

Philip Balko is an internationally published and award-winning portrait and wedding photographer. When not engaged in providing personalized custom-designed photographic art for his individual and commercial clients, Phil can be found wandering local hills, valleys, and towns, recording the daily life and natural beauty of the Allegheny Highlands. Phil's commissioned work can be found at www.philipbalko.com and his landscapes and lightscapes can be viewed at www.laurelight.com.

Ben

Cover artist and graphic designer Ben Baldwin is a self-taught freelance artist from the UK who works with a combination of traditional media, photography, and digital art programs. He has been shortlisted for the British Fantasy Award for Best Artist for the last four years and has also been shortlisted for the British Science Fiction Association Award for Best Artist. In 2013, he won "Best Artist of the Year" in the annual This Is Horror Awards. You can find out more about Ben and his work at www.benbaldwin.co.uk and https://www.facebook.com/pages/Ben-Baldwin/343132594365

Bibliography

Baumbaugh, Pat. Phone interview by Robert Jeschonek. Digital recording. June 28, 2015.

Baxter, Barbara. Phone interview by Robert Jeschonek. Digital recording. June 24, 2015.

Blough, Shirley. Phone interview by Robert Jeschonek. Digital recording. September 3, 2015.

Corbin, Dick. Phone interview by Robert Jeschonek. Digital recording. August 31, 2015.

Corbin, Dick. Phone interview by Robert Jeschonek. Digital recording. September 1, 2015.

Falk, Glenn. Phone interview by Robert Jeschonek. Digital recording. August 30, 2015.

Gasior, Bill. Phone interview by Robert Jeschonek. Digital recording. September 2, 2015.

Ghantous, Albert. Phone interview by Robert Jeschonek. Digital recording. September 16, 2015.

Ghantous, Betty. Phone interview by Robert Jeschonek. Digital recording. September 16, 2015.

Gorham, John. "The man who bags grocery chains." *Forbes*, April 5, 1999.

"History of Penn Traffic Company." Reference for Business. Accessed July 1, 2015. http://www.referenceforbusiness.com/history2/24/Penn-Traffic-Company.html#ixzz3hWEi0YA5

Holsopple, Darrel. Phone interview by Robert Jeschonek. Digital recording. July 11, 2015.

Jeschonek, Marge. Phone interview by Robert Jeschonek. Digital recording. September 7, 2015.

Jucha, Jean. Phone interview by Robert Jeschonek. Digital recording. September 7, 2015.

Kellar, Paula. Phone interview by Robert Jeschonek. Digital recording. September 1, 2015.

Kennell, Eleanore. Phone interview by Robert Jeschonek. Digital recording. July 12, 2015.

Kinley, Gary. Phone interview by Robert Jeschonek. Digital recording. September 21, 2015.

Kohan, Eleanor. Phone interview by Robert Jeschonek. Digital recording. June 21, 2015.

Kriak, John. Phone interview by Robert Jeschonek. Digital recording. May 16, 2015.

Moser, Katherine. Phone interview by Robert Jeschonek. Digital recording. June 30, 2015.

Neff, Marie. Phone interview by Robert Jeschonek. Digital recording. August 15, 2015.

O'Herrick, Virginia. Phone interview by Robert Jeschonek. Digital recording. June 27, 2015.

Penn Traffic Co., Inc. *Penn Traffic Company 1854-1907.*

Penn Traffic Co., Inc. *Penn Topics.* Johnstown, 1954.

Penn Traffic Co., Inc. *Penn Topics Christmas Edition.* Johnstown, 1954.

Penn Traffic Co., Inc. *Annual Report of Penn Traffic Co.: Fiscal Year Ending January 31, 1967.* Johnstown, 1966.

Penn Traffic Co., Inc. *Annual Report of Penn Traffic Co.: Fiscal Year Ending January 31, 1968.* Johnstown, 1967.

Penn Traffic Co., Inc. *Annual Report of Penn Traffic Co.: Fiscal Year Ending January 31, 1969.* Johnstown, 1968.

Penn Traffic Co., Inc. *Annual Report of Penn Traffic Co.: Fiscal Year Ending January 31, 1970.* Johnstown, 1969.

Penn Traffic Co., Inc. *Annual Report of Penn Traffic Co.: Fiscal Year Ending January 31, 1971*. Johnstown, 1970.

Penn Traffic Co., Inc. *Annual Report of Penn Traffic Co.: Fiscal Year Ending January 31, 1972*. Johnstown, 1971.

Penn Traffic Co., Inc. *Annual Report of Penn Traffic Co.: Fiscal Year Ending January 31, 1973*. Johnstown, 1972.

Penn Traffic Co., Inc. *Annual Report of Penn Traffic Co.: Fiscal Year Ending January 31, 1974*. Johnstown, 1973.

Penn Traffic Co., Inc. *Annual Report of Penn Traffic Co.: Fiscal Year Ending January 31, 1975*. Johnstown, 1974.

Penn Traffic Co., Inc. *Annual Report of Penn Traffic Co.: Fiscal Year Ending January 31, 1976*. Johnstown, 1975.

Penn Traffic Co., Inc. *Annual Report of Penn Traffic Co.: Fiscal Year Ending January 31, 1977*. Johnstown, 1976.

Penn Traffic Co., Inc. *Annual Report of Penn Traffic Co.: Fiscal Year Ending January 31, 1978*. Johnstown, 1977.

Penn Traffic Co., Inc. *Annual Report of Penn Traffic Co.: Fiscal Year Ending February 3, 1979*. Johnstown, 1978.

"Penn Traffic Maintains High Rank In Near-Century of Merchandising." *The Tribune-Democrat*, April 18, 1953.

"Penn Traffic Store Air Conditioned." *Today in Penelec* 3, May-June 1955.

The Story of a Store. Johnstown Centennial 1900.

Whittle, Randy. *Johnstown, Pennsylvania: A History, Part One: 1895-1936*. Charleston: History Press, 2005.

Photo by Heather Corbin

Gift shopping made easy!

Our greater-than-ever

lingerie selection . . .

Second Floor

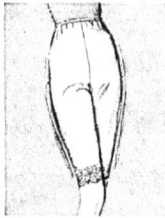

Baby doll pajamas
A. Baby-doll pajamas of flower strewn sheer over opaque with self cording. Delightfully soft and feminine! Sizes small, medium, large. White with turquoise, petal pink with rose, lemon with coral.
6.95

Pettipants
B. Lace-trimmed pettiskirt in white or black is one of the newest and most delightful lingerie fashions. Petite, small, medium, large, extra large.
5.95

Tailored Pajamas
C. Classic pajamas in 40-denier opaque nylon tricot with nylon satin trim. Comfortable, easily laundered and so feminine. White, pink, blue or aqua. Sizes 32 to 40.
$9

Pajama Set
D. Another Artemis favorite! Nylon tricot pajama set with nylon satin trim can be worn with or without belt. White, pink, blue, aqua. Sizes small, medium, large.
$11

Hostess Robe
E. A luxurious hostess robe aglitter with sparkling buttons to accent the rich tones of gold or jade quilted nylon tricot. Sizes 10 to 16.
$30

Quilted Duster
F. Saybury's quilted nylon tricot duster has jewel button closing, nylon satin trim and, like the robe, it's completely washable. Small, medium, large in blue or jade.
$20

Artemis Slip
G. This Artemis slip is one of dozens of luxuriously trimmed gift-perfect designs. It's nylon tricot with applique trim at the bodice. Proportioned 32-38 short, 32-40 average, 34-38 tall. White, black, pearl, red, blue.
$6

matching half slip . . $4

Lingerie, Second Floor

Santa's on our 4th floor today 1 to 4 p. m.

Penn Traffic

SHOP TODAY 1 TO 9

Bonus Gallery

1920 Penn Traffic Christmas Catalogue

THE THRIFTY SHOPPER

CHRISTMAS 1920

All catalogue pages courtesy of Dick Corbin

The Mail Order Division—
A Friendly Service of
PENN TRAFFIC COMPANY

Shop for Christmas Now

NO one, except those who have and do use this service would ever believe the amount of thought and personal attention this store gives mail orders. That division of Penn Traffic service is not a desk filled with a lot of printed forms, filled out and sent about the store by one of its staff. It consists of real thinking people—especially trained to understand your wants by means of a letter. The mail order is a co-operative, friendly medium representing you here at this end and the store.

Each letter after it is carefully read and recorded, receives the attention of very particular shoppers who are selected for knowledge, good taste and judgment. For it takes far higher degree of ability to fill an order for a customer miles and miles away than it does when the customer is present to consult and assist with her own opinion.

Every effort is made to fill every mail order complete, and send out the very same day it is received. We do our utmost to please and to render a service of value to you.

When you mail your order feel assured that it will receive our immediate attention and it will be filled to the best of our ability.

Please address all letters and cards to the

MAIL ORDER DIVISION
PENN TRAFFIC COMPANY

A New Confidential Gift Service

If you have a friend whom you wish to remember Christmas and are puzzled over just what to send—write us, giving your name and your friend's name and address. We will learn just what they would like to receive and notify you.

We will not reveal your name.

This service does not obligate you to buy here—neither is there any charge for the service.

Don't guess gifts.

Please address such correspondence to

THE CONFIDENTIAL GIFT SERVICE
PENN TRAFFIC COMPANY,
JOHNSTOWN, PA.

The Thrifty Shopper
Published by The PENN TRAFFIC CO.

JOHNSTOWN'S LARGEST AND BEST STORE

DECEMBER   JOHNSTOWN, PA.   1920

CHRISTMAS
And the Reconstruction Period

THERE are many things contributing to a Merrier Christmas than for the last few past. Now, we can look back two or three years and visualize restless struggle, and absence of loved ones, sorrow here and sorrow there—at times no merriment seemed in store and the holiday season was rather dull.

But, today—what cause is there for unhappiness? The long-looked-for reconstruction period is well on its way. The old-time normal basis is speedily returning—family members are reunited, sorrows are few, merry voices, smiling faces, jest and laughter are everywhere. The real Christmas spirit is prevailing.

Gift things are assuming a more normal price figure—gifts are more plentiful—the reconstruction period has brought about a readjustment that will enable the purchase of more. It is making better qualities for a price and this good store—over 66 years old—is aiding in every possible way to give you quality, always high quality at the lowest possible price.

The aim of this booklet is to simplify the shoppers task: to bring right into your home the vast storehouse of gifts that are to be found here; to permit you who cannot come to the store to make selections. Select the thing you want, write a letter in your own way, mail it and experienced, painstaking shoppers will buy for you. If not satisfactory, return it.

Penn Traffic Wishes You A Merry Christmas

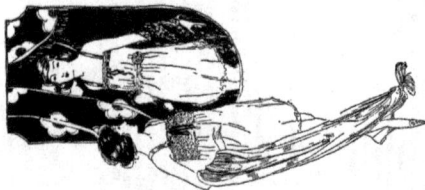

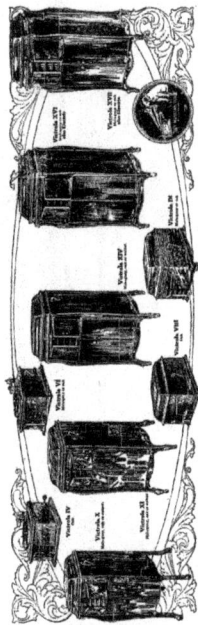

Holiday Gift Suggestions

For Women

Colored Silk Umbrellas, $7.50 to $16.50.

Fancy Boudoir Caps, 50c to $6.50.

Angora Scarfs, $3.50 to $9.

Silk Mules and slippers, $3 to $20.

Silk and Wool Stockings, $3.50 and $4.75 a pair.

Fancy and plain Silk Stockings, $1.25 to $5 pair.

Georgette or Crepe de Chine Blouses, $5 to $40.

Solid Gold or Platinum Lavalieres, $4.75 to $300.

Handkerchiefs, Silk or Linen, 25c to $4.50.

Purses and Hand Bags, $1.25 to $65.

Manicure Set in leather roll cases, $3.50 to $25.

Tourists Rolls and Cases, $32.

Electric Toasters, $6.50.

Percolator, $8.50 to $17.50.

Chafing Dishes, silver plated, $5.75 and up.

Electric Irons, $6.50 and $7.50.

Silk Nightgowns, $5.50 to $16.50.

Silk Envelopes, $2.98 to $13.50.

Gold Mesh Bags, $12.75 to $100.

Kid or Silk Gloves, 90c to $6.50.

Veils and Veiling, 50c to $3.

Negligees or Kimona, $6.50 to $40.

Sewing Baskets, $5 to $25.

For Men

Leather Bill Folds, $2 to $16.

Slippers, $2 to $8.

Traveling Bags, leather or composition, $2 to $70.

Suit Cases, leather or Composition, $2 to $50.

New Style Felt or Velour Hat, $3 to $25.

Latest Shape Cap, $1 to $5.

Men's Cuff Links, $1.75 to $150.

Thermos Bottes and Carafes, $2 to $20.

Cigarette Cases, $3.75 to $35.

Waldemar Vest Chains, $1.75 to $75.

Fountain Pens, $1.50 to $48.

Silver or Gold, always sharp pencil, $1 to $35.

Gold Pocket Knife or Chain Knife, $1.75 to $25.

Smoking Stand, $5 to $30.

Smoking Jacket, $10 to $25.

Suit of Clothes, $25 to $85.

Evening Dress Suit, $50 to $100.

Fancy Vests, $5 to $12.50.

New Winter Overcoat, $25 to $100.

Heavy Sweater Coat, $2 to $18.

Pure Silk Shirt, $7.50 to $18.

Fine Grade Pajamas, $3 to $15.

Solid Leather Belts, 50c to $5.

Garters, 40c to $1.

Desk Clock, $2.75 to $25.

Scarf Pin, $2 to $200.

Skating Cap, $1 to $2.

For Little Girls

Kid Gloves, $1.75 to $2.25.

Middy Blouses, $2.25 to $5.

Winter Dress Coats, $7.50 to $30.

Hats, adorably trimmed, $2.25 to $10.

French Dresses, cotton or wool, $4.25 to $22.

Play Aprons, $2.25 to $3.50.

Linen or silk handkerchiefs, 25c to $1.

Pure Silk Hosiery, $1.75 to $2.

Infants Toilet Sets, $2.25 to $5.

Carriage Robes, $3 to $13.50.

Celluloid Rattles.

Daintiest of Apparel from fine little dresses and baby caps to bibs and things.

For Little Boys

Pocket Knives, 50c to $2.

Wash Blouses, $1 to $2.50.

Knitted Toques, $1 and $1.50.

Smart Little Wash Suits, $2 to $7.50.

Dress Shoes, $4 to $6.

Rain Coats, $4 to $7.50.

Dress or Play Gloves, 50c to $2.50.

Fine Suit of Underwear, $1 to $2.50.

Overall Suits, $1 and $1.75.

Bath Robes, $5.95 to $7.95.

New Hat or Cap, $1 to $10.

Winter Overcoats, $7.50 to $25.

Suit of Clothes, $5 to $20.

Erector Toys and other toys.

Christmas Novelties Will Solve Your Gift Problems

The Art Department is brimful of the most Christmassy little gifts that call forth happy surprise when you see how practical, useful every-day needfuls are made artistic and most giveable.

Coat Hangers, so designed and hand painted that they resemble a pretty girls' head and arms—$1.75.

Darby & Joan Needle Cases are two little French wooden dolls holding needles—50c.

Kitchen Sets of three pieces for cutting, slicing and pealing, attractively boxed—85c.

Cuff Bands of white celluloid—to keep cuffs in place—75c.

Insence Burners and holders in many shades, 35c to $3.

Pin Cushions in so many novel effects, $1.50 to $1.75.

Telephone Shields that transforms your telephone into something quite unusual that blends with your room color scheme, $1.25.

Sweater Hanger Rings, prettily painted, $1.35.

Cretonne Work Boxes, all completely fitted, $1.75 to $2.25.

Work Boxes for Children, brightly painted and fitted with small sewing accessories, 50c.

Sachets of lavender flowers, daintily boxed, $1.25 to $1.75.

Powder Puff Receivers in all sorts of silky creations, $1.50.

PENN TRAFFIC COMPANY

A Host of Adorable Gifts—That are Useable, Too

For The Children's Christmas

If there is any doubt in your mind as to what would make the right holiday greeting for that wee baby, small boy or girl of yours or those little ones very dear to you—visit our

Children's Isle on the Second Floor

There will be so many just right sort of gifts there that you'll have little trouble in your selection.

When Sending Mail Orders

It may simplify your shopping to send a description of what you want—being sure to quote size, color and amount you want to pay. Trained shoppers will fill your order.

Gifts for That Little Girl

She may be at the age when she is quite "particular" in her likes. That is why we are careful to suggest and offer just those wearables that most please little girl fancy and those "fixings" that are very dear to her heart because of their real loveliness.

A Great Selection of Adorable Little Dresses

For Dress Occasions—There are sheer and fresh little voiles with a bit of embroidery, dainty batiste frocks with just enough lace trimming or those exquisite little French dresses, hand made. Perhaps for winter she prefers a taffeta or all wool Jersey. These are to be had in many youthful styles and colors, sizes 2 to 6 years, $5 to $20.

For School or Play—are navy or other dark colored serges or Jerseys and little house dresses of gingham or novelty wash materials artistically fashioned and trimmed.

She Would Surely Like

Jap Silk Kimonas, silk lined and quilted hand embroidered designs.

Dainty Undergarments,

Middy Blouses.

Becoming little hats of felt, velour, velvet or beaver.

For Tiny Girls and Little Boys

COATS

of broadcloth, silvertone, serge, velvet or chinchilla. Good colors and right lines. $7.50 to $30.

White chinchilla or corduroy coats in sizes 6 months to 4 years, $4.50 to $12.

SWEATERS

All wool, Zephyr link and link weave and bells and pockets, sizes 2 to 6 years, $3.50 to $8.50.

Slip-over models in sizes 1 to 6 years, $3.98 to $8.50.

Brushed wool sweater sets, sizes 1 to 4 years, $10 to $16.50.

For Your Boy

Wash Suits—that little fellow like—Tommy Tucker, Oliver Twist, Middy or Peter Thompson styles in white, white trimmed with colors or white blouse and trousers of different color.

Rompers for the very small boy—made of durable gingham with bloomers or straight pants and attached to the waist. Made with drop seats, belts and pockets. Wide range of moderate prices.

To Give the Baby

Carriage Strap and Clamps—made of ribbon with hand painted finish—$1.50 to $3.98.

Comb and Brush Sets in very attractive boxes, 98c to $3.98.

Celluloid Rattles and gay carriage toys, 39c to $2.50.

Novelty Dolls that baby's want to hold, $1 to $5.

Hot Water Bottles with or without fancy hand painted covers, $1 to $3.50.

Ribbon Rosettes for adding a bit of daintiness to hood or dress, 79c to $1.50.

Large Fancy Carriage Bows of ribbon, $1.50 to $3.50.

Infants Hand Embroidered Dresses, plain or quite elaborate, $2.25 to $8.50.

Infants White Silk Caps with linings, $1.25 to $5.

Infants Lace and Embroidery Trimmed White Dresses or slips, 89c to $5.

Infants Long Coats with hand embroidered cape and collar, $5 to $12.

Rompers and Creepers, $1 to $5.

Hand Embroidered Pillow Tops and sheets, $2 to $8.98 each.

Bibs, lace trimmed or plain, 39c to $1.60.

Infants Flannelette Petticoats, 50c to $1.25.

Infants Flannelette Gowns and Kimonas, 50c to $2.

Infants All Wool and Silk and Wool Hose, 69c and 75c.

Vanta Vests, Binders and Bands, all wool or silk and wool, 75c to $1.75.

Vanta Cotton Vests and Bands, 75c to $1.35.

Vanta Gowns, $3.

Baby Rubber Jiffy Pants, 50c and 75c.

Infants Blankets in plain white or colored, $1.50 to $3.50.

Infants Shawls, $3.50 to $6.50.

Infants all Wool Sacques, $1.50 to $3.98.

Infants White Sweaters, $2.00 to $6.

Fancy Wool Toques and Caps, 89c to $5.

Infants Woolen Leggings, $1.75 to $3.

Iceland Lamb Carriage Robes and imitation wool robes, $7.98 to $15.

Japanese Quilted Robes, Baby Bunting, hand embroidered, $3.50 to $12.

PENN TRAFFIC COMPANY

Handkerchiefs—One or a Boxed Dozen

ONE is tempted to buy a dozen! For the little gift, just a remembrance at the Christmastide, what can take the place of a Handkerchief? For the more pretentious gift, where there is doubt as to what to give, one may always rely upon the kerchief. You may buy one or a dozen or more.

ERE are Handkerchiefs in great big assortments —from over the sea and from the nimble fingers of our own needleworkers— colored, part colored, neatly embroidered and just plain. For women, for children and for men—countless styles for everyone.

'Kerchiefs for Women

Crepe de Chine—White with embroidered corners; others in pink, blue, rose, maize and other wanted tints; some are in sport design; lace or hemstitched edge. 25c to 75c each.

Maderia—hand embroidered, open work design, pure linen. $1 to $1.50 each.

Pure Linen—from Spain, hand embroidered corners and hemstitched edges. $1 to $4.75 each.

Linen, Batiste, Lawn—a great collection, embroidered or lace corner effects or white with colored corner. 50c to 75c each.

Pure Linen—beautifully embroidered, Venice lace corners; other hand embroidered. 85c to $2 each.

Initial Corner—of soft Cambric with hand embroidered initial and fancy border effects in white. 25c each.

Lawn and Batiste—wide variety in white with colored or white embroidered corners. 3 to 6 in a box. 50c to $1.50 a box.

Pure Linen—white with hand crochet or tatting around edge. $1.50 to $1.65 each.

Pure Linen—white with full size embroidered corners, hemstitched border. Special 25c each.

Lawn—white with colored or white embroidered corners, rolled or hemstitched edge. 10c to 20c each.

Batiste or Lawn—Colored or white with embroidered corners; lace, scalloped or hemstitched edge. 25c each.

'Kerchiefs for Boys and Girls
Boys—Initial handkerchiefs of cambric, embroidered initial corners. 25c each. White.

Boys—Handkerchiefs with colored effects, plain or colored borders. 25c each.

Girls—Boxed handkerchiefs with comic or kindergarten designs. 3 in a box. 50c to $1 a box.

Girls—Handkerchiefs of lawn with comic or kindergarten designs, rolled or hemstitched edges. 10c to 25c each.

'Kerchiefs for Men
Plain — Cambria Handkerchiefs with ¼ or ½ inch hem, plain or barred effects, white only, 18c to 50c.

Initial—White with embroidered corner, initial, hemstitched borders. 25c to 50c each.

Handkerchiefs are good Envelope Gifts—Easy to Send by Mail for They will Fit Almost any Envelope

Comfort Footwear—The Good Christmas Gift

Easy-to-put-on kinds of felt and leather in pretty colors, fur trimmed or plain, high or low tops. Their real purpose is to solve the gift question—besides being most acceptable and useful. State size, number and color.

FOR CHILDREN
No. 101—Felt comfy slippers, Alice blue, cadet blue and red. Sizes 5 to 11. $1.25 pair.

No. 103—Felt comfy slippers with Pom Pom, American Beauty. Sizes 5 to 8. $1.75 pair. sizes 8 to 11½. $2 pair.

No. 104—Felt comfy slipper. Peacock blue, Alice blue and old rose. Sizes 5 to 11. $2 pair.

No. 105—Felt cavalier. Peacock ,lue and American Beauty. Sizes 6 to 11. $2.50 pair.

No. 106—Misses comfy slipper in Alice blue, cadet blue and red. Sizes 11½ to 2. $1.35.

No. 107—Misses' Comfy slippers with Pom Pom in American Beauty Red. Sizes 11½ to 2. $2 pair.

No. 110—Misses' cavalier comfy or rose ribbon trimmed. American Beauty and Peacock blue. Sizes 11½ to 2. $2.50 pair.

FOR WOMEN
No. 112—Felt. Coral, purple and Alice blue. Sizes 3 to 8. $2 pair.

No. 113—Felt Juliettes. Gray, black, fur trimmed. Sizes 3 to 8. $2.50 pair.

No. 114—Ribbon trimmed Juliettes in wine color. Sizes 3 8. $2.75 pair.

No. 115—Comfy in Alice blue, wisteria, rose and wine. Sizes 3 to 8. $2.50 pair.

No. 116—Comfy in ecru, Peacock blue, taupe, Alice blue and rose. Sizes 3 to 8. $3 pair.

No. 117—Comfy with cuff and button in taupe. Sizes 3 to 8. $3 pair.

No. 118—Cavalier comfy in taupe. Sizes 3 to 8. $3 pair.

No. 119—Ribbon trimmed Juliette in taupe. Sizes 3 to 8. $3.50 pair.

No. 120—Fur trimmed Juliettes in taupe. Sizes 3 to 8. $3.50 pair.

FOR MEN AND BOYS
No. 124—For boys. Brown felt comfy. Sizes 11 to 13½. $1.75 pair. Sizes 1 to 5½. $2 pair. Blue, sizes 2½ to 5½, $1.75 pair.

No. 127—Men's Felt gray Everetts. Sizes 6 to 11. $1.50 pair.

No. 128—Men's Black felt Faust slippers. Leather soles. Size 6 to 11. $1.75 pair.

No. 129—Men's blue felt comfy. Size 6 to 11. $2 pair.

No. 131—Men's brown felt comfy, cushion soles, sizes 6 to 11. $2.50 pair.

No. 132—Men's gray felt slippers with cushion soles and plaid band. 6 to 11. $3 pair.

BOOTS FOR BOYS
At $3—Gum boots, red tops, fleece lined, sizes 6 to 10½. $3 pair.

High top, storm style, fleece lined. Sizes 6 to 10½. $3 pair.

At $2 and $2.50—Black gum boots, knee length. Sizes 6 to 10½ and 11 to 2.

THIS is a place for children and those who love children—those who love to make a child's heart the lightest of all the year on Christmas morning, early. No one hardly could dream of such a wealth of toys—new kinds and old kinds. It appears the Santa's little gnomes have answered the hearts desire of every little girl and boy.

It's a great place—this Toyland and it's an adventure to stroll through there and stop and play—it sort of carries one back years and years.

We cannot tell on this page of all the things to be found there—there's such a great collection.

Toyland

The Greatest Time of All The Year —When Santa Shows His Toys for Little Girls and Little Boys in Toyland at Penn Traffic

THERE are beautiful dolls with almost human faces and dolls that walk and have real hair; dolls with coquettish eyes and alluring smiles. Blocks with big letters in all sorts of pretty colors; toy soldiers that stand as straight and erect as big brother when he wore his uniform; animals of all kinds—cows, pigs, elephants, Teddy bears, horses and tens of others. Toys you can wind up and they will dash around the room, trains going swiftly on tracks into tunnels, out again; building toys, doll trunk—oh, so many, many things, and such an interesting display.

The Lionel Line of Electrical Toys

We show the Lionel Brand of electric toys exclusively. There are no better on the market. The line includes trains, street cars, motors, semiphores, arc lamps, transformers, etc., which can be operated from the lighting circuit by the aid of a transformer or by dry batteries. Every toy is guaranteed, and we'll be glad to mail full information regarding the line upon request.

Sets from $7.50 to $37.50.

Carts, trucks, fire engines and hook and ladder wagons. $1.35 to $2.65.

Iron banks, $1.25.

Toy Irons, 25c.

Doll Carriages—Reed Carriages—brown or natural color; rubber tires, hood, etc., at $5.75 to $25.75.

Construction Blocks—builds almost everything the child or grown-up can conceive. Sets complete at $1.50, $3, $5, $7.50 and $10.

Drawing Master—may be used as a table or on an easel, folds when not in use. $12.50.

Moviegraph—a real moving picture machine, 13½ inches high, base 12x6x¾ inches. Equipped with socket, plug and cord for electricity. Models at $8.50 and $15.

Artificial Snow—at 10c per package, 3 for 25c.

Blackboards on Easel—opens up to use as desk, has chart of instruction at top—at $3.25 to $12.50.

Toy Horses on platform—a wide variety of styles and sizes—50c to $2.65 each.

Rocking Hobby Horses—extra well built, strong and durable—at $4.50 to $14.75 each.

Paint Boxes—all guaranteed non-poisonous and of high grade water colors—at 25c to $3.75. **Chemcraft**—The boys chemistry outfit. Educational, entertaining and absolutely harmless. Sets at $1.50 to $10.

Stationary Electric Engine—of stationary horizontal engine design with moving parts and main features of a horizontal. A faithful reproduction. $4.25 and $5.25. Countershafts $3.75 and $4.75.

Mechanical Trick Auto—Travels forward, backs, turns around and goes in circles. A very clever toy. 75c.

Elektro Electric Toy Range—cooks and bakes—set includes 4 pure aluminum cooking utensils. Complete $10.

Nested Blocks to build up in tall pyramids large nest—at 20c to $1.35 nest.

Embossed Blocks — embossed with letters and animals burnt or embossed in the wood, no paper or paint to come off—at 35c, 45c and 65c.

Electric Transformers for reducing the voltage of street current to suit the toys. Every one guaranteed—the "Lionel" make at $6.65, $10.00 and $11.95 each.

Fancy Tin Horns in different sizes and styles—15c to 50c each.

Electric Motors—for use with battery or regular current—at $2.25, $3.25, $5.00, $5.75, $6.25.

Electric Christmas Tree Outfits—at $2.50 to $6.25.

Electric Track for train sets, extra pieces, 25c to 50c.

Switches for train sets $5.90 and $7.50 set.

Electric Lamps for train sets, 35c and 50c.

Toy Washing Day Needs—

Dolls and Dolls—our stock of dolls presents an assortment found in few toy departments. From the small cellilose 15c doll to the large dressed dolls for $15.00.

Tea Sets and Cooking Sets—China Tea Sets 50c to $4.75.

Enamel Tea Sets, $4.20 to $10.

Aluminum Tea Sets, $1.35 to $2.50.

Enamel Cooking Sets, 85c to $1.50.

Aluminum Cooking Sets, $1.85 to $2.65.

Pull-Apart Animal Circus

There's heaps of fun in Pull-Aparts, but one of the best things about them is that they are instructive as well as amusing. The animals are just as cute and funny as can be, real animal in shape, color and features. You can buy Pull-Apart Circus Sets in five different sizes or you may buy separate animals and actors.

8 piece set $2.

12 piece set, $3.

17 piece set, $4.35.

20 piece set, $5.25.

27 piece set, $6.35.

Extra animals and actors 75c ea.

Ouija Boards—Answer quickly through a glass opening in the table as it moves over the board. Two sizes. $1.25 and $1.50.

Toy Vacuum Cleaner—"Hercules," highly polished cast aluminum. Really sweeps. 24 in. tall, bright color dust bag, hard wood handle, just like mothers. $1.75.

Carrom Board Games—Fun for the long winter evenings.
Type E—Plays 57 games, $5
Type D—Plays 59 games, $5.25
Type B—Plays 100 games, $8.75
Type A—Plays 65 games, $10

Sherwood Steeroplane Sleds—The kind of sled that brings the greatest coasting pleasure is undoubtedly the one that steers. The easier and more effectively a sled steers the more fun the children have with it. Grooved runners grip the snow, prevent side-slipping, and hold the sled on its course. $4.00, $4.75, $5.25 and $7.25.

Just like mothers. Wash Boards, 25c. Wash baskets, 50c.

Mechanical Trains—spring wind, colored, various sizes with coaches, tenders, switch and engines. $2.35 to $5.35 set.

Ten Pin Sets—including pins and balls, 50c to $1.95 set.

Games of All Kinds

Parcheesi, $1.25.

Magic Sets, $2 to $5.50.

Musical chimes, 25c to 75c.

Geographical Lotto, 65c.

Puzzle sets, 85c to $2.65.

Lottoes, 25c.

Dominoes, 25c.

Needle Work Sets, 40c to $1.65.

Paint Set, 25c to $2.

Wash Sets, 50c to $2.

"Pony" Wagon—solid hard wood wheels—steel tired—size of body 11x30 inches—constructed of hard wood—varnished—Price $4.85.

"Teddy" Wagon—the strongest wagon made for any where near its price and nothing stronger at any price—size of body 14x36 inches, malleable iron spindles—a solid cast iron hub—spokes are sunk in hub—hickory wheels—¼-inch steel tire—8¾-inch wheels—coaster brake—hard wood—Price $9.25.

"Coaster Express" same as "Teddy" except larger—size of body same, but wheels are 11 inches and bed is roomier—Price, $10.25.

"Big Four" Wagon—size of body 18½x42½—suitable for small grocery or meat delivery—built to "stand the racket"—Price $12.25.

"Racer" Wagon—a strong coaster wagon that will delight the boy—size 12x32—has ⅝ inch steel axles and wheels that can't come apart—Price $8.50.

CHILDREN'S CHAIRS AND ROCKERS

Reed Rockers, $4.50.

White Chairs at $4.95.

Kindergarten Chairs extra strong—at 65c.

Oak Chairs at $2.65, $3.65, $3.75.

Red Rockers at $1.00.

White Rockers at $3.25 to $3.50.

Oak Rockers at 60c, 98c, $2.00, $3.00.

Children's Desks—Comprising flat tops, roll tops, door tops, etc., in Oak, Mission, White Enamel finishes. $11.50 to $25.50.

Children's Tables—Natural Oak, White Enamel—Foldmor, $2.65 to $18.75.

Good Books are Right Gifts

It would hardly be Christmas without them. Even in the midst of the festive Christmas day itself there is the anticipation of quiet hours and the new or favorite book that brings the merry Christmas message of some friends.

The wise selection of books for your Christmas list is quite as important as the giving of the books themselves. Finding the book that will particularly appeal to individual taste is simplified in—

The Penn Traffic Book Section—Here in the midst of the widest selection of Fiction, Essays, Drama, Poetry, Philosophy, Religion, Science and Childrens' Books especially adapted to young readers-you will be able to find the gift books that will give the greatest pleasure.

For Children

Books for Boys and Girls each in a very Christmasy box or jacket

Tom Swift Series ...... 65c each
23 separate titles.
Motor Boy Series ...... 75c each
21 separate titles.
Rover Boy Series ...... 85c each
24 separate titles.
Tom Shade 65c

Typi al Girl Books

Corner House Girls ...... 75c each
7 separate titles.
Ruth Fielding Series ...... 65c each
16 separate titles.
Dorothy Dale ...... 65c each
12 separate titles.
Motor Girl ...... 75c each
10 separate titles.

For Tiny Readers

Garis Bed Time Stories
25 different titled volumes
85c each
Burgess "Quaddies"
Cloth bound volumes—20 titles
75c each
Mother Goose—$2, $2.50
Linen Books—25c to $1.50
Rag Books—25c to $2

New Fiction

A Man for the Age $2
  Irving Bachelor
Resurrection Rock $1.90
  Edwin Balmer
The Trumpeter Ewan $2
  Temple Bailey
Returned Empty $1.75
  Florence L. Barclay
The Big Town Round-Up... ...... 65c
  Wm. McLeod Raine
Harriet and the Piper $1.90
  Kathleen Norris
The Drums of Jeopardy... ...... $1.90
The Man with Three Names... $1.75
  Harold McGrath
The Devil's Paw $1.90
  E. Phillips Oppenheim
No Defense $2
  Sir Gilbert Parker
The River's End $1.75
The Valley of Silent Men $2
  James Oliver Curwood
Hidden Creek $2
The Branding Iron $2
  Katherine Newlin Burt

Reprints of Popular Fiction

Dawn
  Eleanor H. Porter
The Leopard Woman
  Stewart Edward White
The Valley of the Giants
  Peter B. Kyne
The Magnificent Ambersons
  Booth Tarkington
Nomads of the North
  James Oliver Curwood
Victory
  Joseph Conrad
By Zane Grey
The Borden Legion
The Last Train
The Rainbow Trail
Spirit of the Border
Desert Gold
Wildfire
By E. Phillips Oppenheim
The Double Traitor
The Hillman
The Malefactor
The Kingdom of the Blind
The Way of these Women
By Eleanor H. Porter
Cross Currents
Michael O'Halloran
The Tie that Binds
Laddie
By Edgar Rice Burrows
The Tarzan Books
Gods of Mars
Princess of Mars
By Grace L. Lutz
The Best Man
Dawn of the Morning

Any of the above $1

The Bubble Books

A unique series of books for little tots. Stories are told on records enclosed between the picture color pages of the book.
All the favorite nursery rhymes are sung and told in verse.
12 different Bubble Books—$1.50

Mail Orders for Books will be promptly filled. When ordering by mail add 6c to list price for postage.

PENN TRAFFIC COMPANY

Wherever There's a Home—These are Most Acceptable
Blankets and Bedspreads

THIS big store specializes each year in both. It features immense quantities and the finer qualities. We dare say more blankets and bed spreads go out from Penn Traffic than any other store in this section.

There's reason a-plenty for that, too. All bedspreads here are made according to our specifications, made especially for this store. The blankets are of most excellent quality, full size and lowly priced.

Wool or Cotton Blankets

Woolnap	66x80	Gray—colored border	$6.00 pair
Woolnap	72x84	Large new plaids	8.25 pair
Beacon	66x80	Fancy plaids	7.50 pair
Beacon	66x80	Fancy plaids	11.00 pair
Beacon	72x80	Plaid designs	14.50 pair
Wool	70x80	Plaid designs	11.25 pair
Wool	68x80	Plaid or plain	12.75 pair
Wool	Army	Khaki	6.75 pair
Wool	Crib	Pink or blue	10.00 each
Beacon	Crib	White—colored border	2.95 pair
Beacon	Crib	White—colored border	4.25 pair
Cotton	64x76	Gray—colored border	3.85 pair
Cotton	72x80	Light plaids	4.98 pair
Cotton	64x76	Heather plaids	4.95 pair
Cotton	72x80	Heather Plaids	5.45 pair
Woolnap	66x80	Plaid designs	5.75 pair
Woolnap	66x80	Gray—colored border	6.50 pair
Woolnap	64x76	Plaid designs	5.50 pair
Woolnap	66x80	Light plaids	7.25 pair
Woolnap	66x80	Broken plaids	8.25 pair

Fall Size Beadspread
No. 1000—White
Madras—$3.75
—Hemmed, two very pretty designs to choose from. Light weight.

Single Spreads
No. 75—White
Crochet Spreads—$3
—Good quality hemmed ends, several pretty designs for choice.
No. 300—White
Crochet—$3.50
—Extra quality, many different designs, hemmed ends.
No. 2025—White
Satin Finish—$4
—Heavy quality, two different patterns, hemmed ends.
No. 2060—White
Satin Finish—$4.25
—Patent satin finish, hemmed ends, two attractive floral designs.
No. 215—White
Satin Finish—$5.50
—Scalloped and cut corners, extra fine finish, floral designs.

Three Quarter Size
No. 310—White
Satin Finish—$5.50
—Patent satin finish, heavy quality, hemmed, pretty floral designs.
No. 315—White
Satin Finish—$6
—Patent satin finish, extra quality, hemmed, four designs.
No. 300—White
Satin Finish—$8.75
—Scalloped and cut corners, extra good quality, two floral designs.
No. 320—White
Satin Finish—$5
—Patent finish, hemmed ends, two attractive patterns.

Just Little Dainty Things

Work Baskets—Cretonne covering. Contains pin cushion and needle case. $3.50 each.
Ribbon Sewing Sets—Safety pin holder and fancy work articles. Various colors. 50c set.
Trays—for sewing room. Covered with pretty cretonne, varicus shapes. 85c to $1.75.
Sewing Cabinets—Cretonne covered. 2 to 4 drawers. 65c to $2.50 each.
Glove Boxes—Covered with vari-colored cretonne. $1.65 each.
Vanity Cases—Silk covered with mirror and powder puff. Assorted colors. 25c to $1.

Novelty Pin Cushions—Covered with silk of pretty colors. A little doll stands on top to hold a thimble. Pink, blue or rose. 40c each.
Small Cabinets—Cretonne covering with two drawers. Assorted colors. $1.65 each.
Work Boxes—Cretonne covering. Contains scissors, needles, bodkin, thimbles, shuttle and thread. $3.50 to $5 each.
Sewing Boxes—Cretonne covering. Fitted complete with thimble, needles and the usual needfuls. $1.65 to $3.

PENN TRAFFIC COMPANY

What Women Wouldn't Find Joy in a New Hand Bag?

—and for the quality one would seek for a gift, where else would one think of but Penn Traffic?

This good store has a well-founded reputation for always having the new things ready—and now the fashionable kinds are in a wide assortment.

There are bags of almost every conceivable shape and color to watch a costume or contract, whichever one would prefer..

This is an age of pretty bags and this Christmas showing is decidedly far above the average.

Sharkskin

Here are truly clever affairs—new and superlatively neat. The grain is fine seal, brown color and each corner is tastefully finished with 14k gold. All silk lined. Bags, $15 to $25. Bil folds, $12.50 and card cases, $7.50.

Velvet Bags

—in various colors, odd and regular pouch shapes, metal and fancy shell tops. $3.85 to $22.50 each.

Reed Craft

—the distinctive bag, matches almost every color, wears longer than any we know of due to its fine quality of calf skin leather. Its beauty and harmonizing qualities can be accredited to the finer hand-tooled effects and the soft duo-tone finish.

Envelope or Vanity Bags—$7.50 to $22.50.

Hand Bags—of various shapes, full lined and fitted with purse and mirror. $12 to $32.50.

Beaded Bags

—soft and pliable, firmly woven to stand hard knocks. A host of beautiful designs—many embracing every color of the spectrum. $10 to $6 each, which is easily one-third below quotations a few months ago.

Children's Bags

—of leather, velvet, silk and beaded. A greater selection than this store has ever before exhibited—which is quite an assertion. 65c to $3.

Other Proper Gift Items

Military Brushes—in leather cases. Ivory, ebony or shell. Single or double brushes. $4.50 to $15 each.

Men's Tourist Cases—fitted with 5 to 12 articles. Black or shell fittings. $4.50 to $32.50.

Women's Tourist Cases—fitted with 5 to 12 white ivory articles. $5.50 to $38.50.

Overnight Bags—bright or dull leather with ivory or shell fittings. $16.50 to $125.00.

Work Baskets—of ivory, reed or leather. Fitted with sewing articles of ivory, shell or horn. $5.50 to $18.

Manicure Sets—a very, very large selection in black and colored leather cases. Pyralin ivory fittings. $3.50 to $32.

Stationery — Highland Linen, Crane's Old Hampshire Bond, Quartered Oak, Early English, Ravel-edge and Crinoline Lawn. 25c to $14 a box.

Leather Photo Frames—from post card size to 5x7 inches. $1.50 to $15 each.

If You've a Friend Who Doesn't Have a Desk Set

—and you wan't to please the young lady or the young man a whole lot—make choice of one of these. They're very pretty, very practical and quite a proper gift thing.

7 piece bronze sets—$7 to $25.

5 to 8 piece brown shell sets—$12.50 to $23.

5 to 8 piece white Ivory sets—$8.50 to $17.50.

Christmas Time is Kodak Time

You are sure to add a large amount of pleasure if you choose to give a kodak—a pleasure that will last long after the happy holiday season.

Kodaks
taking pictures from 1⅝x2½ to 3¼x5½—fitted with single or double lenses—$9.49 to $83.

Box Brownies
that simplify picture taking for children, sizes 1⅝ square, 3¼x4¼—$2.86 to $5.90.

Folding Cameras
Premo cameras for convenience in carrying, sizes 2¼x3¼ to 5x7—$10.26 to $86.50.

Cartridge Premos
These are also folding and hold cartridge films—sizes 2¼x3¼ to 3¼x5½—$9.20 to $22.63.

Folding Brownies
Taking pictures in sizes 2¼x3¼ to 3¼x5½. Splendid for snap shots—$10.18 to $19.95.

Kodak Film Tank
for home development of negatives. According to size: $4 to $8.50.

The Autographic
An arrangement fitted on Eastman kodaks for recording the dates of negatives.

Kodak Juniors
Easily operated and thoroughly reliable for the beginner or experienced photographer.

Do All Your Friends Have Umbrellas?

THERE are times when one would think no one had an umbrella—but we know that isn't the case. However, we'll all agree that comparatively few have more than one and because they are so needful and their necessity occurs at such unexpected times—two isn't too many. One for home, the other at one's place of occupation.

Now, if you really want to give a practical gift—here it is.

For Men, Women and Children for Rain and Snow and Sunshine

All Purpose Umbrellas for Women

Highly colored affairs, plain and fancy, in new shapes and with unique handles of ivory, natural wood, bakelite in colors, agate and leather wristlets. Often ferrules and tips match the handles which may be had in almost any colors. Various lengths and sizes—$8.50 to $22.50.

Rain and Snow Umbrellas for Women

With very practical coverings of silk and cotton mixtures, plain or carved wood handles. Some have fancy tips and ferrules. Ivory or bakelite handles in black or colors. A very wide selection. Priced at $4.50 to $8.

Men's and Women's Cotton Umbrellas

Black only, plain mission or carved handles, many with cord wristlets and white ivory rings—$2.50 to $3.50.

Children's and Misses' Umbrellas

One group in black only, of cotton, are in sizes for girls and boys. Plain mission or carved wood handles at $2. Others of linen with silk taped edge with fancy handles—$3 to $3.75.

Silk and Linen Umbrellas for men

All kinds of handles suitable for a man—some mission, others carved and still others with sterling, gold and ivory for engraving. Silk and linen or all-silk taffeta—$6.75 to $12.

Chinaware is Suggested—For a Woman or a New Bride

If she's a bride of recent date or one of a year, her collection of china is not yet what her "air-castle" pictures of it were. So it's a happy newlywed who receives such useable gifts and such pretty ones as are to be found here. Shower her with these prettily decorated pieces.

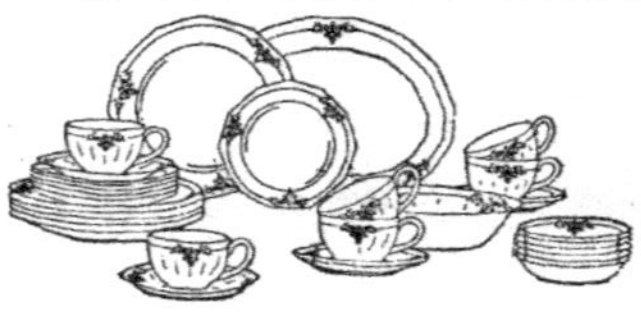

All the way from Nippon came these bowls, plaque, vases and unique little sets—all decorated and finshed in a way that only Japs can do. And, too, with all their beauty and unusualness, they're lowly priced.

There is a wide collection here now especially for holiday choosing.

Dresden China

First to come over since the war. Pure white body with beautiful floral decorations.

High Cake Stand, $7
Medium Cake Stand, $6
Comports, $5
Oval Bon Bon Dishes at $1.25, $2, $4
Round Bon Bon Dishes at $2, $2.50 and $4.
Square Bon Bon Dishes at $2.
Tea Pots, $5
Sugar and Cream Sets, $5

Miscellaneous Pieces and Sets

Sandwich Tray—Oblong shape with ivory border and rose decoration, $4.

Asparagus Dish—Ivory border with gold floral decoration, $5.25.

Hot Cake Dish—Ivory border with gold flowers. $3.75.

Biscuit Jars—Ivory border with rose decoration. $4.25.

Nut Bowl—Square shape with ivory border and flowers. $3.

Tea Strainer and Plate—Small pink floral decoration. $1.25 set.

Mustard Jar & Spoon—Small pink flowers. 85c set.

Tea Cups and Saucers—Pretty violet decoration. $6.75 dozen.

Floral Decoration

—with pretty ivory border and gold decorations.

Celery set, 7 pcs., $5.25 set
Bread and butter plates. 85c ea.
Spoon Tray, $1.85 each.
Pickle Dish, $1.85 each
Oval Cake Dish, $3.75 ea.
Round cake dish, $4.50 ea.
Handled Nut Bowl, $2.50 each.
Square Nut Bowl, $3 ea.
Handled, square Bon Bon, $2.65 each
Hdld, Round Bon Bon $2 each
Hdld., Square Salad, $4.25 each
Hdld., Round Salad, $4.50 each
Salts and Peppers, $1.75 set

THE THRIFTY SHOPPER

23

Furniture Gifts for The Home

GOOD furniture lives a long life—select the good kind from the immense stocks in the good old store. Furniture is a gift to the home—and every one in the home shares and cherishes it.

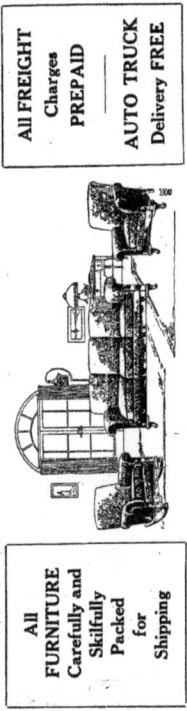

Penn Traffic devotes an entire floor (about one acre) of its great building to the showing of furniture. That section alone is a large furniture store and its rapid growth is due to the firm foundation of real value giving.

All FREIGHT Charges PREPAID

AUTO TRUCK Delivery FREE

All FURNITURE Carefully and Skilfully Packed for Shipping

SUGGESTIONS

Solid Mahogany Book Blocks—in many shapes and designs. $3.50 to 10.75

Polychrome Book Blocks—various odd, new shapes. $3.75 to $12.

Candle Sticks—A choice selection mahogany and polychrome. $2.50 to $23 the pair.

Living Room Suites

—are in an especially wide selection. Almost every imaginable kind is in thees assortments—for large rooms and small rooms.

Cane and Upholstery Combinations

—in fine velours and tapestry coverings find perfect harmony with modern interior decoration. All suits have spring seats, some with loose spring cushions and attractive pillows. All suits consist of 3 pieces.
$350, $405, $425, $450, $475, $515, $550

Overstuffed Living Room Suites

Full spring arm construction with Marshall spring cushions resting upon deep-sinking, upholstery springs.

Tapestry & Velour Suits $415.
Tapestry & Velour Suits $515.
Tapestry & Velour Suits $535.
Tapestry & Velour Suits $560.
Tapestry & Velour Suits $620.
Tapestry & Velour Suits $650.
Extra Fine Tapestry $675
Tapestry and Velour Suits $700.
Imported French Tapestry $700.
Plain Blue Mohair $750.
Ultra Quality Mohair $750.
Blue Figured Mohair $800.

Mahogany Sewing Cabinets—Solid mahogany and veneered. Practical gifts for a woman. $17 to $35.

Boudoir and Desk Lamps—in a wide assortment of bases and shades. $3 to $27.

Gate Leg Tables—Several sizes, colonial designs in Jacobean oak and mahogany. $30 to $85.

Pedestals—Various heights, in mahogany and oak. $9 to $14.50.

Gift Cedar Chests—Natural, Mahogany and Walnut

The cedar chests are plain or artistically adorned with copper bands. Those of mahogany and walnut are plain or in period design to harmonize more closely with furniture you may already have.
Cedar Chests, $26 to $55
Mahog. or Wal. $55 to $100.00

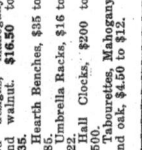

SUGGESTIONS

Oak Trays—In sets for smoking parties or singly. Mahogany with glass centers or metallic kinds. $1.75 to $12.50.

Candle and Small Lamp Shades—Suitable for all kinds of bases. $1 to $10.

Table Lamps—various base styles of mahogany and polychrome. $12 to $60. Shades included.

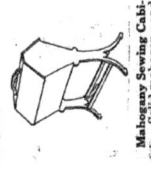

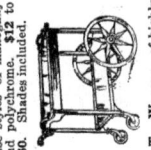

Tea Wagons—of highly polished mahogany or reed. Many with removable glass tray tops. Mostly rubber tired. $20 to $65.

Piano Lamps—many base styles with beautiful silk shades to match. With shade $23.50 to $85.

Davenport End Tables in half round shapes. Period designs, mahogany and walnut. $16.50 to $35.

Hearth Benches, $35 to $85.
Umbrella Racks, $16 to $22.
Hall Clocks, $200 to $500.
Tabourettes, Mahogany and oak, $4.50 to $12.

PENN TRAFFIC COMPANY

THE THRIFTY SHOPPER

22

Happy is the Mother or Wife Who Receives a Rug for Christmas

—for it means more cheerfulness, more attractiveness to her home—her home. You've touched her heart, you've pleased her to an almost inexpressible degree when you try to make her home life more pleasant.

Here are rugs of all sizes—for oddly shaped rooms, little rooms and big rooms. Then there are sizes and various kinds for just dropping here and there—in the bath room, in front of the open fireplace, by the door—anywhere.

Cretonne and Rag Rugs

—in the very popular 27x54 inch size are quite the thing for a bath room or bed room and easily ordered and chosen by mail.

Comes in blue, rose, brown, green and lavender. Priced at $4.75.

When ordering ask for Hampshire Cretonne rug. Give color.

Finest Wiltons, Bengals, Oriental and Turkish Kinds

Washable Cotton Rugs

—in size 27x54 inches are reversible and are fashionable for bedrooms, bath and guest rooms. Plain centers with band borders of blue or rose colors. Priced at $5.25.

When ordering ask for Balmoral 502.

Heavy Chenille Rugs

—for bath rooms. Blue with white line borders.

24x36 inches	Price $3.75
27x54 inches	Price $5.85
27x72 inches	Price $7.50
36x72 inches	Price $10.50

A Helpful Home Gift—Bissell's Sweeper

FEW housewives who wouldn't appreciate a gift that will lessen her house work. Perhaps she has a Bissell—well, a new one will please even more, she knows its value.

AMERICAN QUEEN $7.50
A handsome gift sweeper of excellent appearance and full efficiency. Suggested as a present for mother or married daughter.

ELITE $8.25
The Bissell grade next to the top in efficiency and finish. A practical, good-looking carpet sweeper with durable brushes.

UNIVERSAL $6.00
The lowest priced of the Bissell sweepers but very effective, although it hasn't the finished appearance of the others.

GRAND RAPIDS $6.25
This is the Japanned Model and very efficient for a sweeper at this price. With nickle finish the price is $7.00.

Photo Standards with Swing Frames

The ideal way and complete way to present a photo. These stand on dresser, dressing tables, chiffonieres or any flat surface.

They come in pretty antique gray, antique and rose, gold, silver and mahogany in these sizes—
2x5 inches, price $2.50
3x4 inches, price $3.50
4x6 inches, price $1.69 to $4.50
5x7 inches, price $4.50
5x8 inches, price $4.50
6x9 inches, price $3.50 to $6
7x10 inches, price $1.59 to $5
8x10 inches, price $1.96 to $5.50
8x10 inches, price $1.88 to $7
9x12 inches, price $10.00
Photos inserted free.

Ever Give Electric Sweepers a Thought?

Gift? Well, just figure it out—imagine the feelings of your mother or your wife if they knew their days of sweeping were over. That all they would have to do would be to direct this

Torrington Sweeper

—and it would suck every particle of dust from the carpets and rugs and draperies—sweep the floor in addition and bright the nap. Gift? Well, you decide.

Torringtons are equipped with General Electric motors. $55.

With full set of attachments, $64.50.

Small Framed PICTURES

Scenes of nature prints, outdoor scenes, woodlands, streams and such—colored by hand giving the effect of a colored photograph. A special holiday number. Each packed in a neat glazed box. ¼ inch gilted moulding.

8x10 inches	Price $1.75
8x12 inches	Price $2.25
10x12 inches	Price $2.75

Square Swing Frame Special $1.69

Gift finish, well-made, complete with glass—ready for photo. Sizes 4x6; 5x7; 6x9 and 7x10 inches.

PENN TRAFFIC COMPANY

FORM OF ORDER

Read Carefully

Use this Blank in making an order

(Spaces are given for two addresses, because customers may write from one place and wish goods sent to another.)

Date.................

THE PENN TRAFFIC CO., Johnstown. Please fill the following order.
(Give here Postoffice address at which you will receive a reply if we have occasion to write in respecting the order.)

Name ....

Postoffice .... County .... State.

Name ....

Express Office .... County .... State.

Write here whether by Express, Mail or Freight.

Send goods by ....

Amount Enclosed $....................

Always state amount enclosed and always pin the currency, draft, P. O., or express money order or stamps to this blank.

Do not write in this space

WRITE ORDER HERE

....

TOTAL.....

PENN TRAFFIC COMPANY

Instructions for ordering by mail

Detach and use accompanying order blank.

Write distinctly. Give your name and address and state amount of money enclosed.

Remit the amount of your order by Post Office Money Order, Express Money Order or Cashier's Checks, which can be obtained at any bank.

If you use currency do not fail to have your letter registered.

If the Post Office Address is different from the express or freight address, give both addresses.

State how you wish goods shipped, whether by mail, express or freight.

In ordering from catalog give page number.

If ordering goods not listed in our catalog, give description, price, and if possible send sample.

Express charge on C. O. D. purchases are paid by the customer, also charges for returning money to us if less than $5.00.

Privilege of examination of C. O. D. packages is not permitted.

When sending for samples state material, color, style and price as near as possible.

WE PREPAY THE POSTAGE ON THESE GOODS:

On all small Packages weighing 4 ounces and under we will prepay the charges anywhere in the United States or its possessions.

We will deliver all Dry Goods and Wearing Apparel FREE to All Points in the first and Second Zones as described in the Parcel Post regulations—the limit of distance being approximately 300 miles.

POSTAGE PREPAID ON THESE IN $5.00 ORDERS OR MORE:

On all other goods, including Stationery, Books, Housefurnishing Goods such as Glassware, Lamps, Furniture, Etc., and other bulky articles transportation charges will be paid within the 250 mile limit when the order amounts to $5.00 or over. We also prepay the freight on Grocery orders amounting to $10.00 or over.

ABOUT RETURNING GOODS.

Goods returned within one week, uninjured, and not used, will be exchanged, except the following items which are not returnable:

Goods made to order, scamped goods, ornaments, holiday cards and calendars and such articles as are not exchanged for sanitary reasons, catalog values, hair goods, toilet articles, bedding, neckwear.

In returning goods wrap securely, address package to us, putting your name and address in the upper left hand corner. Write us a separate letter, giving full particulars of the goods returned. All claims and complaints must be made within 5 days of receipt of goods.

Address All Communications to

Penn Traffic Company
JOHNSTOWN, Pennsylvania.

MAIL ORDER DEPARTMENT

PENN TRAFFIC

Is Johnstown's Greatest Store

It is the Christmas store of friendly service, on good terms with thousands in the City and State.

Penn Traffic is the largest store in the State, outside of Pennsylvania's two largest cities. The store's facilities are modern, its resources great. Visitors are always welcome and we take pride in showing the special features that enter into modern merchandising. Some of these are interesting:

The Model Bakery (second floor) where 7000 loaves of fine bread are made daily.

The Refrigerating Plant with its 6000 feet of piping which keeps the cold-rooms of the Grocery and Meat Market at a desired temperature.

The Ice Cream Factory (Basement) and the Candy Factory (fifth floor).

The Private 'Phone Exchange, with its 46 stations and Telephone Desk for Grocery Orders. On busy days, 'phone calls into the store average one every ten seconds.

The Mail Order Division, where salespeople "go to school" daily. Manufacturing our own candy lowers the price which will be noticed readily upon comparison.

The Educational Room, rated the most careful and painstaking in the State.

The Special Conveniences for patrons—branch Post Office, Rest Room, Writing Facilities, Information Booth, Emergency Hospital.

Use a Shopping Card

When Buying in more than one Department

The Shopping Card permits you to go from one department to another without having to wait for each purchase to be handled separately.

It saves time for you, when time is valuable; it saves the annoyance of many small bundles and simplifies shopping generally.

When you reach the store, apply at the Exchange Desk, first floor, for a Shopping Card. Use it per the printed instructions, and when you've finished shopping, all your purchases will be waiting for you, to be sent anywhere you direct.

Use the shopping card, buy anywhere in the store and save yourself the annoyance of looking after small bundles.

Christmas Candies

PENN TRAFFIC is well-known for its good candies, its pure, wholesome candies. We maintain our own candy factory, expert candy makers are employed and sweets are made fresh daily from pure sugar. Manufacturing our own candy lowers the price which will be noticed readily upon comparison.

Chocolate Covered Candies

	Pound
Chocolate Drops	45c
Triple Vanilla Creams	45c
Mint Creams	45c
Wintergreen Creams	45c
Assorted French Creams	45c
Cream Cherries	65c
Nut Clusters	60c
Chocolate Coated Almonds	80c
Chocolate Coated Brazil Nuts	90c

Fancy Chocolate Candies

	Pound
Maple Creams	50c
Coffee Creams	50c
Honey Creams	50c
Orange Creams	50c
Peanut Chips	40c
Lemon Creams	40c
Peanut Caramels	50c
Peanut Clusters	50c
Fudge Patties	45c
Chocolate Nut Dainties	60c

Hershey Milk Kisses	65c
Vanilla Bitter Sweets	60c
French Cream Neapolitans	60c
Walnut Tea Vanilla Creams	60c
Chocolate Caramels	60c
Milk Filbert Clusters	60c

Hard Candies

	Pound
Pure Sugar Stick Candy in Assorted Flavors	40c
Assorted Rock Candy	30c
Peanut Brittle	30c
Christmas Mixed Candy	30c
Ribbon Candy, assorted	40c
Mint Pillows	40c
Clove Pillows	40c
Wintergreen Pillows	40c
Assorted New Wafers	40c
Cocoanut Caramels	35c
Butter Scotch Wafers	45c
Vanilla Taffy	60c

Special 5-Pound Box—$3 Box

Selected from our very best grade of Penn Traffic chocolates, neatly packed and especially chosen for true goodness.

Fancy Gift Candy Packages

—in prettily ornamented boxes, many tied with colorful ribbon, others with transparent paper. Three kinds selected from well-known sweet-makers.

Reymers Candies—½, 1, 2, 3 and 5 pound boxes—40c to $12.
Russells Candies—½, 1, 2, 3 and 5 pound boxes—40c to $9.
Lovell & Covel Candies—½, 1, 2, 3 and 5 pound boxes—40c to $10.

If you do not see what you want on these pages—write us about it. We have it.

PENN TRAFFIC COMPANY

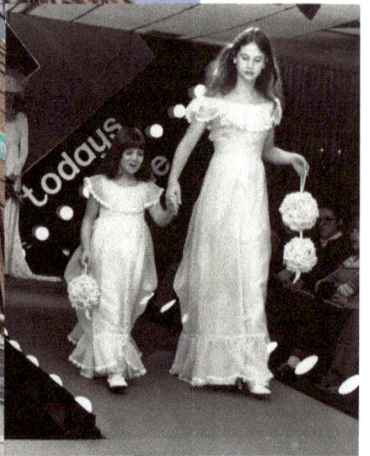

Can you smell the roasting peanuts?

The Glosser Bros. Department Store has reopened, just for you, just in the pages of this one-of-a-kind book. For the first time, the whole true story of Glosser's has been told, on the 25th anniversary of the fabled department store's closing. Step through the famous doors on the corner of Franklin and Locust Streets and grab a brown-and-white-striped shopping bag. You're about to embark on a journey from the humble beginnings of Glosser Bros. to its glory days as a local institution and multi-million dollar company…and the thrilling battle to save it on the eve of its grand finale. Read the stories of the executives, the employees, and the loyal shoppers who made Glosser Bros. a legend and kept it alive in the hearts and minds of Glosser Nation. Hundreds of photos, never before gathered together in one place, will take you back in time to the places and people that made Glosser's great. Experience the things you loved best about the classic department store, from the roasted nuts to the Shaffer twins to the Halloween windows and the amazing sales. Discover secrets and surprises that have never been revealed to the general public until now. Relive the story of a lifetime in a magical tour straight out of your memories and dreams, a grand reopening of a store that never really closed in your heart and will open its doors every time we shout…

Long Live Glosser's

Other Johnstown and Pennsylvania Books
By Robert Jeschonek

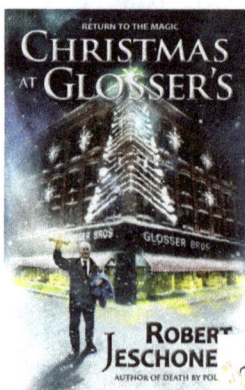

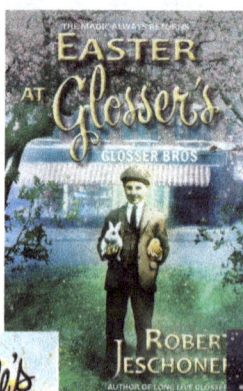

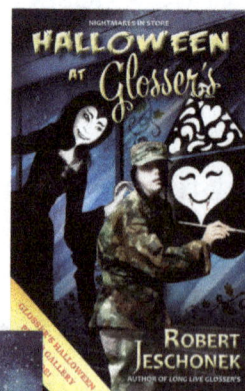

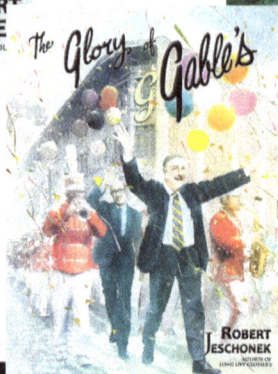

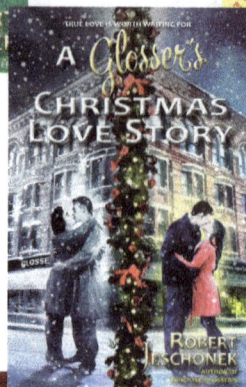

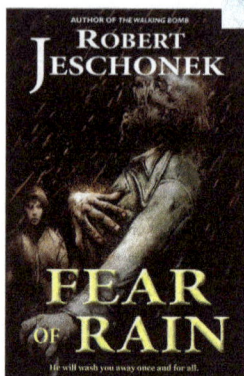

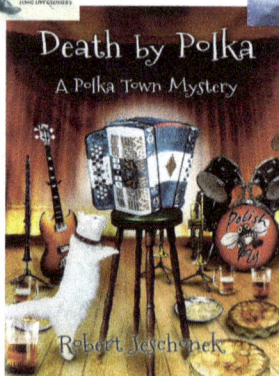

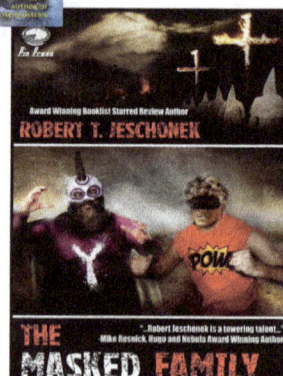

(A Johnstown Flood Story)   (A Johnstown Mystery)   (A Cambria County Adventure)

Order from Amazon, Barnes and Noble, Books-A-Million, or any bookstore or online bookseller.

Ask your book dealer to search by title at Ingram or Baker and Taylor.

Also available from Pie Press at www.piepresspublishing.com or call (814) 525-4783

PIP

pie press publishing

www.ingramcontent.com/pod-product-compliance
Lightning Source LLC
Chambersburg PA
CBHW050637150426
42811CB00052B/931